States and Power

DATE DUE

*Dedicated to the memory of my sister
Susan Margaret Lachmann Humphrey*

States and Power

Richard Lachmann

polity

Copyright © Richard Lachmann 2010

The right of Richard Lachmann to be identified as Author of this Work has been asserted
in accordance with the UK Copyright, Designs and Patents Act 1988.

First published in 2010 by Polity Press
Reprinted 2011

Polity Press
65 Bridge Street
Cambridge CB2 1UR, UK

Polity Press
350 Main Street
Malden, MA 02148, USA

ISBN-13: 978-0-7456-4538-4 (hardback)
ISBN-13: 978-0-7456-4539-1 (paperback)

A catalogue record for this book is available from the British Library.

Typeset in 11 on 13 pt Sabon
by Servis Filmsetting Ltd, Stockport, Cheshire
Printed and bound in the United States of America, by Edwards Brothers, Inc.

The publisher has used its best endeavours to ensure that the URLs for external
websites referred to in this book are correct and active at the time of going to
press. However, the publisher has no responsibility for the websites and can
make no guarantee that a site will remain live or that the content is or will
remain appropriate.

Every effort has been made to trace all copyright holders, but if any have been
inadvertently overlooked the publisher will be pleased to include any necessary
credits in any subsequent reprint or edition.

For further information on Polity, visit our website: www.politybooks.com

Contents

Preface

This is a book about power: the power to tax, the power to build public works and to deploy thousands or millions of workers, the power to make soldiers fight and die in wars, even the power to make children sit in rooms for years and listen to teachers. It is also about the power of citizens to demand services from their government and to replace a government they don't like with a new one.

Power, as Max Weber wrote, is the ability to make others do what you want them to do and what they wouldn't do otherwise. Parents can exercise such power over children, as can criminals with guns over passers-by, and cult leaders through force of personality over their disciples. Those sorts of power are worthy subjects, but they are not what I will discuss here. Instead, I will focus on how enormous organizations claimed ever stronger and more varied power over all the people in a territory and how subjects and citizens pushed back either to weaken that power or to exert collective counter-power against state rulers.

State power is a relatively recent human creation. Humans first appeared on Earth no more than 200,000 years ago. Agriculture, which made possible the first sedentary societies larger than a few hundred people, began 10,000 years ago. The first written records are 6,000 years old. The first empires appeared in the Middle East 5,500 years ago. Few states existed until 500 years ago. It is only in the twentieth century that virtually every territory on Earth (except for Antarctica) became an independent state, replacing the empires, city-states, tribes, and theocracies that once ruled most humans and the lands on which they lived.

All of you reading this book, and your parents, and probably your grandparents as well, have spent your entire lives as citizens of a state. Moreover, you also have spent your lives in a world in which everyone you could ever meet also is a citizen of a state (or a refugee from a state). If we want to think about states sociologically, that is, as creations of humans who both are shaped by and in turn remake the institutions in which we interact, we first must be able to envision a world in which states do not exist. That act of imagination is easy because until 500 years ago states did not exist in most of the world; indeed, had never existed. As we recover the historical world of tribes, city-states, empires, and theocracies we will be able to see states for what they are: a relatively recent European creation that simultaneously with capitalism has come to dominate the world.

Only when we see states as neither natural/inevitable nor static can we ask the critical questions that this book seeks to answer. Only when we realize that states have not always existed can we realistically analyze whether states will continue to dominate the field of power in the future and to consider which other institutions and forces actually might rival or supplant states.

Chapter 1 asks: what is a state and how does it differ from the political forms that existed until 500 years ago? In order to understand how unusually dynamic and powerful states became, we need to see why the other, long-enduring forms of power, from tribes to empires, had such limited influence on the ways in which their subjects lived, worked, and thought.

The second chapter begins by asking why Europe was the place where this new form of state power first developed and supplanted rival institutions of power. The process of state formation is a much studied and debated topic, and this chapter is where I will review the range of existing explanations and show the insights and limitations of each. My goal is not to hand out kudos and criticism to various scholars. Rather, I will mine these theories and the debates surrounding them to formulate the best synthetic explanation for the emergence of states that I can derive from our current store of historical understanding.

Once states gain monopolies on the means of coercion within their territories, they deepen the control they exert over their citizens' bodies, minds, and property. Chapter 3 catalogues the range of capacities states have amassed over centuries. I am concerned in that chapter with explaining how states sought to achieve control in four domains: the appropriation of resources through taxation, the conscription of citizens into the military and the targeting of enemy nations' citizens in wars, the creation of national identity among its citizens, and the development of national cultures. The timing and dimensions of state capacity in each domain were the combined products of officials' ambitions and of citizens who variously resisted and collaborated with the state.

States dominated Europe and then the world at precisely the same time as capitalism supplanted all other modes of production. Chapter 4 looks at the role states have played in capitalist development. I begin by looking at the mercantilist strategies early modern European states adopted in varying forms, and then at post-colonial states' attempts to develop their economies. I am concerned both with how state officials formulated policies and the extent to which they had to respond to demands from domestic capitalists, foreign powers, and popular forces within their own nations. I also consider why some developmental policies were effective and others less so, and finally why, in recent years, many states have moved away from efforts to shape their economies directly in favor of neoliberalism, and why some states have resisted that trend.

Elections and other forms of democratic politics restrain many states, their rulers, and their capitalist allies who would like to make policy without popular interference. Chapter 5 examines the reasons for the spread of democracy in a series of waves beginning in the late eighteenth century and continuing to the present, and for countervailing waves of dictatorship in the decades before and after World War II. It is important to go beyond the mere existence of elections and examine the extent to which classes and other groups in civil society are able to affect state policies through electoral and non-electoral means. I do that in chapter 5 by focusing on social benefits and exploring how mass mobilization, through electoral and other means, has affected the variations in social policies over time and among nations. I explore the reasons why the United States, a leader in social benefits before World War II, has fallen far behind other wealthy nations, and why in recent decades so many nations have embraced neoliberal revisions of social benefits to a greater or lesser extent.

The growth of state power and capacity has been challenged, blocked, and reversed in some parts of the globe. Chapter 6 looks at the consequences of revolutions, colonialism, and military defeats on states, and why in recent decades some states, mainly in Africa, have become so vulnerable to disintegration.

Recently, it has appeared that state power is weakening, being displaced by the reach of multinational corporations, the anonymous workings of global financial markets, or the dictates of international organizations including the International Monetary Fund, the World Bank, and the World Trade Organization. The seventh and concluding chapter of this book assesses the future of states. I ask whether the US's loss of economic and geopolitical dominance is inevitable, and if China or another power will replace the US as hegemon, or if the world will, for the first time in 500 years, enter an era with no hegemon. I explore how other states would be affected by a world with no hegemon, and if competition among powers would cause a world or regional wars. Finally, I consider how states will respond to environmental disaster and resource shortage, and how citizens can influence state policies under those conditions.

As I wrote this book in the first decade of the twenty-first century, the power of the state was demonstrated anew to those of us who are citizens of the United States as well as to those affected by American policies elsewhere in the world. A president, chosen by a minority of the popular vote and only after the unprecedented intervention of the US Supreme Court, quickly convinced Congress to enact the largest tax cuts in the country's history, which had the effect of transferring hundreds of billions of dollars to the richest citizens. On the basis of fraudulent intelligence, he was able to commit the

United States to an invasion of Iraq, which, by the end of his presidency, had resulted in the deaths of almost a million Iraqis. In that same decade, the United States has stood alone among the major industrialized nations in refusing to ratify or implement the Kyoto Protocol, and has used its full diplomatic weight to stymie efforts to negotiate a successor treaty to prevent global climate change. Ultimately, that decade-long delay in reducing carbon emissions almost certainly will result in more deaths than the war in Iraq. The tax cuts and Iraq war would not have occurred if the 2000 election had gone the other way, while the Bush Administration's rejection of Kyoto merely reinforced an existing Washington consensus, reflected in a unanimous 1997 Senate resolution in opposition to that Protocol. More recently, governments around the world have intervened to counteract the effects of the 2008 financial crisis with as yet undetermined consequences for the banking, automobile and other industries, and perhaps for the distribution of wealth and power in those societies.

The United States, as we will see, is not unique in the power it exerts over its citizens, even as its power to affect world events remains unparalleled. As I finished this book in 2009, President Robert Mugabe of Zimbabwe had just secured another term in office through a fraudulent election and open attacks on the opposition party. No other government intervened, and the citizens of that nation, despite the highest inflation and unemployment rates in the world, have not attempted to overthrow the Mugabe regime.

Citizenship remains one of the most important determinants of someone's life chances. Stand at the US–Mexican border, at the wall dividing Israel and the Palestinian territories, or on the beaches of the European islands in the Mediterranean to see what efforts governments make to secure their borders and the risks non-citizens take to pass through those divides. Jobs, civil rights, social benefits, physical security, and even water are kept on one side of those borders. More than 30 million humans today are refugees, fleeing from one country to another in an effort to survive.

States and their futures matter because, at the outset of the twenty-first century, they remain, by far, the most significant repositories of power and resources in the world. The vast majority of violent deaths are caused by wars between states, by states' violence against their own subjects, and by armed attempts to seize state power.

Politics is almost entirely about states. People mobilize to influence state policies, and to gain control of states through elections or with violence. Where states are weak, as in much of Africa, citizens' life chances and life spans are drastically reduced. Every realistic plan for economic growth, for reductions in poverty, hunger, disease, and environmental degradation, and to slow or reverse global warming depends largely on initiatives that are directed by governments alone or in concert.

At the same time as recent events demonstrate state power, the importance of citizenship, and the vulnerability of state rulers to voters at some moments and their vast autonomy in other instances, a chorus of recent commentators has claimed that states and political ideologies no longer matter and that the world is flat (i.e., without meaningful borders). Nations and their governments, in this view, must submit to the inexorable dictates of technological innovation, the global economy, and universal desires for more material goods.

Francis Fukuyama (1992) claims that since the fall of the Soviet Union no ideology or political movement offers a credible challenge to liberal democracy and consumerist market economies. Communism is discredited, as are fascism and fundamentalist religion. Governments that cling to religious, socialist, or authoritarian ideologies are condemning their citizens to repression and economic backwardness. Liberal democracy, in Fukuyama's depiction, is not a program of social reform or even a basis for collective decision-making but merely a framework to allow the pursuit of profit by corporations and consumer spending by individuals. Fukuyama's book, which provides a veneer of Hegelian analysis to American triumphalism, merely asserts the ideological consensus around liberalism and offers no historical account or causal analysis for why competing ideologies and social systems declined in some places but not others, nor for how bastions of fundamentalism and state economies will convert to liberalism.

Political actors are almost entirely absent in Thomas Friedman's *The World Is Flat* (2005). Instead, he identifies ten "flatteners" that allow and force all individuals, firms, and states to compete in a global economy. Only one, the fall of the Berlin Wall, is a political development. The other nine are technological or organizational innovations to which all must adapt if they are to avoid bankruptcy or poverty. Like Margaret Thatcher, Friedman is convinced that "There Is No Alternative" to neoliberal market economies. He asserts that, with the demise of the Soviet Bloc, states no longer are capable of shielding themselves and their citizens from competition. State policy now can be effective only at producing educated citizens and infrastructure, the inputs that will attract investment from globalized firms.

Fukuyama and Friedman reflect, as they provide intellectual pillars for, a consensus in the United States and increasingly elsewhere. In this view, politicians are helpless to control events and so are citizens. Elections and protests are virtually meaningless. These premises justify a journalistic approach to politics that largely ignores issues and presents those who seek public office as motivated by a corrupt desire to enrich themselves or by an obsession with fame. Too much writing about politics has become gossip and biography instead of historically grounded analysis.

I have written this book in part to address the widening divergence in journalistic and academic analyses of politics. This reflects an academic's usual disgust that thinly researched and theoretically untenable works receive such wide and respectful attention merely because they reach politically convenient conclusions. The proper response is not for academics to join the game of political posturing in the guise of public intellectuals. Rather, I hope that by offering an account of what historians and social scientists know about states, I can provide the basis for a counter-analysis to the ahistorical and confused thinking that passes for profundity in many journalistic and governmental circles. Only when we are aware of and have gained intellectual command over the existing base of historical knowledge and the techniques for analyzing states can we understand the actual choices open to officials and citizens. There are alternatives. We have the theoretical bases to figure out what those are and in that way to determine when, where, and how citizens can become public actors in the making of their political world.

Acknowledgments

One of the pleasures of writing a synthetic work like this is that it allows me to recall advice, insights, and suggestions for reading from many teachers and colleagues over decades. Their assistance is reflected throughout this book in my arguments and citations, many of which build on their own innovative work. Several friends offered specific advice on this manuscript. I am pleased to acknowledge Georgi Derluguian, who read the entire manuscript, and Denis O'Hearn and Sam Cohn, who commented on chapter 4. Jonathan Skerrett and Emma Longstaff at Polity Press guided me from proposal to finished manuscript.

1

Before States

A state is a claim and the power to make that claim a reality. States, in Weber's ([1922] 1978: 54) definition, claim a "monopoly of the legitimate use of physical force in the enforcement of its order," to which Mann adds the crucial qualifier, "in a territorially demarcated area, over which it claims a monopoly of binding and permanent rule-making" (1986: 37). The key words in those phrases are "legitimate" and "monopoly."

States are mechanisms for the definition and generation of legitimacy as well as organizations that accumulate resources to enforce those claims of legitimacy. States claim the authority to define all rights, and each individual's rights are defined in relation to the state itself. That is a claim broader and more fundamental than those contained in either Weber or Mann's definitions. States don't just use violence and make rules, and they don't just aspire to monopolies in both realms. States seek to create a social reality in which each subject's property claims and their civil rights and liberties, including their very right to life, exist only in the context of their legal status in a particular state. Successful states have the force, the organizational reach, and the ideological hegemony to enforce those claims upon all who live within its territory.

States do not have to treat all of their subjects equally. For Carl Schmitt [1922] 1985, the state or "sovereign is he who decides on the exception." In other words, states have the power to define certain individuals or categories of people as outside the law, and

1

certain periods of time as emergencies when normal laws don't apply. The US Constitution explicitly defined slaves as property rather than citizens, a categorization reaffirmed by the Supreme Court in its 1856 Dred Scott decision which denied slaves the standing to bring suit in a Federal court even if they were brought by their owners or had escaped to a "free" state. Slaves were and remained the exception to US citizenship rights until the post-Civil War Constitutional Amendments. In 1944, the Supreme Court ruled in *Korematsu* v. *United States* that citizens of Japanese descent could be interned. That latter decision justified the government's racial distinction by drawing a temporal distinction between wartime emergency and normal times of peace. Giorgio Agambem, in *State of Exception* (2005), argues that the Third Reich was a regime that declared a state of exception, an emergency that lasted from its first day of power to its last, and which allowed the regime to legally define whole categories of citizens as without rights and deserving of extermination. More recently, Agambem finds that George W. Bush's "war on terror" is a new attempt to establish a long-term state of emergency that allows the state to override "enemy combatants'" civil rights under the US Constitution and their rights as prisoners of war under the Geneva Conventions. Most states in their histories have declared that some times are exceptional and therefore some of their citizens fall outside the rules and rights the state confers in normal times.

States differ from all other political forms in that they assert and often achieve a monopoly on both violence and legitimacy within a territory. City-states, empires, tribes, and theocracies usually didn't attempt to assert a monopoly on the legitimate use of violence, nor on most other forms of legitimacy, and when they made such claims they were unable to enforce them. Those polities didn't define exceptions or declare emergencies, in the sense that Schmitt and Agambem mean, because they lacked the capacity to assert regular and enduring rules that applied to all those who inhabited their realms. Indeed, the boundaries of those polities, as we shall see, were shifting and vague, and their powers and claims varied across time and space and in relation to their subjects.

States, thus, are unprecedented in their ambition and capacity to divide the world into territories each ruled by a single political entity. In order to appreciate the state's unique identity and operation we first must examine the reality of power, and its distribution, in tribes, theocracies, city-states, and empires. Once we have done that, we will be better able to appreciate the originality and the audacity of the claims states have put forward and sought to enforce.

The Long Pre-History of Politics

Power, until around 10,000 years ago, was confined within kin groups. Beyond such extended families no human was able to exercise long-term control over others. Links between kin groups involved exchange of goods and of adults (mainly women) for reproduction. Groups attacked one another but were unable to parley victory in battle into permanent domination. Indeed, Michael Mann in his review of archeological and anthropological evidence (1986: 63–70) can find no instances in pre-literate societies where chiefs (headmen, big men, elders) were able to permanently take resources from others or to force others to work for them. Chiefs adjudicated disputes among followers and with neighboring tribes, but they could not compound that authority and prestige "into permanent, coercive power" over others (ibid.: 63), and certainly could not create institutionalized power that they could pass onto successors.

William Cronin (1983), in his sweeping study of the ecology created by the Indians who inhabited New England before the arrival of British colonists, describes how sachems (chiefs) negotiated with one another on behalf of their tribes to decide the boundaries of land that each village could use for farming and hunting. However, that land wasn't property, and the sachems didn't derive special material advantage through their role as representatives of their tribesmen. Although Cronin doesn't reach this conclusion himself, his examination of the evidence makes clear that states did not exist, nor did anyone exercise power outside their kin groups, in New England prior to the arrival of Europeans.

3

Evidence for politics in non-literate societies anywhere is elusive at best. Anthropologists for the most part examine societies that already have been transformed by conquest, colonialism, and markets. Edmund Leach's classic work of political anthropology, *Political Systems of Highland Burma* (1954), analyzes an elaborate network of links among village polities in which the strategies of rulers in each locality affect the overall structure of social relations among units and thereby push the entire highland region through cycles of greater egalitarianism and hierarchy in which particular rulers achieve temporary dominance beyond their home territories. Leach's analysis of struggles over land and office proceeds with virtually no mention of the fact that Burma had been under British control for 120 years and had just passed from Japanese occupation to renewed British rule to independence in the decade before Leach published his book. Leach's blind spots don't take away from the elegance of his structural analysis; indeed, they make it possible. However, they show the difficulty of turning to anthropology, which after all is a discipline that confines itself almost exclusively to the study of peoples who were colonized by Europeans and their descendents, for a realistic picture of prehistoric or pre-literate politics.

The Origins of Civilizations and Politics

Coalitions among kin groups were weak and shifting because it was possible for a family or even a larger lineage to exit from the tribe. Scale was kept small by the absence or limited nature of agriculture. Groups had to move from place to place to find food. Hunter-gatherers lacked the permanent habitations or economic surplus that would support rulers and the armed retainers who could control and coerce subjects.

The era of pre-politics and pre-history came to an end with the development of agriculture in river valleys. Irrigation, and the larger-scale agriculture it made possible, provided the bases for the first permanent and hierarchical political structures. Mann argues that irrigation mattered because it "caged" humans within river valleys. "Their local inhabitants, unlike those in the rest of the globe, were constrained to accept civilization, social stratification, and the state. They were trapped into particular social and territorial relationships, forcing them to intensify those relationships rather than evade them. This led to opportunities to develop both collective and distributive power. Civilization, social stratification and the state resulted" (1986: 75).

But what sort of power and "state" developed in these river valleys? Cities in Mesopotamia beginning 5,000 years ago were governed by leading families and at times headed by kings who were able to force subjects to build irrigation canals and walls to protect the cities in which they lived, and to serve in "a 'citizen army' of all free, adult males" (Mann 1986: 101). Most spectacularly, Egyptian pharaohs headed a government that controlled trade along the Nile and with neighboring peoples, using the resources gained in trade to support masses of laborers to build the Pyramids and other monuments that are the outstanding relics of the ancient world. Egypt created an army big enough to capture and control slaves, although they were a minority of the workforces that built the Pyramids. Slaves and other forms of forced labor were even more limited in all the other ancient empires from China to the Americas.

In sum, ancient civilizations were highly limited in their forms of power. Rulers usually were coordinators of leading families. Even autocrats who claimed divinity, as in Egypt, had limited power, and their monuments were artifacts of their capacity to coordinate and control trade far more than the fruits of conquest and coercion. Most subjects, even those who lived a few kilometers from the "capital," carried on their lives in extended kin groups that were aware of their ostensible rulers mainly through their involvement in trade networks, when they participated in religious rituals at central temples, or when armed men came and looted their goods or took away captives. Rulers mattered to their subjects mainly for what they took, and had little impact otherwise. Most power and legitimacy remained within kin groups.[1]

For these reasons, Weber ([1922] 1978: 1006–69) was justified in describing patrimonialism as the main form of power in the world prior to the advent of capitalism and states. To the extent that rulers were seen as legitimate rather than just violent wielders of power whom subjects must obey or evade, it was because they called upon traditions of paternal authority and extended family links to justify their control over both kin and unrelated retainers. Households expanded to include followers as well as relatives. Just as a patriarch could duplicate and transfer his authority to sons, allowing them to rule wives and children as their father had done, so too could a chief, manor lord, pope, or monarch grant "benefices" to followers, allowing them to claim authority and income rights over underlings. In return, the patrimonial benefice-granter claimed a share of the benefice's income and offered varying, though generally highly limited, help in pacifying the land and people ruled by the follower.

Weber equates benefice-holders with the ruler's staff, but rulers in fact exerted only limited control over followers with benefices. The benefices which rulers offered to entice retainers into service then "made the officials. . .practically irremovable. . .The officials who had legally or factually appropriated the benefices could very effectively curtail the ruler's governmental power, above all they could vitiate any attempt at rationalizing the administration through the introduction of a well-disciplined bureaucracy and preserve the traditionalist stereotyped separation of political powers" (Weber [1922] 1978: 1038).

Patrimonialism was a highly decentralized form of authority. Rulers' control over their staffs was less consistent and less intrusive than that of the heads of government in the states we will examine in subsequent chapters. Less revenue flowed up from benefice-holders to patrimonial rulers than from taxpayers to states, and rulers were only able to demand limited military or administrative service from their staffs.

Rulers, thus, could extend their authority in two sorts of ways. One was to grant benefices to followers, which empowered and entrenched those officeholders as much as it did their patron. Such a strategy of extended patrimonialism could expand the nominal reach of a kingdom or church but did not deepen control over subjects. The other was to use violence to extract resources and obedience. The limits of that strategy, or of a combination of both techniques, will become apparent in the next section.

The Limits of Ancient Power: The Roman Empire

We can best understand the limits of power in the ancient world by focusing on the Roman Empire, which was the most successful political entity of the ancient world, rather than attempt a vast or schematic survey of all empires.[2] By understanding how Rome formed an empire, what that empire accomplished, and why after its demise it left only a limited impression on its former dominions, we can comprehend how empires differ from and lack the transformative capacity of states. As we will see, the Roman and other ancient empires relied mainly on armed force to exert power, and so in studying the limits of Roman power we will be able to gain a sense of the limits of organized violence as a means of control.

At the same time, it is important to distinguish between ancient and modern empires and to be careful of taking lessons from Rome and applying them to the empires created in the past 500 years. The latter were formed by nation-states, existed in a capitalist world, and therefore had much greater capacities than their ancient counterparts. That is why works that attempt to offer a general model of empires, most notably S. N. Eisenstadt's *The Political Systems of Empires* (1963), conflate radically different systems of political control, albeit ones with the same label, and as a result are unable to explain the dynamics of imperial formation and decline in the modern world. Max Weber didn't fall into that error. He recognized that politics in the modern era of capitalism, rational action, and nation-states operated very differently from all that came before. We need to understand the Roman Empire on its own terms, and to refrain from translating its dynamics into later millennia. The Roman Empire offers lessons about political actors' limited reach in the ancient world. We will need to analyze the empires of the past 500 years separately to understand what empires in conjunction with capitalism and modern technologies can accomplish.

Rome, like all other ancient empires, created its dominion through violence. Roman armies, like all those anywhere in the world until a few centuries ago, faced severe logistical limits in waging campaigns more than few days' march from home. Their capacities for transporting provisions were highly limited, especially at sites not directly accessible by ships from sea. Animals, like humans, ate more in a week than they could carry. As a result, armies had to feed themselves and their animals by pillaging farms and urban storehouses as they fought. This restricted war and conquest to settled agricultural areas with surpluses capable of producing enough food to support both the farmers and the marauding troops. If an area produced too little food, then military seizures would cause the local population to starve and the area wouldn't yield a surplus for tribute in future years. That is why the boundaries of the Roman Empire ended at the sparsely populated Germanic woodlands in the northeast and at the desert south of its African territories. Similarly, deserts surrounded the Chinese Empire. Once armies had ventured more than a few days from home, they and their animals ran out of the food they had brought along and had to plunder their way forward or back home.

Rome did not surmount the technological limitations faced by ancient empires. However, through organizational and political innovations it built and sustained a vast empire for more than half a millennium, from roughly 100 BC to 400 AD. During that era China was beset by civil wars, conflicts between rival kingdoms, and periods of severe decentralization as local elites and landlords appropriated virtually the entire surplus for themselves, leaving little to flow to the center (Scheidel 2009). The best indicator of the Empire's capacity to funnel resources to the capital was Rome's population, which reached a peak of one million in 100 AD, and sustained that level for more than 200 years. During those centuries Rome had more than twice the population of the largest Chinese city, even though the nominal boundaries of the Roman and Han Chinese Empires contained almost the same number of people and amount of land. Neither Chang'an nor Luoyang, the two cities that alternated as the Chinese imperial capital, topped

500,000 inhabitants until 500 AD, the first time a Chinese city was the largest in the world since 1,000 years earlier (Modelski 2003: 39–56, 219). China became the largest and most prosperous polity in the world only with the consolidation of the Tang Empire in 618 AD.

My purpose is not to rank empires, and pass out a gold medal to Rome and a silver to the Han. Rather, what is at issue is the extent to which any ancient empire could exert control over conquered peoples and extract resources from them and deliver those resources to the capital. In fact, the Roman and Chinese Empires faced the same limits and pursued similar strategies to overcome these, albeit with more success on the part of the Romans.

Julius Caesar famously wrote, "I came, I saw, I conquered," to which he, and all other ancient generals, could have accurately added, "I looted, I left." In search of food to survive and more booty to bring home, armies kept marching on, sometimes for years and thousands of kilometers. What distinguishes Caesar and the other Roman conquerors is what they left behind after their conquests, which was much more than any other ancient empire-builders: roads, garrisons, and a universal language and culture that bound the elites of the conquered lands to the empire politically and socially.

The army was the Romans' key institution, as it was of all other ancient empires. The highest officials of the Roman Republic and, in later centuries, the emperors came largely from the military. The army was the institution that ensured the territories remained conquered, that tribute flowed to Rome, and that wealthy citizens of the empire were able to exploit and trade with the provinces. Because the Roman army was different from all other ancient military forces, its empire was more substantial too, but as we shall see it remained limited in crucial aspects and ultimately was destroyed. To understand the dynamic of Rome we must first analyze its military's innovations and effect on Roman politics.

The Roman Republic's army was a citizen army. That meant Roman soldiers maintained their loyalty to Rome because they expected to return home after they completed their military service, and therefore opposed any effort by their generals to establish breakaway kingdoms in the territories they controlled. Conquering generals had to maintain their loyalty to Rome to ensure that their soldiers remained loyal to them. To be sure, the number of Roman soldiers who remained in each territory was small. Rome always depended largely on local elites to administer each locality and province. Then how did a few Romans, far from home, keep local elites and the masses of farmers and townspeople pacified? Two factors were paramount: terror and trade.

The Romans did not stint in their use of violence. Indeed, they managed to hold territories in part because their use of extreme violence created memories of terror that served to keep defeated populations subservient long after their conquest. Most spectacularly, the crucifixion of 6,000 rebellious slaves after the defeat of Spartacus in 71 BC ensured that the Roman Empire never again had to face a major slave uprising. Terrorism worked.

Trade bound Roman generals and administrators as well as local elites to the empire. Trade was facilitated by one of the great Roman innovations: its use of the army to construct roads, fortifications, and provincial capitals. As a result, the Roman Empire was far better integrated than any other ancient empire. Local elites in each province came to have an interest in maintaining their locales' allegiance to the empire since that gave them access to investment, trade, and luxury goods produced in Rome. Similarly, ease of trade allowed Roman military commanders and administrators to profit on a continuing basis from their positions. Local elites as well as Romans got richer inside the empire than they would have outside.

Economic and political ties across the empire were further reinforced by legal and linguistic commonalities. Rome created a system of civil and property law that was the same throughout the empire.[3] Roman law provided local elites a source of protection for their accumulated wealth, as well as ease in selling property or conveying it to heirs, giving them a compelling reason to maintain loyalty to the empire. Law thus joined trade and the threat of military terror to bind provincial and Roman elites together, dampening the centrifugal forces that induced civil wars, rebellions, and decentralization that verged on autonomy in other ancient empires, including those of China. Commercial and legal integration were deepened as they fostered linguistic and cultural cohesion across the empire. All elites – but only the elites – Roman and provincial, spoke and read Latin and received similar educations that focused on Latin language, rhetoric, and literature (Mann 1986: 313–17).

The only other empire that created a greater degree of cultural integration was China, with its uniform written characters (which coexisted with significant regional differences in oral language), and then with Confucianism which was the basis for the tests that selected government officials and thus of the schools in which the sons of wealthy parents prepared for the tests that selected the next generation of officials. Even though China achieved cultural integration under the Han (contemporary with the Romans), the Han and their successors were unable to maintain control over provincial officials or the landed gentry to the extent that the Romans did, largely because the Chinese imperial armies were less centralized than the Romans and China lacked a uniform legal system of property and civil law. Roman imperial cohesion, thus, was the product of multiple factors, while Chinese cultural-religious unity was undermined until the Tang dynasty by gentry autonomy, which fostered economic autarky, which, in turn, created incentives for local officials to collaborate with the gentry in withholding resources from the imperial court.

Eisenstadt (1963) argues that imperial power in all empires depended on the creation of what he labels "free-floating resources," i.e., resources not tied to local institutions. The Roman legal system made the property of local elites and the loot of army officers into genuine private property, the ultimate free-floating resource. Confucianism made the education of wealthy Chinese into a resource that could be converted, through competitive exams, into income-producing offices anywhere in the empire. However, office was not as fungible as Roman property and China remained a collection of autonomous locales held together only lightly and episodically by dynastic regimes until the Tang created a more centralized military, governmental administration, and economy similar to what the Romans had achieved 600 years earlier.

11

The Roman Empire, then, was better integrated, commercially and culturally, than any of its ancient contemporaries. Yet we should not exaggerate the cohesiveness or efficiency of even this largest and most capable of ancient empires. The greatest challenge to the Roman Empire, as it was to all other ancient empires and, as we will see later in this chapter, to feudal monarchies as well, was its lack of bureaucratic or other mechanisms for directly controlling territories. The Roman Empire had few administrators and, even with universal Latin literacy among elites throughout the empire and the most advanced system of roads in the ancient world, communications between provincial administrators and the capital was slow and uneven. The army, therefore, was the main organ of administration. Each legion took responsibility for ensuring that its subject territory didn't rebel and also that it paid tribute to Rome.

The organizational and logistical limits to Roman geopolitical cohesion were further constricted by internal contradictions in the empire's system of conquest and control. Imperial cohesion was confined to the army and to the administrative and commercial elites, so their interrelations and dynamics were the key to the fate of the empire. Rome was undone by political conflicts among the ruling elites that manifested themselves in fiscal crises and vulnerability to internal rebellions and barbarian invasions.

Rome's military was transformed by its imperial success. As the empire grew in size, ever more legions were needed to maintain Roman rule. At the same time, the potential supply of citizen-soldiers shrank. Slaves brought to the Italian heartland and agricultural products imported from the provinces undercut peasant farmers. Roman smallholders were driven into bankruptcy and then could no longer afford, nor were they obligated, to serve in the military. Many flocked to Rome to live off the dole; others entered the military but as mercenaries rather than citizen-soldiers. Mercenary forces, as we will see in later eras as well, allow rulers far more autonomy than when they have to depend on citizen-soldiers. As long as the Senate and then the emperors could come up with enough cash, mercenaries – whether or not they were citizens – could be kept fighting and loyal to the empire without the political concessions that citizen-soldiers demanded.

Fiscal crises undermined and eventually destroyed the Roman Republic and later weakened the empire. Rome's budget grew, as it had to field ever more legions to control its expanding territories. The only surviving budget figures, from Emperor Augustus's reign at the beginning of the first century, show 70 percent of spending went to the military and an additional 15 percent for the "dole," the food subsidies and entertainments needed to keep the growing number of landless and unemployed plebeians in Rome loyal to their rulers (Mann 1986: 273). That left little to pay imperial officials or for public works. As the military pressures on the empire became worse, even more of the budget went to the armed forces. When a government has little money to pay officials, they support themselves through corruption, weakening central control. The main solution to fiscal crises was to make the legions self-financing by allowing generals to keep war booty and provincial tribute in return for paying and supplying mercenaries. When money runs short and troops don't get paid regularly, they support themselves through shakedowns, and, when times become even more desperate, looting. As the Senate lost control of military payrolls, they also lost control of the armies themselves and of their generals, resulting in the series of coups that marked the imperial centuries.

The Roman imperial government had no way to solve its fiscal crisis. To increase revenues would have required a larger and more honest bureaucracy, and the ongoing fiscal crisis ensured that the money needed for such reforms would never be found. Even if the money had been there, provincial governors, generals, and their mercenaries had become so closely tied to local elites that they no longer had a motive to divert local resources (which the Romans and local elites shared) to the center. The empire's common language and culture, which once bound local elites to the center, now facilitated the melding of Romans and locals at the provincial level, and eventually within each town and small region.

Local elites' ability to withdraw resources from the imperial administration further reduced the Romans' weak influence on their empire's overall economy and limited the amount of trading profits as well as tribute that flowed to the capital for Romans' consumption and for military ventures. Trade, as far as we can measure it with the few records that have survived, stopped growing in the second century. Slaves – which were both a major source of saleable capital for generals and a crucial source of labor for public and private construction, and to operate the great plantations that increasingly supplied food to the capital – began to decline in number at the same time. The real, but limited, stimulus which imperial trade gave to both Italy and the provinces was reversed as the flow of tribute and slaves declined.

As Rome became starved of resources, emperors, generals, and Senators turned on one another and the masses became restive whenever the dole was reduced. The weakened empire, then, was easily shattered and overrun by barbarians in the fourth century.

The fall of the Roman Empire revealed the limits of its, or indeed of any ancient empire's, capacity to transform social, economic, or political relations in its conquered territories. Class relations and the ways in which farmers and tradespeople carried out their work changed little in the centuries of Roman domination. Technological innovation under the Romans was slight. The list of inventions under the various Chinese Empires is longer, as Joseph Needham documents in his magnificent multi-volume, *Science and Civilization in China* (1954–2004), but still progress was slow in China and there are many centuries in which there were virtually no advances in farming, engineering, or science in either empire (Goldstone 2008: 136–44). Most of the inventions in both the Roman and Chinese Empires affected mainly urban elites. Little changed in how farmers farmed, builders built, physicians doctored, or most people thought about themselves and their physical and moral worlds during the long centuries and millennia of Roman and Chinese imperial rule.

Nor did techniques of power change much in those empires and, as a result, central control remained shallow. Empires were built on violence, meted out by mercenaries or citizen-soldiers. The former were limited by an empire's ability to raise funds, which was meager at best, and always in danger of declining. Citizenship was limited in number, and empires created flows of slaves and booty that undermined the economic independence of citizens, reducing that supply of soldiers. All empires relied on local elites, whether warlords, landlords, or priests. The relationship between local elites and the imperium was one of tribute and nominal allegiance won through military violence with the added benefits for local elites of protection from external and popular threats and the enticement of trade.

Most humans in the ancient world became aware that they had new rulers only in the moment of conquest. Otherwise, they continued to farm or practice their crafts and surrender part of their production to a local ruler. Subjects left their villages and traveled to other parts of the empire only when they were taken as slaves or forced laborers. It was only in the capital, and to some extent major provincial cities, that the cosmopolitan nature of imperial life was revealed. And, with the fall of Rome, the political and cultural distinction and most of the material wealth of the empire was gone.

Feudal Politics

The fall of the Roman Empire had little effect on local social relations. Elites remained relatively unchanged after the demise of the empire. Roman governors and legionnaires retreated home or transformed themselves into provincial elites. European localities oscillated between the almost total absence of central authority and the arrival of armies that were able to demand a fraction of the allegiance and tribute that Roman legions once extracted. Those conquering armies also left much less of an imprint than had the Romans.

Feudalism emerged in the absence of imperial power. Feudalism systematized social relations among the highly autonomous elites of Europe in the Dark Ages that followed the fall of Rome. To an extent, feudal lords were heads of mini-states. They commanded armed forces, often, in the case of knights in manor castles, armies of one. Lords used their violence to extract resources from peasant farmers. Hierarchies of lords formed in many regions of Europe. Nobles with bands of retainers amassed the force to compel lesser knights to offer allegiance and a small amount of tribute to their overlords. Some lords at the top of those hierarchies crowned themselves kings.

Medieval kings had little power. They often couldn't get their nominal underlords to join them in war, and when lords and knights came to battle they remained in command of their own forces (Gelete 2002: 10–41; Finer 1975). As a result, medieval battles were disorganized and almost always inconclusive. The most revealing indicator of medieval kings' weak capacity to amass force was their usual inability to capture territory. Although kings made grandiose claims to sovereignty over vast territories, their actual zones of control were small. Nor could kings draw much revenue from the lands they supposedly ruled. Revenues, even for the rulers of the largest medieval kingdoms, were barely enough to support a modest court.

Kings often weren't the biggest landlords, masters of the largest courts, or commanders of the strongest armed force in their supposed dominions. Provincial nobles often rivaled or surpassed their putative rulers. In every kingdom, groups of allied nobles could overpower the king; hence the frequent changes in dynasties in most European kingdoms. Even when a king remained on the throne and successfully passed the Crown to his heir, disgruntled nobles could withhold resources, both cash and armed men, when a king angered them.

Wars in medieval Europe usually had the effect of undermining elite cohesion and weakening great nobles' control over lesser seigneurs and kings' power over all lords. Kings and nobles simply lacked enough armed men to simultaneously fight their rivals and maintain control over underlings. The main way for a medieval ruler to increase the size of his army was by carving new fiefs out of his domains and granting them to underlings in return for their loyalty and presence in battle. Thus, wars more often than not led to further "subinfeudation" rather than consolidation of land and power. Poggi concludes "the 'feudal state' is one that undermines itself, making unified rule over large areas increasingly difficult" (1978: 26). When wars diverted kings and nobles and fragmented their powers, peasants, at least temporarily, gained a degree of insulation from demands by kings, landlords, and clerics. Elite efforts to reassert their claims to rents, taxes, and tithes were reconstructed with difficulty in the aftermath of wars. Only when great lords were secure from external attack could they devote their limited armed forces to ensuring obedience and demanding tribute from lesser nobles.

Kings and nobles both were undercut by a second system of power: the clergy. In most of Western Europe, the Catholic Church was the largest landlord, controlling at least a quarter of all manors. In addition, the Church collected tithes and other dues from most of the lands controlled by lay landlords. The Church operated a system of clerical courts that claimed jurisdiction over peasant land rights under the guise of guarding tithe rights. The Church was decentralized, in fact, despite its formal hierarchical structure. Most tithe and manorial revenues remained with locally based bishops, monasteries, and other institutions. Relatively little made it to the Pope and his court. Both clerical and lay hierarchies were disrupted by cross-cutting alliances between clerics and nobles. Many bishoprics and clerical Orders throughout Europe were under the control of noble families that had the de facto right to place their younger sons in clerical offices and who then siphoned off much of the income from those positions. Aristocratic clerics used the legal and political authority of their offices to insulate their noble-born families from interference by rivals. Locally dense links between clerics and aristocrats acted as firewalls against efforts by kings and rival elite families to assert authority over lay domains and clerical offices, guarding offices, lands, and revenues from appropriation and consolidation from above.[4]

Multiple elites and their cross-cutting hierarchies kept feudal class relations static and power decentralized. Efforts by landlords to deepen their control over land and/or the labor of their tenants were blocked by the competing interests of rival elites. Land tenure and peasant labor in much of Europe was regulated by multiple legal systems: the king's royal court, the regional courts of great aristocrats, manorial courts in which both seigneurs and tenants were represented, and clerical courts. Victory by king, noble, or local landlord in one court could be blocked in another venue. Peasants rarely had the resources to bring cases anywhere beyond the manorial court, but, when one elite's demands on peasants impacted the incomes and rights of rival elites, those other elites brought court cases to protect the status quo. Thus, even when and where peasants were disorganized and weak, landlords were usually unable to deepen their control because that would have undermined the income interests and political influence of rival elites, and those rival elites used their legal authority to prevent change.

Feudalism, then, was a more fragmented version of the decentralization we saw in the Roman and Chinese Empires. Where local privileges were protected in the Roman Empire by the bureaucratic weakness of the imperium and by civil property rights, local autonomy was actually institutionalized under feudalism by parallel legal systems, hierarchies of authority and privilege, and by multiple armed forces.

Max Weber ([1922] 1978: 1086) therefore was justified in describing feudalism as "a chronic condition," but he was wrong in attributing its stasis to Catholic theology. Catholicism mattered far more as an institution, with its courts, tithes, estates, and even armies, than as a belief system that counseled passive acceptance. Indeed, a very different ideological worldview coexisted with and supported feudalism in Japan. Structurally, Japanese feudalism was almost identical to that of Europe. Local landlords exploited peasant tenants and used the surplus they extracted to arm themselves and, in the case of larger landlords, bands of armed retainers. Regional blocs cross-cut hierarchies of nobles, and monasteries held land and regulated land tenure. Japanese monarchs were weak and, as in Europe, were rivaled and often overpowered militarily and politically by magnates who amalgamated local nobles into regional coalitions.[5]

Most Europeans and Japanese, like the inhabitants of the rest of the world, lived in rural villages until the eighteenth century. Urban Europeans, that is, residents of towns with at least 5,000 people, made up less than a tenth of the population in 1500 (de Vries 1984: 11). In Japan, only 5 percent of the population lived in cities of over 5,000 in 1600 (Farris 2006: 247–8). The other 90+ percent dealt almost exclusively with the local landlord and parish priest. Outside forces – kings, great nobles, high clerics – mattered mainly in their ability to weaken local lords' power over tenants. Most of the revenue collected by manor lords and parish priests stayed at the local level. Kings, great nobles, and high Church officials lived off their own estates more than from the revenues they were able to compel lesser lords and clerics to pass up to them. No outside force was able to force peasants to labor away from their homes on public works or in the military, or to enforce criminal laws. The Catholic Church's control over individuals' beliefs and behavior was limited. The medieval Church had almost no knowledge of their parishioners. We know how weak Catholicism's ideological hold over its parishioners and its parish priests was because the Church, following the conclusion of the Council of Trent in 1565, sent missions to study the state of religious practice through Western Europe in an effort to strengthen devotion and block further inroads by the Protestant Reformation. Church missions found that most Europeans practiced an ad hoc amalgam of Catholicism and pagan superstition. Priests claimed supernatural powers and used the sacraments to cure diseases, blessed cattle to increase fertility and milk production, and poured holy water on fields. A majority of priests couldn't recite the Lord's Prayer and were ignorant of most Church doctrine, which perhaps explained why many were found to be living with common-law wives.[6]

Rural Europe was an archipelago of isolated islands. Many villagers spoke languages or dialects that were unintelligible a few miles away (Robb 2007; Muchembled [1977] 1985). Most people spent their entire lives a few miles from where they had been born. News traveled slowly. Neither kings nor popes, nor great nobles and bishops, had much influence on how their nominal subjects worked, married, fought, thought, or prayed. When hunger, disease, flood, drought, fire, or invaders arrived, Europeans got no help, nor did they have any reason to expect help, from outside elites. Families, kin groups, and villages were largely on their own, and they provided few resources to elites who lived more than a day or two's walk from their homes. Feudal Europe and Japan

19

were constellations of weakly linked and largely autarkic villages. The small sizes and pathetic capacities of royal, clerical, and aristocratic courts were evidence of elites' narrow reaches into the hinterlands of their "dominions."

City-States and their Limits

The greatest concentrations of power and resources in Europe before the sixteenth century were found in cities. The largest cities in Europe in the fourteenth century were commercial centers in what are now Italy and Belgium. Paris and London were smaller than Venice or Florence. Paris became the largest city in Europe only in 1500 (Lachmann 2000: table 3.1), the moment when the French monarchs began to gain the capacity to extract revenues from throughout their kingdom.

City-states gained autonomy where they could take advantage of divisions among feudal elites. Urban wealth was a product of the economic backwardness of most of Europe. In other words, medieval and Renaissance cities were strong because everyone else in Europe was weak. The Italian peninsula, and especially Tuscany, was the site of the greatest elite divisions and conflict in Europe. French and Burgundian kings, popes and rival ecclesiastics, and German emperors fought each other for control over Italy. None of those monarchs had the armed force or the revenue base to mount a sustained campaign that could capture and hold Tuscany, not to mention the entire peninsula. As a result, Tuscan nobles were able to play competing invaders against one another and win recognition of their land rights with autonomy for their towns. Instead of the single and autarkic feudal lords that exercised power over small fiefdoms, power devolved in Tuscany upon corporate bodies of nobles and untitled families living in cities.

Towns gained autonomy elsewhere in Europe only when elite conflict intensified. Thus, Champagne fair towns gained concessions from the Counts of Champagne who were battling to maintain their independence from French kings and the papacy. When that conflict was resolved with the incorporation of Champagne into the kingdom of France in 1285, the fair towns lost their autonomy and merchants, despite their wealth, lost their privileges (Abu-Lughod 1989: 55–67). London and other English towns never gained autonomy since English kings and nobles divided control over territory with little conflict in the medieval era. Indeed, London and the other English towns were so weak, and their merchants so insignificant, that English kings granted most trade concessions to Italians (de Roover 1963: 71). This pattern held throughout Europe: where a single elite dominated the territory in which a town was located, the town and its merchants came under the noble, king, or bishop's domination and were relatively poor and powerless. Where elite conflict was intense and unresolved, urban nobles and merchants gained autonomy for themselves and their towns. That is why Poggi (1978: 36–42) is wrong to view urban autonomy as a grant from kings seeking to win financial support in their efforts to subdue the aristocracy. Towns won whatever power they had by defeating or outmaneuvering fragmented and conflicted feudal elites.

The ruling aristocracies of autonomous medieval towns were a feudal elite with a crucial difference. In addition to their fiefs (tiny urban neighborhoods and small rural estates), which they controlled as individual families, they also were part of collective bodies (their town governments). Urban nobles had to act collectively to block efforts by monarchs and great nobles to revoke their privileges. At the same time, noble families fought with one another for a greater share of urban offices and the revenues they yielded. Urban factions at times sought powerful external allies in their internecine struggles (for example, many Northern Italian factions claimed allegiance to the Pope or the German emperor), but that carried the risk of falling under the control of powerful overlords. More often, urban factions recruited allies from below, from among newly wealthy merchants and guildsmen. This created a far more dynamic politics than in rural Europe. Florence, along with Venice the richest and most powerful city in medieval Europe, was renowned for political intrigue. It probably is the place where ballot stuffing first was practiced. At the same time, the competition for allies created opportunities for

non-aristocrats and guildsmen to claim political rights (to vote
for some offices, to own and convey property, freedom of association and limited freedom of speech, access to courts in civil and
criminal cases) that were unprecedented for non-elites in ancient
or medieval Europe.

What did town officials do with their autonomy? First, they
schemed to protect the offices they controlled, and the revenues
those offices yielded, from rivals. Thus, urban politics in medieval
and Renaissance Europe was factionalized and was mainly about
electoral and armed battles for control over all or part of city
governments. Occasionally, a single faction achieved sustained
control over a city, or factions devised a long-lasting system for
rotating offices among families and alliances, and the city government acted with unity to project its interests. Thus, some cities
conquered limited agricultural areas beyond their walls, allowing
urban families to accumulate rural estates, which they exploited
much as rural aristocrats did.

More significantly, city merchants used their autonomy from
feudal polities to establish networks of trading offices beyond their
home territories. The Florentines became bankers for English kings
and exported English wool to generate revenues to service that
debt. Most lucratively, the Florentines leveraged their neutrality in
fourteenth-century Italian wars to assume the role of bankers to
the papacy. Florentines established offices across Western Europe.
(There even was a Florentine outpost in Krakow, Poland.) Venice
seized and negotiated for a constellation of forts and trading posts
in the Eastern Mediterranean.[7]

A new sort of polity began to emerge in the interstices of feudal
Europe. It did have a territorial base in an autonomous city, but it
also had limited sovereignty over territories distant from its home
city. Often its greatest powers were in control over trade routes
and flows of revenues rather than land. Florence, Venice, and
lesser city-states gained leverage over portions of other polities
by exploiting conflicts between nobles and the towns, kings and
aristocrats, and popes and bishops. Florence got the papal banking
concession because the Medici and a few other Florentine families
established links to popes looking for allies in their efforts to pry

revenues from dyads of bishops and the noble families to whom they were related.

City-states did well less because they were powerful than because kings, popes, and nobles were so weak. English kings' willingness to bank with Florentines rather than local financiers was a reflection of elite conflicts within England far more than Florentines' banking skills or stores of capital which, as the subsequent bankruptcies of both the English monarch and the bankers themselves made clear, were limited. Popes relied upon the Medici mainly as political allies, rather than as financiers. Indeed, the flow of revenues was from Pope to Medici, not the reverse.

Europe, of course, did not become a continent ruled by city-states. The glorious era of Florence and Venice ended quickly for two reasons. First, the resources that those city-states could mobilize, from their own citizens and from the outposts and networks they controlled, were limited. No city-state accumulated the armed forces or corps of officials needed to consolidate control over significant territories. The resources those cities did command were mobilized in ways similar to those of kings: through temporary and shifting alliances among leading families, and by acknowledging that those families enjoyed autonomous control over lands, offices, and their armed retainers. Whenever alliances within a city-state broke apart, the ability of that city's 'government' to project power externally was lost, and feuds and uprisings erupted within the city walls.

Second, each alliance between a city merchant, on the one hand, and a king or Pope, on the other, lasted only as long as both counterparts retained their positions. Feudal instability, as we have seen, led to frequent changes in monarchs. Even if a king retained his crown, uprisings or resistance by nobles and peasants could cut off a ruler's revenues, leading to both his bankruptcy and that of his bankers. Royal and papal finance was a risky business, and feudal warfare reverberated in fiscal crises and commercial depressions in the city-states, which in turn created political turmoil within those urban enclaves.

It was far safer, if somewhat less lucrative, for urban merchants to attempt to 'feudalize' their official and commercial positions.

The Medici and all their lesser imitators bought offices and rural estates, and increasingly confined their speculations to the bonds of their city-states. Such rational investments sapped the capital available for trade or the development of manufacture. As those merchants turned rentiers became more secure in their urban compounds and country houses, they sought to undercut the collective power of the urban commune, which threatened to regulate or challenge their familial interests.

City-states, therefore, never became viable sites for the accumulation of significant armed or administrative resources. Their declines largely preceded the rise of powerful states in Europe. How some isolated and underfinanced monarchs created the first consolidated polities in Europe since the fall of the Roman Empire is the subject of the next chapter.

2

The Origins of States

Europe, like the rest of the world, was highly decentralized at the outset of the fifteenth century. Political institutions either were localized, controlling groups or places of at most thousands of inhabitants, or were vast entities that asserted religious, cultural, and patrimonial claims over millions but in fact were able to command little of their subjects' incomes, labor, or attention. All the political entities we examined in the previous chapter – tribes, city-states, empires, and feudal kingdoms – were hampered by severe limits in their capacities to compel loyalty from either their agents or their subjects.

Those limits were transcended first in Europe, beginning in the sixteenth century, and with ever greater breadth and depth in subsequent centuries as political forms developed by Europeans were copied, adapted, and further transformed by politicians throughout the world. This chapter focuses on the origins of states. I examine the strategies rulers adopted to increase their power, and explore why formerly autonomous elites, communities, churches, towns, and families were compelled or enticed to bring ever more of their resources and powers within states.

State formation is a much studied and debated topic. Any plausible explanation needs to answer the following three questions:

1. How did states increase their control of the peoples and lands over which they claimed sovereignty? (the *methods* of state formation)

2. Who took the actions that made states more powerful? (the *actors* of state formation)
3. Why were states able to gain power in the sixteenth and subsequent centuries when they had failed to achieve those objectives previously? (the *timing* of state formation)

Existing theories differ in the answers they give to these questions. We can gain a sense of the theoretical fault lines surrounding research on state formation by seeing how key authors understand and address the questions of methods, actors, and timing. Let us review the most influential and incisive theories.

Weber

Marx and Weber set the contours of debate on state formation, much as they did in other realms of sociology. Both saw the emergence of modern states as by-products of other dynamics that are central to their general social models: for Marx, capitalist development; for Weber, the emergence of rational action in the Protestant Reformation. Remember that Weber saw feudalism and patrimonialism (of which absolutism was just a final manifestation) as "chronic conditions," incapable of being transformed through their own internal dynamics.

Weber begins *The Protestant Ethic and the Spirit of Capitalism* ([1916–17] 1958) by observing that capitalism, states, and sustained scientific advances emerged at the time of the Reformation and initially were concentrated in Protestant regions. Weber then offers an explanation for how Protestantism created a psychological shock that disrupted old ways of thinking and behaving, and ushered in modern social action.

Calvinism (and what Weber contends are the psychologically equivalent doctrines of Pietism, Methodism, and Baptism) created anxiety among believers over their eternal fates. Calvin challenged medieval Catholics' confidence that they could depend on the Church and its rituals and prescriptions to ensure salvation. Calvin's doctrine of predestination meant that neither any church nor one's actions in this life could affect God's judgment because everyone's fate was predetermined in God's eternal plan at the instant he created the universe.

Only the notion of the Calling, that God's plan included opportunities for the few who had been saved to serve and honor God, provided any relief to the anxiety created by belief in Calvin's doctrine of predestination. In their eagerness, which really was psychic desperation, to assure themselves they were among the elect, Protestants engaged in systematic work. To Freud, this is anal compulsive behavior, and it is no accident that Martin Luther found the "knowledge [of the doctrine of salvation through faith] the Holy Spirit gave me on the privy in the tower" (quoted in Brown 1959: 202). Weber calls this rational action, and in the economic realm it became capitalism, the systematic organization of production for regular markets to maximize profit in the long term. In the intellectual realm, this became science, carried out by trained specialists who engage in experimentation to develop comprehensive theories about the entire natural world. Theory-making extends to history (as in Marx and Weber's work), and even to theology. In the political realm, it led to the creation of bureaucratically organized states with a monopoly of legitimate authority in a defined territory, which is to say states.

Weber, thus, sees the increase in state capacity in the sixteenth century as a direct result of the Reformation. The creators of states were those Protestants who directed their psychic compulsion to fulfill their calling to the political realm. States, then, suddenly became more efficient at collecting taxes, mobilizing armed force, and administering territories. Once these new modes of political and economic action became established in a few places, people elsewhere in the world had to imitate capitalism and bureaucratic states. Those who failed to do so, presumably because their ethic did not foster rational action, were eliminated in economic competition with capitalists, or were conquered and absorbed or colonized by rival polities. That is what Weber means by the "iron cage." He recognized that Protestantism, like any other faith, quickly becomes routinized and loses its fervor. Once that happens, the rigors of geopolitical competition, not fear of Judgment Day, keep state rulers rational and their governments bureaucratic.

Sociologists and historians regard Weber's Protestant Ethic thesis very differently. The former, generally unschooled in early modern European history, take it at face value. It still is presented as valid in most sociology courses. In contrast, "all historians," writes Fernand Braudel, "have opposed this tenuous theory . . . it is clearly false" (1977: 65–6). The historians are correct. The problem with Weber's model is that political actors have diverged widely in how they understood their interests, approached their official duties, and organized their regimes to achieve control over their subjects and fend off rivals. Later authors have mined the history Weber didn't know or ignored to show the range of action Protestants pursued, and identified parallels between post-Reformation Catholic and Protestant capitalists and politicians. The Protestant calling inspired varied political programs, while European Catholics and Japanese Shinto-Buddhists pursued similar schemes of state-building, conquest, and imperialism.

Michael Walzer challenges Weber by noting that Puritanism "led to a fearful demand for economic restriction (and political control) rather than to entrepreneurial activities as Weber described it" (1965: 304). Mary Fulbrook (1983) found that English Puritans and German Pietists adopted economic and political ideologies only when, and to the extent that, their institutional freedoms were challenged by rulers. Christopher Hill (1972) shows that English Protestantism gave rise to a libertarian communism, as well as to a politically repressive and capitalist ideology. Hill traces how the ultimate political stance of each Puritan denomination was formed as its adherents struggled with rival sects and against the monarchy and Church of England. At the same time, the Catholic Church in France and some other parts of Europe found justification for bureaucratic rationality and capitalist enterprise by reinterpreting Catholic doctrine, while Catholic clerics elsewhere upheld pre-Reformation practices (Delumeau [1971] 1977).

In other words, the varied state forms that emerged in the centuries following the Reformation do not correlate directly with religious tenets. There is no single or necessary connection between religion, rationality, and state formation. Universal theories miss the variable and contingent nature of state formation. Weber's historical shortcomings are even more extreme in the work of sociologists, such as S. N. Eisenstadt who advocates "the search for equivalents of the Protestant ethic in non-Western societies" (1968: 17), and assumes they are to be found in the places that experienced the most rapid economic development and came the closest to European state forms. Eisenstadt's analysis is post hoc; he looks at the religions of successful "modernizers" and argues that they, like Protestantism, promoted "autonomy in the social, cultural, and political orders" (p. 14).

Weber's Protestantism and Eisenstadt's functional equivalents are reduced, in modernization theory, to a general "interest in material improvement" (Levy 1966: 746). Once Europeans demonstrated that such improvement could be achieved, people "will always seek to implement that interest if the opportunity seems afforded" (ibid.). The question of when and how such opportunity affords itself could be an entrée into the study of state formation, but, as Charles Tilly noted, modernization theory, with its notion of steady, orderly evolution, "seems unlikely to yield statements about the conditions under which a given political structure will disintegrate, stagnate, combine with others, or transform itself into a variety which had never been seen before" (1975: 615).

Tilly's critique of modernization theory can be applied with even greater force to the work of John Meyer.[1] Meyer claims that "in the West, since at least the seventeenth century, nation-states have claimed legitimacy in terms of largely common models; this commonality led them to copy each other more freely than is usual in systems of interdependent societies" (1997: 163). In other words, Meyer asserts that early modern European states were able to demand that subjects pay taxes, serve in the military, and obey laws by evoking a European (and in later centuries a world) culture that "allocates responsible and authoritative actorhood to nation-states" (p. 169). Meyer, and the amazingly large corps of students and followers who have signed on to develop his model, have little to say about how subjects who didn't hold state office and, as was discussed in the previous chapter, had almost no contact with such officials came to share this "world culture." As we will see in the next chapter, states were only partially successful in making demands on subjects in the seventeenth century, and the eighteenth and nineteenth centuries as well. Contrary to Meyer's notion of a world culture, states varied in the sorts of claims they were able to sustain and in the institutional mechanisms they employed to extract resources and obedience from their subjects.

Meyer and his followers are guilty of historical anachronism, as well as of constructing a universal and unidirectional model similar to the modernization theory that Tilly critiques. To the extent that Meyer et al. present empirical evidence, it is for the twentieth century, and focuses on the adoption by governments of practices and forms borrowed from the most successful states. This "institutional isomorphism" certainly plays a role in explaining why contemporary governments conduct censuses, adopt constitutions, join international agencies, establish ministries of education, and (at least until recently) all had a national airline as well as a flag. However, his claim that states' common culture allows for "greater penetration to the level of daily life" (p. 146) is not supported by the evidence he presents, which is confined entirely to showing commonalities among state symbols and organizational charts. In any case, his twentieth-century evidence cannot be used to claim that subjects regarded states as legitimate in earlier centuries.

That is why religious and cultural factors need to be examined as part of a more nuanced understanding of states. Philip Gorski (2003) assigns Calvinism a more limited role in state formation. In his analysis, Calvinism unleashes a desire for discipline, in the faithful themselves, and more vitally by the faithful as government officials over their subjects. States, in Gorski's model, become more effective and more ambitious in their plans to supervise and direct subjects, because of Calvinist doctrine. Gorski acknowledges that other Protestant denominations, and Catholicism, also fostered somewhat different and often lesser disciplinary impulses. Gorski doesn't offer a comprehensive model of state formation because, while he recognizes that religion interacts with institutional variables, he does not identify or analyze those non-cultural factors in a comprehensive way. Nevertheless, Gorski's work is a model for how to conceptualize the interaction of culture and structure.

Similarly, Eiko Ikegami (1995) traces how Japanese religion and samurai notions of honor were transformed as the samurai were incorporated into the developing Japanese state (and later into capitalist enterprises as well). Like Gorski, her goal is to explain cultural changes and show how they affect and interact with structural developments in state and economy. This is quite different from Eisenstadt, who sees Japanese religion as the "equivalent of the Protestant Ethic" (1968: 17), and therefore assumes it has a sudden and total effect on all aspects of Japanese behavior, thereby propelling a rapid transition to modernity in economy and polity.

Gorski and Ikegami show how religious reforms and cultural transformations can be specified and made part of a causal model of state formation. They provide a needed antidote to the universalistic and historically ignorant models offered by Weber himself, and by his successors, including Eisenstadt, Meyer, and modernization theorists. Yet, Gorski and Ikegami, in their necessary focus on culture, do not examine the organization and operation of states with the specificity needed for a comprehensive theory of state formation. Fortunately, all the other scholars who have addressed state formation, beginning with Marx himself, emphasize structural factors. We must now turn to those models, and evaluate their strengths and weaknesses, before we can formulate a theory that specifies the interactions among cultural meaning and structural interest that propelled political rulers and their subjects into states.

Marx

Marx views all states as instruments of dominant classes. While feudal states were manned by the aristocrat ruling class whose interests they guarded, capitalist states often though not always are run by managers who are not themselves capitalists. Marx and later Marxists offer a variety of explanations for how capitalists maintain control over non-capitalist state managers and have debated whether state rulers can achieve significant autonomy for themselves by playing classes and class fractions against one another. Marx at different times argued that the ruling class itself staffed the state, while in other works, most notably *The Eighteenth Brumaire of Louis Bonaparte* ([1852] 1963), he analyzed how splits among capitalist fractions and with remnants of the aristocracy provided an opening for Louis Bonaparte to achieve enough autonomy to become dictator and then emperor, at the expense of capitalists' civil liberties and even of their material interests. Marx is concerned with who runs the state, and in whose interests they act, and not much with how they come to acquire the resources and powers they deploy.

Marxist state theory recognizes that, as capitalism develops, capitalists come to rely ever more on the state to guard their property rights, control and train workers, reproduce the means and forces of production, and gain access to resources and markets throughout the world. Marxists contend that when capitalists see the need for a stronger state, they fairly unproblematically cede their direct powers to state managers, or to fellow capitalists who man state agencies. Thus, Marxists assume that whenever capitalists delegate power to the state, the state generally is able to accomplish the missions it is assigned by the ruling class, although neither Marx nor his successors identify the mechanisms through which capitalists' or capitalism's functional needs lead to changes in state capacities.[2]

Marx himself in *Capital*, and Lenin in *Imperialism: The Highest Stage of Capitalism* ([1917] 1996), noted that capitalists seek to surmount the internal contradictions of capitalism by seizing trade routes and colonies to expand the scale of exploitation to encompass the entire world. This insight has been developed most fully by world systems theorists, most notably Immanuel Wallerstein (1974–89) and Giovanni Arrighi (1994; 2007). They argue that a world system emerged during the seventeenth-century crisis. That economic and demographic crisis could not be resolved, as previous ones had, within the confines of feudal polities. Capitalists ceded power to political rulers organized into states, which they acknowledged as the superior authority in each territory, in return for recognition of their property rights and protection of commerce. Capitalists depended on states to guide and protect the key innovations that allowed the seventeenth-century and subsequent crises to be resolved: (1) the development of settler colonies beyond Europe; (2) slavery organized as a capitalist enterprise; and (3) economic nationalism which made national governments the main actors in the contest for colonies and trade networks. Each of those innovations allowed capitalism to expand in scope and to realize new opportunities for profit. Each of those innovations required ever stronger states to provide the legal regulation and military muscle to sustain those forms of capitalist exploitation. In this respect, world system theory is functional. When capitalists need stronger states, those states gain strength. Why some states do so, while others fail, is not analyzed, beyond pointing out that core regions have the strongest states. However, since core regions maintain their centrality through strategies that require strong states, this argument becomes tautological. Similarly, peripheral states appear to be weak from the perspective of residents of the periphery. However, from the perspective of the entire world system, and of the core capitalists who reap the greatest profits, peripheral states function very well at facilitating exploitation of labor and resources in the periphery and the flow of profits to the core.

Despite world systems theory's contribution to understanding how states with different capacities contribute to the division of labor, profit, and power in the capitalist world system, this model has little to say about how those different states, especially the strongest ones in early modern Europe, were established and amassed the powers that facilitated capitalism at home and imperialism abroad. Instead we are left with a series of unanswered questions. How did capitalists decide to surrender powers to states? Did all capitalists understand the necessity of that concession and, if not, how did some capitalists convince or force others to go along? How did state rulers come to make it their mission to further the interests of their local capitalists, and in the case of peripheral states, of capitalists from core regions? In chapter 4 we will analyze state managers' efforts to affect economic development and examine whether and when states and their rulers or citizens have enough autonomy and capacity to move their territories from periphery to core or vice versa.

A different thread of Marxism, concerned with the transition from feudalism to capitalism, does address the original formation of states. In their analysis of how capitalists gained power and property at the expense of aristocrats, Marxists offer answers to questions such as who strengthened states, how they accomplished that, and why this occurred first in sixteenth-century Europe.

The most sophisticated Marxist analysis of how class struggle affected state formation is that of Perry Anderson. His *Lineages of the Absolutist State* (1974b) situates the origins of states in the crisis that followed the Black Death of the fourteenth century. Feudal lords in the wake of that demographic catastrophe were no longer able to control peasants at the local level. "The result was a displacement of political-legal coercion upwards towards a centralized, militarized summit – the Absolutist state. Diluted at village level, it became concentrated at national level" (p. 19). Even though "for many individual nobles" absolutism "signified indignity or ruin, against which they rebelled" (p. 47), "no feudal ruling class could afford to jettison the advances achieved by Absolutism, which were the expression of profound historical necessities" (p. 54). Aristocrats, in Anderson's view, had no choice but to remain loyal to absolutist monarchies upon which they depended for the power and legal legitimacy necessary to extract resources from peasants. That is why no European aristocracy "ever was wholly or mainly won to the cause of revolt" (p. 54).

How did localized aristocrats first go about reorganizing themselves into absolutist states? Anderson suggests, without offering much historical detail, that nobles ceded power to a leading aristocrat, often one who already held the nominal title of king, who organized a collective military response to rebellious peasants. Aristocrats united into an absolutist state were able to extract more resources from peasants than isolated nobles ever had. As a result, the collective capacity of the aristocracy increased.

Absolutist states at first were strong only in comparison to isolated feudal nobles. Just a few of these monarchies developed into states with substantial capacities in the sixteenth century. How and why did they do so? Anderson's answer centers on the development of a bourgeoisie, which he presents as the inadvertent outcome of absolutist state policies designed by aristocrats to safeguard their collective interests. Where a bourgeoisie formed, states became more powerful. Both state and capital grew and profited from the monetization of taxes and rents, the sale of state offices, and the establishment of protected monopolies domestically and of colonial ventures abroad. Anderson explains the different trajectories of Eastern and Western European states and between England and France in terms of the strength of aristocrats' organization within estates, the extent of town autonomy, and the results of military competition.

Even though European bourgeoisies were able to coexist and prosper under absolutism, those monarchies, in Anderson's model, were governments of, by, and for the aristocracy. In this Anderson differs from Charles Tilly and Michael Mann (discussed below) who view absolutist state rulers as self-interested and willing to work with any class as long as it helped them to aggrandize state power. Anderson also differs from Engels in *The Origin of the Family, Private Property and the State* ([1884] 1972) and Marx himself in *The German Ideology* ([1846] 1970) and from Poulantzas ([1968] 1975), who contend that absolutist monarchies played off equally powerful aristocracies and bourgeoisies against one another. That argument suffers from the inability to explain where such strong bourgeoisies come from, a problem Anderson solves by showing their slow emergence as a privileged though subordinate class under absolutism.

Anderson's great accomplishment is to explain why states developed in Europe when they did, in the centuries following the Black Death, and to identify actors – feudal aristocracies engaged in a self-directed reorganization to re-establish control over peasants – as the mechanism of state formation. Anderson's shortcoming is that he is unable to account for the subsequent bourgeois revolutions in seventeenth-century Britain, and in France in 1789, that transformed absolutism into much more powerful modern states.

35

Anderson's reliance on broad Marxist class categories – aristocracy, peasantry, and bourgeoisie – leaves him unable to explain why bourgeoisie and aristocratic interests became opposed. The sites of bourgeois class formation he identifies – state offices, autonomous towns, Crown monopolies, manufacture, foreign trade – also were inhabited by aristocrats. How can we impute different class identities to occupants of the same sites? What factors allow us to know when actors realign their interests away from those of the states that once privileged them?

Anderson never addresses those questions directly. Readers of *Lineages* never learn how distinctions among aristocratic and bourgeois actors and their interests could be made within or across states. Anderson suggests that differences among class fractions created political tensions within states, but never works out how that led to revolutionary conflict. Instead we are treated to summary sentences at the end of the British and French chapters which merely assert that "[t]he aristocratic reaction against Absolutism [in France] . . . passed into the bourgeois revolution that overthrew it" (pp. 111–12), or "English Absolutism was brought to crisis by aristocratic particularism and clannic desperation on the periphery: forces that lay historically behind it. But it was felled at the centre by a commercialized gentry, a capitalist city, a commoner artisanate and yeomanry: forces pushing beyond it. Before it could reach the age of maturity, English Absolutism was cut off by a bourgeois revolution" (p. 142).[3]

Anderson's analysis falls short because he is unable to specify the agents who strengthened absolutist states. His commitment to Marxist categories prevents him from seeing the crucial divisions between actors who occupied the same class positions but who, by virtue of the offices they held, were parts of different elites. As we will see at the end of this chapter, elite and class conflict interacted to transform states and to create capitalism. When even the most historically informed and theoretically sophisticated Marxist analysis can't account for the development of some absolutist monarchies into more robust and complex states, we need to look beyond a pure class analysis.

The Fiscal-Military Model

The dominant sociological model of state formation, developed by Charles Tilly, breaks with Marxism in seeing state officials as self-interested rather than as agents of a class. Tilly seeks to explain why from "something like 500 states, would-be states, statelets, and statelike organizations" in 1490, Europe's polities consolidated into "a mere 25 to 28 states" by 1990 (Tilly 1990: 42–3 and passim). Note that Tilly takes the Marxist problem of how power was transferred from feudal lords to states and reframes it as a question of consolidation from many small polities into a few large ones.

In Tilly's model, the initiative is with rulers rather than capitalists. Some early modern European monarchs managed to defeat rivals, absorbed their territories, and "empowered existing, relatively autonomous local and regional authorities to collect taxes, gather troops, administer justice, and maintain order on their behalf" (Tilly 2004: 49). Successful rulers made deals that gathered more capital (which could be used to buy weapons and to hire mercenaries and administrators) and more coercion (armed men) to their side than neighboring polities, which they then defeated. Rulers' success depended partly on their political skills in building alliances and winning support from rich and powerful subjects, but more decisively was determined by the relative concentrations of capital and coercion which rulers found in their territories and which varied across Europe. At first, the advantage lay with capital rich polities. Mercenaries could be mobilized more quickly, and were better armed, than bands of feudal retainers. In the sixteenth century, "the increasing scale of war and the knitting together of the European state system . . . gave the warmaking advantage to those states that could field great standing armies; states having access to a combination of large rural populations, capitalists, and relatively commercialized economies won out" (Tilly 1990: 58). As a result, dominance passed to states that combined capital and coercion, most notably France and Britain.

The fiscal-military model sees state formation as path dependent. States, once launched on their particular trajectories, are not diverted by later contingent events. The initial deals rulers struck with capital or coercion-controlling subjects shaped the organization of each state and its ultimate success in defeating and absorbing rivals, as well as its capacity to suppress subjects' tax strikes or rebellions. Other scholars follow a similar path-dependent logic while giving emphasis to different factors than Tilly. Ertman (1997) distinguishes states along two dimensions: their absolutist or constitutional political regimes, and their patrimonial or bureaucratic state structures. He argues that states became embedded in their typological cell when they were drawn into geopolitical competition; thus the timing of their entry into European wars is crucial. Ertman's argument in this regard parallels Wallerstein's (1974–89) contention that states' characters and their class relations become fixed at the moment when they are incorporated into the world system. Similarly, Porter (1994) and Downing (1992) argue that wars forced rulers to reach accommodations with subjects that then set the future social and political arrangements of each state.

Tilly (1990, 2004), much more than Ertman, Porter and Downing, emphasizes how slowly and with what difficulty states established bureaucracies that bypassed the estates, corporations, venal officeholders, autonomous towns, and other privileged intermediaries between rulers and subjects. Even when states gained the organizational capacities to deal directly with subjects, their political systems still were shaped by the initial mixes of capital and coercion and by the political deals that marked their emergence.

Tilly's focus on resources and political alliances is a studied and successful effort to avoid engagement with Max Weber's emphasis on Protestantism. Tilly manages to avoid cultural factors and still offer a clear answer to the two questions of who initiated state formation and how they amassed power for themselves. Tilly's actors are self-interested rulers, who gained territory and power through divide-and-conquer strategies, coopting some elites, and then used the men and resources those new allies provided to intimidate and defeat others. Tilly, and Downing and Porter as well, are less clear on why rulers were able to increase the size and resources of their kingdoms in the sixteenth century when their predecessors failed

to do so in earlier centuries. Tilly suggests that new military technologies made conquest easier, an argument developed by some
military historians. In particular, they point to the development
of more powerful artillery, which could knock down castle walls,
making it impossible for nobles to resist royal forces. However,
such artillery was quickly countered with the *trace italienne*,
stronger fortifications that could withstand artillery.[4] Such walls
enabled Italian, Spanish and French Huguenot cities, and the
entire Dutch Republic to resist Spanish and French royal armies.

Most cities and provincial elites took a different path and
decided to tie their fates to states rather than seek to guard their
autonomy with forts and private armies. We then are left with the
question of why various elites made, or were forced into, different political decisions in the sixteenth and subsequent centuries,
some maintaining autonomy while others sought position and
privilege within states. Tilly's model traces the consequences of
those choices, but he does not really explain how states enticed or
compelled elites to abandon military and political independence.
Ertman rightly points to "representative institutions," the collective bodies of nobles, clerics, and wealthy townsmen, as key sites
at which monarchs either enticed those local notables to subordinate themselves to the state or where elite resistance was organized
and mobilized. Unfortunately, Ertman doesn't develop that insight
(one raised by numerous historians in their narratives of particular conflicts in individual countries) into a model of how and
when elites decided to resist or submit. Thus, Ertman, – like Tilly,
Downing, and Porter – doesn't really take us inside the workings
of those early modern states in formation, nor into the collective
minds and maneuvers of once formerly autonomous elites.

Poggi (1978) argues that feudal estates and autonomous towns
were weakened from within rather than subdued by kings through
armed force. As the scale of war increased, neither towns nor aristocrats could afford to purchase the new sorts of arms and field
the larger forces needed to compete. Medieval forms of military
training and combat became obsolete and nobles either had to
retire from combat or enlist in royal armies as officers. Nobles
and towns, no longer able to defend themselves, were especially

terrified by the religious wars that erupted with the Reformation, and Poggi claims they looked to kings as adjudicators of sectarian conflict. Kings, in Poggi's view, further enticed towns and estates to surrender their autonomy by promulgating uniform national laws that guarded both urban merchants' commercial interests and aristocrats' privileges. Poggi ignores towns and estates' massive resistance to such royal efforts to usurp their powers. Instead, Poggi believes that aristocrats were eager to become passive rentiers and state officeholders, and therefore were willing to convert their positions as members of estates into mere tax exemptions and privileges, "enjoying them exclusively as components of patrimonies" while surrendering "the ability to initiate collective action" (p. 68).

The fiscal-military model offers a plausible account of the seeming centralization of fiscal resources and military power within states at the expense of taxpayers, draftees, and self-sufficient communities. However, it leaves much unexplained because it makes the mistake of reifying states and assuming that all revenues collected by state officials were used for ends desired by the monarch. In fact, absolutist states and their successors were diffuse entities, staffed by multiple elites with different and often opposed interests, each often capable of withholding resources from other "state" officials. Armies didn't fight in unison. Until the late eighteenth century, military officers – almost all of whom inherited or bought their positions – commanded armed men and ships with a high degree of autonomy, ignoring orders from their nominal superiors when they preferred not to fight or rejected their monarch's military plans, or saw an opportunity to enrich themselves through looting or piracy. That is why there is so little relation between the size of a state's budget and its ability to conquer territories within Europe or colonies in the rest of the world. The richest power of each era (Spain, from the 1560s to the 1600s, and France, from the 1630s to 1789) did not add territories during most of its years of fiscal supremacy, and the powers that accumulated territories (the Netherlands and then Britain) as often as not had smaller budgets than rivals who failed to add to their holdings or lost lands to poorer powers.

National budgets, whose growth is the key indicator in the fiscal-military model, are as poor predictors of domestic state capacity as they are of military success. Much of the "state revenues" measured by scholars of fiscal history never made it to the central treasury. Not only were provinces and towns given high levels of autonomy and immunity from taxes in return for nominal allegiance to the monarch, but many provincial officials were able to keep the tax revenues they did collect in the state's name. As a result, the biggest or most populous territories, or the ones with the largest budgets, often were less able than smaller or poorer states to increase their capacity to tax subjects and enforce laws, just as they were less successful in adding to their territories.

State capacities and domains didn't expand gradually but rather in sudden jerks. States did not advance on a single path, unimpeded. State capacities were lost in some instances. State formation was contingent and reversible. We need a more nuanced theory to explain what happened within states and how deals were constructed with non-state elites. We need a theory that can open up states and look within them to see how state rulers made decisions and how resources and authority were divided up among the factions that vied for power. We also need to see state formation as a series of contingent events, not as a path – whether of universal modernization or a set of divergent developments – molded just by world position or pre-modern heritage. Important insights come from two directions: rational choice theory and Michael Mann's theory of power.

Rational Choice

Rational choice theorists bring an element of contingency to the fiscal-military model's relentless interaction of bureaucratization and war as propellants of fiscal growth. The key contributors to this strain of scholarship – Kiser and his collaborators, Rosenthal, and Greif – differ from Tilly in their analysis of how rulers and subjects choose whether to use cooperation or confrontation in their respective efforts to increase or minimize taxation. Rulers weigh the benefits of increasing taxes, which could finance potentially profitable wars, with the risk that subjects might rebel. Taxpayers can choose whether to submit to higher taxes, use bribery or subterfuge to reduce their personal tax burdens, or engage in collective action to roll back tax increases.

Rulers' and subjects' decisions on whether to cooperate or fight were based on their (often inadequate) information about "the anticipated reactions of other actors" (Kiser and Linton 2002: 889). Past experience guided decisions. If a ruler was successful in raising taxes in the past, he was likely to try again when he wanted or needed to fight the next war. Subjects evaded taxes if the ruler's agents lacked the information to calculate the tax burden, or enough personnel to collect what was due. As kings built bureaucracies capable of gathering such information, subjects then had to either pay what was demanded or rebel. Bureaucratization spurred rebellion.

Failure resulted in learning. Kiser and Linton (2002) describe repeated or catastrophic failures as "hinges of history," which forced actors to change strategies and led states down different paths of state formation. Successful revolts led kings to scale back tax demands or, in extreme cases, to recognize representative institutions. Thus, episodes like the Great Revolt of 1381 in England "defined the limits of taxation (specifically, an invasive tax like the poll tax would not be tolerated)" (p. 906). Conversely, the Spanish Crown's ability to crush the Communeros revolt of 1520–1 taught subjects that the costs of rebellion were too high and the odds of success too low. "After that point, the Cortes was marginalized, administrative centralization and taxes increased, but there were no more revolts in Castile against the power of the crown" (p. 906). French tax revolts achieved mixed results, until the Frondes of 1648–53. After the Crown's victory in that rebellion, the largest until the 1789 Revolution, French subjects resigned themselves to rising taxes. Rebellions abruptly fell off, even as taxes began a sustained rise.

Rosenthal (1998) describes England and the Netherlands, polities where king and elite[5] learned to cooperate, as parliamentary, and Spain and France, where king and subjects continued to

42

struggle over war and taxes, as absolutist. Key rebellions, in this model, were moments of contingent structural change, transforming relations between kings and subjects, and altering the subsequent forms of state development. However, once actors adopted their post-rebellion strategies, states were then launched on paths from which they never diverged.

Rosenthal tracks Kiser and Linton (2002) in describing the benefits, for both kings and subjects, in agreeing to cooperate in setting tax rates and collecting revenues. Such agreements lowered the costs of tax collection, ensuring that more of the taxes subjects paid ended up in the hands of the state rather than being lost to corruption. Such relatively non-corrupt polities were seen by creditors as safer places to make loans, reducing interest rates.

Rational choice theorists argue that agreements on the levels of taxes often extended, at least implicitly, to the decision of whether or not to go to war and also to how the spoils of war were to be divided. Both king and elite could, potentially, benefit from pooling their resources to fight wars that would take territories or trade routes from rival polities. The elite hesitated to contribute its resources because it feared that the king would monopolize the spoils of war. When the king and elite agreed on rules that gave the elite a say in the decision to start a war, and in the distribution of the spoils of war, then the elite was more willing to approve taxes and also to loosen restrictions that preserved elite control over the economy. Elite economic controls retarded economic growth and so when such controls were loosened the economy grew, making it easier for the polity to afford wars.

Cooperation between kings and subjects over taxes and wars increased domestic tranquility as well. When parliaments approved wars, or at least the tax increases needed to pay for wars, rebellions and tax evasion were less likely. Kiser and Linton (2002) note that even in "absolutist" France, rebellions were less likely when the Estates General or provincial estates voted in favor of war taxes, and also when wars were "defensive" responses to foreign attacks rather than "offensive" wars to take new territories.

The rational choice model suffers from an inability to explain why actors learn from some rebellions, or from some rival polities' military victories or bureaucratic innovations, but not in other similar instances. Kiser and Linton (2002) offer no clear criteria to identify turning points. Learning is not explained; it merely is posited from otherwise unexplained changes in behavior. "[T]hese events can rarely, if ever, be predicted, but they can be recognized by their consequences after the fact" (p. 893). Further, Kiser and Linton (2002) are not always clear on what is learned and by whom. They note "the aftermath of the Fronde was marked not just by repression but by concessions and co-option as well" (p. 897), but don't explain why the Crown learned to make concessions after it was supposedly so successful at repression. In fact, the Crown practiced repression on some elites and made concessions to others, but because Kiser and Rosenthal build their analyses on highly simplified games, with a monolithic elite or "taxpayers" facing off against a unified monarchy, they are unable to explain why actors adopted divergent strategies. As a result, they can't account for strategic decisions that resulted in a decline in state fiscal capacities; indeed, such declines are not addressed in their work. For Rosenthal, parliamentary and absolutist are descriptive terms. He is unable to explain why some states went down one path and not the other.

The main contribution of rational choice theory is that it recognizes that rulers and those outside of states had choices, and therefore examines the strategic thinking of the actors who vied for power in the centuries during which rulers drew elites and their resources into states. As with the other theories we have considered, rational choice is weakest on the problem of timing. It has nothing to say about why the rules of the game changed in the sixteenth and seventeenth centuries, nor why elites, which previously refused to cooperate with their nominal rulers, became more willing to surrender money and power to a central political institution.

Michael Mann's Theory of Power

The theories we have examined so far regard power as fungible: money can be used to hire armed men, and armed men can be used to extort taxes. Political office can be used to control peasants and workers, and control over land and labor can be parlayed into governmental position. In fact, as many of these authors recognize when they write in detail about specific historical cases (though not in their general theories), the exchange of money, military might, and office is not at all seamless. Power won at one site often cannot be redeployed elsewhere. Subordinates who follow, or submit to, a leader's dictates in one sphere may not accept direction in another realm. Tilly, in his contrast between coercion-rich and capital-rich states, recognizes differences in two forms of power, but he uses that distinction mainly to draw comparisons *between* polities in order to explain why states that win wars in one era lose in later centuries. We need a more comprehensive theory to explain how power-holders *within* a territory amalgamated their different forms of power into states in some parts of Europe in the sixteenth century, but not elsewhere and not in earlier centuries.

Michael Mann makes a huge contribution to such a theory when he recognizes that "societies are not unitary," but instead "are constituted of multiple overlapping and intersecting sociospatial networks of power . . . A general account of societies, their structure, and their history can best be given in terms of the interrelations of what I will call the four sources of social power: ideological, economic, military, and political" (1986: 1–2). As Mann traces the exercise of power from ancient Mesopotamia to the beginning of the twentieth century (we looked at his analysis of ancient civilizations and the Roman Empire in the previous chapter), he attempts to explain how political rulers institutionalized their power, and how they interacted with other power-holders whose sources of power were located in different places and varied in the mix and volume of ideological legitimacy, productive resources, armed force, and administrative organization they combined.

Mann's key insight is that social change occurs in the "interstices" of the institutions in which power is held and exercised. Changes in the distribution of one type of power affects the other three types as well. In other words, when one power-holder manages to coopt or seize the power resources of others, the entire character of a society changes. Power-holders can find that their ability to dominate subordinates or to apply their power within a territory is newly constrained by transfers of power among others in which they did not directly participate.

Mann, in the final chapters of the first volume of *The Sources of Social Power*, uses that general insight to trace the formation of states in Europe. He shows how political, economic, and military power in medieval Europe was decentralized among feudal manors and in the territories dominated by great nobles. At the same time, ideological power was held by the Catholic Church, whose power in that realm encompassed all of Western Europe.

Mann traces the British state's growing revenues and military might as archetypal of the reorganization of power in Europe. He argues that less territorially centralized polities, such as the Duchy of Burgundy, could not mobilize the force needed to defend itself from the new centralized states like England or the Paris-based French monarch. Mann, like Tilly, sees the growing budget of the British monarchy, and the military power it bought, as the prime measure of state formation. Like Anderson, Mann believes that aristocrats had to join the newly strengthening states, even at the cost of their political and military power, to maintain their economic power over peasants. Mann contends that aristocrats' depoliticization smoothed the way for capitalists to gain state protection of their property rights and thereby furthered capitalist development. Where aristocrats had been weakened and capitalists were strong, kings took a constitutional path, granting capitalists parliamentary representation in return for higher taxes. Where aristocrats hadn't been sufficiently depoliticized, kings were more absolutist, granting powers to various corporate bodies in an effort to undermine the still powerful landed magnates. Thus Mann, unlike the rational choice theorists, has an answer to why states became parliamentary or absolutist. Yet that merely pushes the problem back in time. He doesn't explain how or why aristocrats in some parts of Europe but not others were depoliticized and, for that reason, he can't account for why states developed when and where they did.

Like the fiscal-military model, Mann sees the state as a unitary entity, assuming that the entire British budget (and presumably those of other states) was at the disposal of the king, either alone or with the consent of a parliament. Similarly, he sees the Catholic Church as a single hierarchical organization, able to propagate Christianity as a consistent ideology throughout Europe. He ignores the very different theology and organizational structure of Orthodox Christianity in Eastern Europe, and he exaggerates Catholicism's capacity to produce cultural uniformity across and within countries. Mann misses Catholicism's actual influence on European politics because he doesn't follow the logic of his overall model and examine Catholic Church officials as power-holders who interact with other holders of political, military, and economic power.

Mann's model analyzes the structure of power without identifying the mechanisms by which actors exercised power. For that reason, Mann is right to acknowledge that "perhaps too much functionalism pervades" parts of his discussion of state formation (1986: 430). He makes an important contribution by showing how the reordering of one set of power relations (between state and Church, among aristocrats, or between capitalists and state) affects the entire social structure. But a full theory of state formation requires that we identify the actors who seized each type of power and specify how they accomplished that at each moment of transformation. That in turn will make it possible to explain why state formation began in the sixteenth century, rather than earlier or later, and in parts of Western Europe and not elsewhere.

Elite Conflict and State Formation

Power, as Marx and Mann in different ways make clear, is relational. The efficacy of an actor's military, economic, organizational, or cultural resources varies as the structural position of the actors holding those resources changes. We have seen that reducing actors to classes (as the Marxists do), or to state and taxpayers (as both Tilly and rational choice theory do), fails to capture the actual relations among power-holders and the masses they dominate, and therefore prevents us from tracing the often multi-step and contingent paths that transformed decentralized political power into states.

Power-holders in medieval Europe, as elsewhere in the premodern world, controlled institutions that exerted political power and simultaneously were imbricated in economic production. Feudal manors were political and economic institutions that gave their lords military power and ideological legitimacy as well. The Church was the largest manor lord in much of Europe. Lay and clerical lords constituted rival elites, which jostled each other for resources and authority while trying to fend off demands by kings and aristocratic magnates for control over their lands and the peasants they exploited.

If manor lords, magnates, kings, and clerics all exercised a mix of economic and political power, combined with varying degrees of military force and ideological legitimacy, how can we differentiate one elite from another? The answer is that each elite inhabited a distinct organizational apparatus with the capacity to appropriate resources from non-elites (Lachmann 2000: ch. 1). According to this definition, elites are similar to ruling classes in that both live by exploiting producing classes. However, elites differ from ruling classes in two significant ways. First, although in Marx's theoretical framework the fundamental interest of the ruling class is to reproduce its exploitative relation vis-à-vis the producing class, in the elite conflict model this interest is complemented by an equally vital interest in extending its power with respect to rival elites. Second, each elite's capacity to pursue its interests derives from the structure of relations among various coexisting elites as much as from inter-class relations of production. Elite conflict is the primary threat to elite capacities; yet the interests each elite seeks to defend are grounded in their relations with the producing classes. Elite *capacities* change primarily when the structure of elite *relations* changes.

Elite institutions assert a combination of economic, political, military, and ideological powers as they seek to guard their interests against both rival elites and the non-elites from whom they extract resources. Aristocratic, clerical, provincial, and urban institutions in early modern Europe made juridical and fiscal claims similar to those of the "state" headed by a monarch. All the authors we examined above assume that when rival elites were defeated, or incorporated into states headed by monarchs, the resources they formerly controlled were available for geopolitical aims set by rulers (in some cases in consultation with parliaments). In fact, control over resources within states cannot be assumed; it needs to be the object of analysis. Just as rival elite institutions can challenge and work at cross-purposes to "rulers," so can elites incorporated within states retain powers and resources from their old organizational bases and seek to appropriate state resources for their own benefit. Let us see how elite conflict played out in Europe, and how it shaped the early development of states that for a long time remained arenas in which multiple elites jostled for resources and power. Once we acknowledge and analyze this historical reality, we will be able to see how states formed and gained capacity as elites combined or were forced into a unified polity.

The Reformation transformed the "chronic condition" of feudal elite and class relations, but not in the way that Weber believed. As we saw earlier in this chapter, the historical evidence does not support Weber's claim that Protestantism compelled rational action, which, in turn, bureaucratized states. What the Reformation did do was to disrupt elite relations, setting in train a series of elite and class conflicts that played out differently across sixteenth-century Western Europe and led to the formation of various types of states in some parts of the continent but not others. Let us trace out the sequences of elite conflict and structural transformation in the four countries that became the main contenders for geopolitical dominance in Europe and later the greatest colonial powers: Spain, France, the Netherlands, and Britain. I will then compare those four path-setters with Russia and the weaker states of Eastern Europe and the autonomous development of the Japanese state, and finally draw general conclusions about the process of state formation.

Spain

Spain's initial state formation was similar to the pattern of territorial consolidation in empires: Castilian kings "reconquered"

Muslim lands. Then Ferdinand and Isabella were the lucky inheritors of multiple crowns from childless relations, creating the largest polity in Europe after Russia. The Habsburgs, like medieval kings and emperors before them, commanded armies that were too small to subdue their domains, and corps of paid officials that were far too few to govern them. How then did Castilian kings maintain control over all of Spain, as well as Portugal, and the Italian, Burgundian, German, Flemish, and Dutch territories that they inherited or conquered in the sixteenth century?[6]

The Habsburgs enlisted mainly aristocratic allies in each of their Iberian territories by offering those nobles total exemption from all direct taxes. As a result, the full burden of taxes was borne by peasants and by towns, which were subordinated to the aristocracies of their provinces. The Church provided an additional source of revenue as popes ceded control over clerical offices and properties to Habsburg rulers in return for the rulers' support of papal foreign-policy objectives. Popes offered unprecedented concessions to the Habsburgs and other secular allies because the Reformation had opened the Catholic Church to challenge from Protestant rulers, aristocrats, towns, and common people in much of Europe. Thus, the Reformation mattered – even in entirely Catholic Iberia – because it altered the continental balance of forces, which led popes to surrender Church powers within securely Catholic lands in order to enlist Habsburg help in recovering ground in Protestant areas.

The feudal pattern of shared sovereignty and divided jurisdiction over land tenure and peasant labor was replaced with rule by unitary elites in each Spanish province. The Habsburgs extended to their other European dominions their policy of trading local political and fiscal autonomy for fealty to the Crown. The transformation in elite relations was less extreme in those lands than in Iberia. Aristocracies gained at the expense of clerics, and towns lost some of their autonomous rights; however, the institutional bases of rival elites survived Habsburg sovereignty albeit in weakened form.

At first, aristocrats were the major beneficiaries of their alliance with the Habsburgs. Nobles gained full control over peasants and over the administrative apparatus of their provinces, no longer having to share sovereignty and control over land and peasant labor with clerics and town merchants. Aristocratic hegemony in Spanish provinces made for a weak central state which was prone to fiscal crises, as aristocrats became ever more successful at preventing the Habsburgs from circumventing nobles and taxing rural production or urban commerce directly. Spain's land and naval forces were controlled by provincial nobilities and could rarely be mobilized to fight abroad, forcing the Habsburgs to rely on mercenaries, even as elite control over revenues created a constant fiscal crisis and spiraling debt.

Yet aristocrats' provincial autonomy depended on provision by the Habsburg rulers of, first, legal recognition and, second, armed assistance at times of peasant rebellions. In that way, Spanish aristocrats became part of a state. Aristocrats were further incorporated within the state as purchasers of venal offices and investors in state bonds. Even aristocracies in the Habsburg holdings beyond Spain benefited from the legal privileges granted by the monarch. That is why most of the empire remained intact long after Spain lost the capacity to vie for European or global dominance. Indeed, the American independence movements were sparked by Spain's late eighteenth-century efforts to increase control over American elites, not by Spain's two-centuries-old military weakness (Mahoney and vom Hau 2005; Lynch 1989: 329–74).

Aristocrats' imbrication within the Spanish state did little for the Habsburgs' continental ambitions. With limited revenues, and multiple strategic interests, Habsburg forces were almost constantly committed on multiple fronts. As a result, the Habsburgs conquered virtually no new territory after their burst of consolidation in the sixteenth century, and then progressively lost almost all of their non-Spanish European holdings. Their conquest of much of the Americas brought ever less revenue to the metropole, as Spanish-American elites established control over land, mines, and Indian labor while Spanish armed forces and administrative resources were committed in Europe.

Yet, as the Habsburgs' imperial holdings and ambitions fell

away, their core Spanish polity became ever more state-like. Aristocrats' control over land and labor became ever more mediated through royal edicts and offices; their status and income derived as much from offices and state pensions and bonds as from titles and estates. Even though the state was the site for competition among aristocratic factions divided by province and political networks, the entire ruling class was drawn within the state in the sixteenth and seventeenth centuries and remained there afterwards. The state was the terrain for conflicts over power and resources at the same time as it was the object of the entire ruling class's plans for self-preservation and familial betterment. As aristocrats joined the king in bringing their powers and assets within the state, they came to share an interest in strengthening their collective capacity through the state for taxing and controlling the mass of Spanish subjects. Spanish elites still came into conflict over the division of state authority and spoils, but after the sixteenth century those disputes were within a polity of defined borders and a legitimacy then accepted by all elites.

France

Catholicism remained the dominant faith in France. Yet the Reformation did spark conflict between Catholic and Protestant, and then among Catholic lay elites desiring to hold or seize the institutional assets of the Catholic Church. That elite conflict created an opening for French kings, who previously had only weak control over the duchies and independent territories which had been claimed for France by the fifteenth century, to pursue a strategy of "vertical absolutism" (Lachmann 2000: 99–102, 118–46). Rather than empowering a single elite in each territory, French kings played off rival elites against one another, granting powers and offices in return for payments. The sale of such venal offices subverted the capacities of great nobles to mobilize lesser elites to challenge the Crown on the national level. Venality created new paths of surplus extraction as each new office was endowed with the authority to extract revenues from peasants or from commerce distinct from existing seigneurial rights.[7]

Vertical absolutism created a dynamic that was almost the inverse of that under the Habsburgs. While Spanish rulers ceded local power and revenues to elites in return for recognition of Habsburg sovereignty, French kings extracted revenues from competing elites eager for royal support in their competitions for provincial authority. By 1633, half of all Crown revenues were derived from the sale of venal offices, and from the *paulette*, an annual fee paid by incumbent officeholders in return for royal recognition of their right to resell or bequeath their venal posts.

The Crown's strategy of vertical absolutism, and the new revenues it produced, were self-limiting. Each office sold created a permanent obligation to divert a particular stream of revenue to the officeholder. Each new office also undercut the authority and revenues of existing offices. The Crown created a small corps of non-venal Intendants in an effort to exert more control over venal officials and the "state" revenues they collected. That, combined with provincial officials' anger at the continuing sale of new offices, sparked off the Frondes, the last significant armed challenge to the French Crown until 1789.

The Frondes demonstrated that vertical absolutism was a successful political strategy for the Crown, even though it limited the amount of control French kings had over revenues. The Frondes encompassed both challenges by nobles and officeholders to the Crown and peasant rebellions directed against seigneurs as well as against taxes. Regardless of the source of peasant discontent or the target of their anger, officeholders and seigneurs were far more vulnerable during the Frondes than was the Crown. Overlapping jurisdictions and conflict among venal officials made them an inviting target for peasant and urban rebels. When venal officials challenged royal authority they also were undermining the legitimacy of their own positions, which were based upon royal grants of "privileges which were subject to differing interpretations and which were defined in reference to the king" (Beik 1985: 219). As a result, provincial seigneurs and officeholders were forced to abort their rebellion, appealing to the Crown for aid in suppressing peasant uprisings. Elites learned from their failure in the Frondes that they had lost the capacity to act independently of the state of which they now were a part and from which they now derived their legitimacy and much of their incomes.

The Netherlands

The Netherlands' political structure was forged in its decades-long war for independence against its Spanish occupiers. The Netherlands had never had feudal agrarian relations and the paucity of elites (few nobles, a weak clergy, and hardly any state officials) short-circuited opportunities for factional conflict. The Netherlands had been a highly decentralized collection of towns and rural hinterlands, brought together only on the basis of Protestant opposition to Habsburg rule and the Catholic repression Spain enforced. Without the Reformation, there would not have been a Dutch revolt and therefore no state. A single dominant elite of urban merchants led the anti-Habsburg rebellion.[8]

Once the Spanish were removed, urban merchants fortified their control over the newly independent towns and provinces, and prevented challenges from upstarts, through Contracts of Correspondence which created a system for rotating offices and dividing the profits from trade routes and merchant companies among elite families. The system also prevented the sort of competition among multiple elites that was rife in France. Nor were there significant challenges from Dutch non-elites in those centuries.

The Contracts of Correspondence, and the overarching constitutional agreements among Dutch cities and provinces, became the basis of a Dutch state, the United Provinces. The rigid protections each Dutch elite secured for itself against potential rivals permanently weakened the central state, ensuring the Republic's defeat at the hands of a poorer and initially less well-equipped Britain. The Dutch Republic never was able to achieve central control over patrimonial officers in the various separate armies and navies maintained by each province. The progress of the Dutch state as an expanding fiscal and bureaucratic entity, and its capacity to compete internationally in trade and war, was sapped by elite tendencies to pursue their own interests and preserve their existing

positions even at the unintended and partially unforeseen consequence of long-term competitive decline.

Britain

The Reformation almost entirely eliminated the Catholic Church
as a distinct institution in England. Yet the Henrician Reformation
did not simply allow the tiny royal government to absorb all the
Catholic clergy's powers and properties. Instead, the Crown, with
only a few dozen officials directly under its control, and dependent
on nobles to collect taxes and provide armed men, was forced to
collaborate with lay landlords in expropriating the property and
powers of the Catholic Church. This transformed the previous
tripartite elite structure of Crown, lay landlords, and clerics into
a dual elite structure in which the Crown was unchallenged at
the national level, while the gentry gained full control over land,
peasant labor, and county and local politics. Henry VIII and his
successors were able to use their national-level hegemony to break
the military and political power of the landed magnates, creating
a monopoly on the legitimate use of armed force in England and
later in all of Britain. In this way, the English dual-elite structure
diverged from that of Spain. The Reformation gave the English
Crown the resources to break the magnates and devolve landlord
power down to the local level, in contrast to Spain where the lack
of a Reformation meant that the Habsburgs had to reach a settlement with each province's aristocracy as a bloc, foreclosing the
possibility of challenging the greatest Spanish nobles.[9]

English kings, despite their safety from national-level military
or political challenges, never were able to escape from their alliance with lay landlords. Unable to create a bureaucracy, kings
continued to rely on largely unpaid local officeholders who served
their own private interests and were controlled by county political
blocs. Unable to play clergy and laity against one another in parliament after most clerics were purged from their seats, the Crown
found it increasingly hard to control the county blocs, which by
the eighteenth century had coalesced into two national parties.
The seventeenth-century Civil War and Glorious Revolution

demonstrated the limits of royal power and kings' narrow room for autonomous action. All royal initiatives, whether to increase taxes, pass legislation, or fight wars, required consent from the Members of Parliament who represented the interests of the dominant elite of county-based landowners, and later of merchants organized into guilds and chartered companies and represented through city governments. The British state remained an amalgam of elites, each with its own institutional base for wielding economic and political power, and with strong ideological legitimacy, well into the nineteenth century. Yet, in conclusively limiting royal power, the Civil War and Glorious Revolution confirmed that national institutions, above all parliament, were the sites at which property rights and political authority were allocated and protected.

Russia and Eastern Europe

Weak kings initiated the sequences of elite conflict that allowed for state formation in Western Europe. Kings were able to do so because the Reformation set in motion a struggle for former clerical properties and powers in Britain, a scramble to protect or seize Catholic holdings in France, geopolitical fissures which the Habsburgs exploited in Spain and beyond, and popular agitation for religious and political autonomy against Catholic rule in the Netherlands.[10]

The absence of a Reformation meant that the Orthodox Church, or – in Poland and Central Europe – an unchallenged Catholic Church, didn't need to surrender resources or ally with the Crown to protect its interests. Kings were symbolic figureheads recruited from abroad (Poland), or elected by aristocrats (Hungary and Bohemia), or heirs to local dynasties, and all were weak. Nobilities were highly decentralized. "Complex chains of rear-vassalage or sub-infeudation were effectively unknown . . . the result was that vertical feudal solidarity was much weaker than in the West" (Anderson 1974b: 223). This meant that great lords were unable to consolidate blocs of supporters to begin the process of concentrating coercion and taking territory from weaker neighbors, as Tilly (1990) posits.

Unlike in the West, the initiative for change came from decentralized aristocrats. As Anderson correctly argues, Eastern nobles had to reorganize themselves within states to maintain their capacity to control and exploit peasants in the wake of the Black Death. Peasants took advantage of the resulting labor shortage by fleeing onerous work and rent obligations for vacant lands further east, or to the estates of other lords who offered better terms. The abandoned lords lacked either aristocrat allies or enough military muscle of their own to hold or recover their missing tenants. At the same time as their capacity to exploit peasants was undermined, lords were threatened by invasion. Successive waves of attackers came from the Khanates of Central Asia, the Tartars and Ottomans in the South, and Sweden in the North. Decentralized aristocrats were unable to mobilize and coordinate enough force to repel the invaders.

The solution to both threats – fleeing peasants and invading armies – was the same. Small, defenseless nobles banded together to fight off attackers. The larger a noble conglomeration became, the more likely it was to defeat and absorb smaller neighbors. Individual nobles, thus, had an overwhelming incentive to join one of these states-in-formation, agreeing to join the "service nobility," that is, to commit themselves to spending their entire adulthood as a military officer or administrator at the service of the state, in return for protection from foreign invaders.

State formation in Eastern Europe thus followed a different trajectory from that predicted by the fiscal-military model. It was not a gradual process in which rulers of small territories amassed modest amounts of coercion, which they then used to conquer a neighboring polity. If that had been the case, Eastern Europe would have been comprised of numerous small states that would have been consolidated only after a long series of wars, as was the case to the West. Nor was it just a response to foreign invasion. If that had been the case, Eastern nobles would have coalesced into states centuries earlier and spared themselves from being repeatedly overrun and looted by invaders. Instead, the pattern fits Anderson's model. Only when they were faced with class extinction after the peasants fled did nobles surrender their autonomy and combine their power within large states. The initiative did not come from ambitious rulers; in fact, as we noted above, Poland had a powerless king, in others the king was elected, and in the rest was weak.

The newly formed states were first instruments of class control: without peasants, there cannot be lords. Yet, once nobles were consolidated within states, it became possible to form armies large enough to repel invaders and then to conquer new lands, even though those states were objectively weaker than their counterparts in the West, as measured in revenues, administrative reach, or bureaucratization, and evidenced in their military confrontations with Western powers. The Grand Duchy of Muscovy became a kingdom and eventually the largest state (in terms of land mass) in the world. How did Russia do it?

Russia and the states of Eastern Europe were quite different from any of those in the West we examined earlier because the room for elite and class conflict was far narrower in the East. Only a small portion of the Eastern population lived in cities, and the level of commerce was pitiable. Merchants played virtually no role in politics. Clerics were secure in their positions and in control over their estates, but excluded from interfering on lay manors and from playing any role in the state. Peasants were pressed into serfdom, and all manors were under the exclusive control of a lay or clerical lord, or the king. There was none of the division of authority or the overlapping legal systems that fragmented control over land and labor in the West. The two elites in the East, nobles and clerics, were almost totally compartmentalized in the institutions of rule and surplus extraction they inhabited.

As aristocrats came together in states, the bases for conflicts within that elite were eliminated. Categories and ranks of nobility were abolished or became merely symbolic as aristocrats all entered the same state service. Nobles seeking to advance themselves competed for high office in the military, civilian administration, or at court. "Nobles henceforth intrigued within the Autocracy, not against it" (Anderson 1974b: 342). Court factions did not have regional or status bases, and therefore could not draw upon allies outside the state, or create divisions that affected class relations or state rule. Even as individual nobles fought for office, they shared an interest in expanding the state's capacity to appropriate resources from civil society. Thus, the nobility backed Catherine II's push to appropriate Church holdings, weakening the clergy as a separate elite. The state's land holdings expanded, until it owned 40 percent of Russian serfs, who then could be conscripted into the army. Nobles, in turn, gained the right to move serfs among their land holdings or to sell them and their labor to other land-holders. Czar and nobility, joined within the state, collectively augmented their control of peasant labor and of clerical lands during the eighteenth century, gains that were not achieved by their decentralized predecessors in earlier centuries.

State formation in Russia and much of Eastern Europe was a process of aristocratic reorganization, both against the peasantry as Anderson argues, and against themselves by eliminating opportunities for nobles to create factions or form alliances with other elites outside of the state. That process was possible because tight regional elites, or factions that spanned provinces or linked up with clerics or urban merchants, did not exist and so no elite was in a position to block state formation.

Poland and Hungary provide a negative demonstration of how elite structure determined the strength and form of emergent states. The Polish and Hungarian aristocracies were tightly organized on the regional level and re-enserfed peasants in the fourteenth century through provincial armed forces that were controlled entirely by local nobles. Kings were elected by Diets, parliaments totally controlled by nobles, which ensured that kings never would be able to challenge aristocrats' local power. These tightly organized regional elites even survived foreign conquest. Hungary came under Turkish and then Habsburg control. Poland was partly conquered by Germans in the fourteenth century. Hungarian and Polish nobles kept their control over peasants and over local government even while under foreign rule. Indeed, Polish nobles continued re-enserfing peasants even as they were being conquered by Germans. The foreign conquerors had hardly more leverage over, or entrée into, provinces controlled by tight local elites than did the Polish or Hungarian kings and their courts. Only in the eighteenth century – when Poland was partitioned among Russia, Prussia, and Austria, and the Polish state lost even its nominal existence – did the conquering powers begin to disrupt local aristocratic power and succeed in levying taxes. State formation was incomplete in Poland and Hungary, even as aristocratic class rule was strengthened, because local elites were tightly organized, as well as being free from challenges by other elites. Weak states were vulnerable to foreign conquest, but that was of little consequence for nobles who sustained their local political and class power over centuries.

Japan

Feudal Japan, as we saw in the previous chapter, was cross-cut by various overlapping elites. The Emperor and the rival shogun both sought to gain advantage over each other by granting lands they had seized in battle to samurai retainers. The shogun's bakufu government was more powerful than the imperial regime, but both their efforts were limited because hereditary lords (daimyo) controlled a majority of land in Japan, which they defended with their own corps of samurai to whom they had granted subfiefs. Clerics derived revenues from their own feudal estates and fielded their own armed forces to protect those domains.[11]

The key moment of state formation came under Hideyoshi, in the second half of the sixteenth century. Hideyoshi was neither emperor nor shogun. Rather, he built a coalition among many daimyo and samurai, which endured for over two centuries (from 1603 to 1868) under the Tokugawa shoguns. Hideyoshi drew support from elites desperate to suppress peasant rebellions. Thus, Japanese state formation at first resembled that of Eastern Europe: diffuse factions of the landed lay elite coming together into a state to preserve their class position against peasants. As in Eastern Europe, peasants were more deeply exploited, and were disarmed, as well as being legally banned from leaving the land or entering into trade or professions. Similarly, samurai spent increasing time in the service of the bakufu government or, in regions where daimyo had a high level of autonomy, to their lord. Samurai were tamed, partly in an ideological and cultural process as Ikegami (1995) describes, and partly because their income came from funds that the bakufu or daimyo administrations appropriated directly from peasants and then allocated centrally to samurai who had become their employees. Samurai then devoted more of their time to administration rather than military training and combat, and lost any rights to, or control over, specific plots of land. Similarly, daimyo spent more of their year at court – pursuing lucrative positions, maneuvering for power, and enjoying the high life of the capital – much as provincial elites did in France.

Tokugawa elite consolidation advantaged the daimyo, high state officials, and some samurai. Trade increasingly was dominated by the daimyo, who controlled towns. Formerly autonomous towns, which had thrived as intermediaries between battling daimyo, now were increasingly marginalized as daimyo and shogun domains became settled. Similarly, daimyo and shogun were able to disarm the clergy and appropriate their lands.

Elite conflict became internal to the state as shogun and daimyo battled for court position and revenues. When those conflicts climaxed in the Meiji Restoration that eliminated the shogun and removed most daimyo from power, those defeated elites were unable to counter-attack. The samurai who once were their political and military base had, during the centuries of Tokugawa state formation, been integrated into a central administration.

The new Meiji government took radical steps that enhanced state power: abolishing feudal fiefs, granting equal citizenship to all Japanese males, and giving the state direct control over capital investment, which it used to foster industry and to forge a massive national military. Those reforms were possible because any elites that could have had the interest or capacity to oppose those policies had been brought within the state (samurai and merchants), or, if they retained autonomy at the end of the Tokugawa era (the daimyo), were left without allies to mount a meaningful challenge to the central state. Once all elites were within the state, they could adopt policies that enhanced Japan's geopolitical and economic position because all elites benefited from those developments.

How States are Made

I'd rather have him inside the tent pissing out than outside pissing in.
US President Lyndon Johnson

Johnson's explanation of why he gave his political enemies positions within his administration reveals the essence of state formation. States were not for the most part created by eliminating enemies on the battlefield, or by sending bureaucrats or soldiers from a capital to tax and control the hinterland. States came into existence when elites and their organizational capacities were combined into a single institution. All the states we examined, in Western and Eastern Europe and Japan, were not created because a king succeeded in using force to make elites and subjects surrender resources to him. Rather, they were instances of elites centralizing themselves. They did so for a range of reasons; state formation often had multiple motives. Elites came together:

- to appropriate the powers and assets of other elites (England, France, Spain);
- to enhance control over peasants (Japan, Russia, and Eastern Europe);
- to protect themselves against foreign invaders (Russia, Eastern Europe, the Netherlands).

Once elites found themselves together in a single state institution they used their new capacities for a variety of ends:

- to exert new controls over peasant labor (Spain, Britain, Japan, Eastern Europe);
- to launch wars against foreigners and to seize colonies (Britain, France, Spain, the Netherlands, Russia);
- to extract revenues from towns (Spain, Russia and Eastern Europe, Japan) and from clerics (Spain, Russia, Japan).

We need to be careful to distinguish between the motives and conflicts that brought elites together in states, and the opportunities and new conflicts that were contingent outcomes of the original melding of elites into states. State formation was not anywhere a single project of aggrandizing rulers. Rather, it was the inadvertent by-product of multiple elites coming together to gain leverage in their conflicts against other elites and peasants. Each victory in elite conflict created a new constellation of elite relations, often altered agrarian class relations, and defined the terrain for the next round of elite conflict.

Amidst all the historical particularities of each case, we can identify some general relationships between the structure of elite relations and the sorts of states that formed. The most crucial factor was the degree of autonomy that manor lords sustained in their ability to extract a surplus from peasants. Where lords were the sole extractors of surplus and regulators of peasant production on their estates – as in most of Eastern Europe, Russia, and Japan – the state was under the control of that single elite. State power was vested in the collective hands of the landed elite – not through representative institutions or through the provisions of a constitution, but through nobles' occupation of military and administrative offices. Over time, factionalism became centered on control of state offices and resources, rather than about the struggles for land and aristocratic rank that had dominated pre-state feudal politics. Clerical and merchant elites in such polities lost their autonomy and were forced to surrender an ever greater share of their land and income to the state. As nobles focused their attention on, and derived ever more of their wealth and status from, state office, kings gained the opportunity to manipulate aristocratic factions. Out of such manipulations kings increased the power of the court in relation to all elites and won growing autonomy, which they could then use to increase state capacity.

In Western Europe, by contrast, multiple elites sustained their own institutions that were capable of regulating land tenure and extracting resources from peasants. States were formed out of such complex feudal politics only when one elite was able to defeat and appropriate powers from another elite. How that happened varied among Spain, France, the Netherlands, and Britain. However, in all four cases, the Protestant Reformation set in train a series of events that transformed elite relations. In England, the effect was most direct, with the king and lay landlords joining to eliminate the clergy as an independent elite and to divide its powers. The dual-elite structure that resulted determined the form of the British state. In France, the Reformation was incomplete, but it sparked inter- and intra-elite conflict. All elites sought to bolster their positions by taking state offices. This gave the French Crown the power of manipulation, but also limited the ways in which kings could use their new authority and revenues since the state now included other elites, which held permanent claims on the revenues and powers of their offices.

The Reformation had an indirect effect in Spain and the Netherlands. The Pope's need for allies in the Catholic war with Protestantism, gave the Spanish Crown leverage over the Catholic clergy. Combined with Habsburg intervention in elite conflicts in its newly acquired territories, the elite structure of Spain became more like that of Eastern Europe, with single elites in each province. Habsburg power came from its ability to bring resources from one territory to intervene in another component of its empire. But such geopolitical leverage was difficult to accomplish and unsustainably expensive in struggles against the single dominant elites in each territory. Similarly, unitary elites emerge in each Dutch province in the struggle against Habsburg rule; yet, as with their former ruler, power in one province could not be applied to subordinate the ruling elite in the next province.

States were artifacts of elite conflict. The form of each state derived from the structure of elite relations that existed in pre-state feudal societies. The clergy mattered for state formation less as carriers of an ideology than as power-holders. They did not just exercise ideological power as Mann contends, but all four forms of power. Clerics shaped the state mainly through their position in the overall structure of elite relations. Where they were vulnerable to appropriation by rival feudal elites, above all in England, their defeat and absorption cast the relationship of the remaining elites that formed the state. Where the clergy were highly autonomous – as in Japan, Eastern Europe, and the Netherlands – they played little role in state formation, even if they were later subdued by the elites unified within the state. In France and Spain, their role was more complex, as clerical powers were partly appropriated by multiple elites even as they retained enough autonomy to shape future elite conflicts. For this reason, past theories that ignore the clergy entirely cannot explain the varying trajectories of state formation.[12]

Feudal elite conflict resulted in the formation of a variety of states. Despite their differences, they all met Weber's definition of a state. All these states achieved a monopoly on the legitimate use of force in a territory, even though they at first accomplished that mainly by admitting other holders of armed force into the state. Increasingly, the rights of all elites and of non-elites came to be defined by the state and in relation to the state itself. How states went about doing that defining, and what rights and obligations they each sought and succeeded in imposing on their subjects, is the topic of the next chapter on nationalism and also of the following chapters, which examine state economic and social welfare policies, and the advent of democracy.

3

Nations and Citizens

All my life I have thought of France in a certain way.
　　　　　　　Charles de Gaulle ([1954] 1955: 3)

But especially the people;
That's America to me.
　　　　　　　Abel Meeropol, lyrics, "The House I Live In" (1943)

Once elites came together within unified polities, they began to develop a common interest in expanding their states' capacities to appropriate resources, to enlist subjects in wars, and to foster a sense of national identity that could create and deepen loyalty to the state. As subjects were compelled or enticed to serve the state, they came to see themselves as citizens and in turn made demands on the state for civil rights and social benefits, and to participate in political decisions.

States and the territories they controlled became more than a set of institutional arrangements within recognized borders. Officials and citizens increasingly identified themselves in national terms and justified their political desires by evoking national ideals and interests. The quotes from Charles de Gaulle and Abel Meeropol both express a sense of nation. For de Gaulle, his idea of France led him to a military career and leadership of the Free French resistance to the Nazi occupation. Indeed, the line quoted above begins his three-volume memoir of "the War Years." De Gaulle's "certain way" is one of collective devotion to nation, exemplified by the willingness to fight and die for France. Meeropol, a New York City high-school teacher, composer, and lyricist (and adoptive father of the orphaned sons of Julius and Ethel Rosenberg), wrote "The House I Live In" for a short film, starring Frank Sinatra, which was produced and shown in the last year of World War II. The lyrics include images of everyday life in America, interlaced with Meeropol's vision of national ideals and aspirations: "democracy . . . all races and religions . . . the right to speak my mind out . . . the dream that's been a growing for a hundred-fifty years . . . my neighbors black and white, the people who just came here . . . the tasks that still remain . . . a land of wealth and beauty, with enough for all to share . . . and it belongs to fighting people." Meeropol's fighting people are not the soldiers of de Gaulle's memoirs, but rather those who struggle for freedom, justice, and equality within the United States. The contrast between de Gaulle's and Meeropol's nations is not just the difference of France and the United States, or even of a conservative and a leftist politics, but between the nationalism of a General, Prime Minister, and future President and that of a teacher and writer who sees himself as part of the working class.

These contrasting visions of national mission and destiny were formed within states, and they shaped and motivated the elites and classes that struggled to control national resources and direct them to further their interests and ideals. This chapter traces how state rulers and subjects developed national identities and fought over the obligations, rights, and meaning of citizenship. I begin by focusing on the two most crucial state capacities: the ability to collect revenues and to enlist soldiers. I then look at how those efforts to mobilize money and men fostered nationalism, which, in turn, led to the creation of national cultures. My attention in this chapter is on the decisions made by state elites and their successes and failures in achieving their ends. State action, of course, provoked and interacted with capitalist development and with popular demands for democratic participation and social benefits, which are the topics of later chapters.

Money

When elites came together into states they brought with them their capacities to extract revenues from the rural villages, urban communes, clerical benefices, and trading concessions that they controlled. Elites tried to maintain their control over local communities even after they were incorporated within the state. A town official, landlord, or cleric might have had some idea of the relative income or wealth of individuals and families under their control, but that information was not conveyed to central state administrators. Often, local elites had neither the right nor the capacity to track the income or assets of their subjects, and instead collected dues based on long-standing formulas that became increasingly distant from subjects' current ability to pay taxes. In either case, states received revenues from communities, through the elites they had incorporated, rather than from individual subjects.

Kings and their closest allies, who were becoming a self-interested state elite, sought to gain a greater share of the revenues appropriated by local elites, while local elites in turn attempted to shield their appropriations from such centralizing demands. At the same time, local elites continued to try to extract more resources from the subjects under their control, and the state elite schemed to establish their own mechanisms for bypassing local elites and directly taxing subjects. Subjects, of course, continually resisted the demands of both state and local elites by forcibly rebelling against taxes, quietly evading taxes, or negotiating with one elite in an effort to win an ally against the demands of other elites.

Most tax revenues were encumbered: the elites that collected those revenues maintained control over their disposition even though they had become "state" revenues. As a result, much of the state budget went to the salaries of venal officials, commissions for tax farmers, pensions, and interest payments, or was dedicated to specific entities or tasks designated by the elite that collected the revenues. Once elites had claimed the revenues under their control, little was left to fund military or domestic projects initiated by kings or legislative bodies. Kings financed wars almost entirely by selling offices or through loans, which then became future obligations to venal officials and financiers.

State elites thus faced two problems: increasing overall receipts and gaining control of the revenues that were collected by other elites. This, ultimately, was a political rather than administrative problem. European rulers long knew how to assess property and compile that information. The Norman rulers of England had enough leverage over their recently conquered subjects to conduct the Domesday survey in 1086, listing landholdings and numbers of livestock. That survey was used by weaker kings to allocate taxes in England for centuries to come. Medieval Italian city-states were able to assess both the fixed (land, buildings) and moveable (ships, commercial goods, gold, jewels, crops) wealth of their residents, most notably in the Florentine *catasto* of 1427 (Herlihy and Klapisch-Zuber 1978). Where rulers failed to get such information, it was because subjects resisted providing it and rulers had neither the personnel nor the political leverage to demand it. So how did rulers manage to find and tax revenue on their own and move beyond the stagnant base of income they derived from their dynastic landholdings? We will answer this question first, and then examine how states gained control of the revenues collected by other elites.

Long-distance trade, and the merchants who conducted it, were the most vulnerable to the demands and enticements of central rulers. In much of Western Europe, and many Asian polities, merchants and towns were outside the control of landed elites, allowing rulers to demand tariffs without significant interference from rival elites. Conversely, as in Russia and Eastern Europe, and Spain after the Habsburgs created their alliances with single elites, local aristocracies controlled towns and so rulers had little entrée and tariff revenues remained low. Elsewhere, elites competed for control over towns and trade by offering charters that granted political and commercial freedoms in return for tariffs. Rulers took advantage of situations where local elites contested one another's jurisdiction to assert authority and grant town charters. Once towns had such royal recognition, they had an interest in sustaining royal authority and blocking efforts by rival elites to reclaim control. Chartered towns became the primary source of royal revenues that could not be appropriated or diverted by rival elites.

Merchants' main leverage against rulers and their tariff demands was flight. They could and did move to other polities where rulers were willing to settle for lower tariff rates in return for the higher volume of trade that arriving merchants would bring. Merchants in the medieval and Renaissance eras enjoyed the most autonomy in the independent city-states of Italy. The concentration of merchants and trade there allowed city-states to compete fiscally and militarily with much larger kingdoms. City-states were the main nodes of trade in Europe until the sixteenth century, and therefore the sites where tariffs could most easily be collected. Trading cities also had the greatest concentrations of individuals with cash incomes and "moveable" assets that could be seized for non-payment of taxes. City-states developed the capacity to assess residents' wealth, and, while they did not levy either income or wealth taxes, they did require citizens to buy government bonds in proportion to their assessed wealth (Lane 1973; Mohlo 1971; Butters 1985). As independent cities were conquered, and as ever larger kingdoms sponsored their own commercial centers which rivaled and eventually supplanted Florence, Venice, and Genoa, trade and tariff revenues shifted to the Netherlands, France, and England.

Tariffs remained the only national tax in most of the world until the nineteenth century. It was the largest source of Federal revenue in the United States until the beginning of World War I. Indeed, tariffs remained the principal revenue source for many third world states in the twentieth century. That is why demands by the International Monetary Fund and the World Trade Organization that states foster "free trade" by reducing tariffs have had such devastating effects on government budgets, and hence on states' abilities to fund education and health care, in so much of the third world since the 1980s.

Tariffs provided a limited and, in time of war insufficient, source of independent revenues for rulers. Nevertheless, the vast bulk of national income remained beyond the reach of central states as other, mainly landed, elites maintained control of the revenues they extracted, and local communities remained closed to the inquiries and demands of central governments. As with tariffs, the main block to state taxation efforts remained political. States could not expand their revenues until they found a way to break the autonomy of elites and communities.

States first gained leverage to collect taxes on land, or on the sale of commodities such as salt, through the practice of tax farming. Financiers would advance money to states in return for the right to collect land and sales taxes in part or all of the kingdom. Kings, in granting tax collection rights to financiers, were creating a new elite, one with national reach. Some members of old elites who invested in tax farms, or bought venal rights to collect taxes, became simultaneously members of the new, state-created, elite, thereby undermining the unity of the old provincial elites.

The size of the new elite expanded further as financiers established their own corps of tax collectors, sometimes on salary, more often by leasing sub-farms, that is, the right to collect that tax in part of the territory where the main tax farm had been granted by the state. The salaried employees and sub-farmers often were recruited from the ranks of landlords, clerics, or urban merchants, adding to the numbers of those whose income and status were derived from royal grants of tax farms.

The revenues realized from tax farms did not increase steadily. Rather, there were sudden jumps in tax receipts when kings succeeded in weakening or eliminating an elite. Tax revenues also fell when elites succeeded in coming together to resist state efforts to appropriate local revenues (Kiser and Linton 2002). In the sixteenth century, France and then Spain collected the most revenues among European states. In the two hundred years from 1515 to 1720, state revenues rose 1,365 percent in Britain, 275 percent in France, 808 percent in the Netherlands, and 182 percent in Spain. By 1720, France was the clear leader among those states, collecting as much as the other three combined, which by 1720 enjoyed roughly equal revenues. Then, in the century from 1720 to 1815, British revenues rose 980 percent, French 190 percent, Dutch 40 percent, and Spanish not at all. Britain became the richest state in

Europe, having been far poorer than the other three in 1515, with France a close second and the other two far behind (Lachmann 2009: table 1).

Spain's fiscal stagnation was due to the Habsburgs' state formation strategy, which we discussed in the previous chapter. Once single elites were ceded exclusive control over a province, there was no leverage to introduce tax farmers. In the Netherlands, tax collection was highly efficient since merchant elites controlled each town and province, but those elites collectively agreed to tax increases or cuts depending on their support for the United Provinces' military ventures, which caused state revenues to fluctuate and eventually stagnate just as the Dutch conflict with the British for European and colonial hegemony reached its peak. French taxes rose in spurts as provincial elites were weakened or incorporated within venal bodies of tax collectors. Britain's dramatic increase in taxes followed the resolution of Crown–gentry conflicts in the Civil War and Glorious Revolution, creating enough elite unity through parliament to support and implement tax increases during wartimes and the professionalization of the Treasury and then of tax collection throughout the kingdom (Kiser and Kane 2001), even as the gentry were able to keep the rate of the land tax low throughout the eighteenth century, fobbing most tax increases onto consumers through tariffs (O'Brien 1988). The 1789 Revolution, in sweeping away many local elites, spurred a similar expansion and professionalization of central tax authority in France. As a result, Britain and France both were able to drastically increase tax collection during the Napoleonic Wars, during which Britain became the first European state to institute an income tax that assessed and taxed individuals.[1] Japan's Meiji Restoration (discussed in the previous chapter) eliminated provincial elites' ability to oppose the central government's land tax reform. Once that political realignment occurred, the new central government was quickly able to assess all agricultural land in Japan and to impose a uniform land tax, vastly increasing state revenues at the expense of weakened landlords rather than peasants (Yamamura 1986).

As autonomous provincial and urban elites were weakened or defeated in revolutions and civil wars, or linked with state elites through chains of political realignments, more revenues came under the control of the central state at the expense of ordinary subjects as well as elites. Peasants and workers found it more difficult to resist taxes when elites were unified since most rebellions took advantage of elite divisions on the local or national levels. Thus, as elites unified within states, tax rebellions declined dramatically in the seventeenth century and largely disappeared in the eighteenth century. Peasants and workers then avoided taxes only to the extent that they could hide their income and wealth from authorities (Charlesworth 1983; Lemarchand 1990; Vovelle 1993; Tilly 1995a). Such avoidance was most successful where peasants, artisans, or other non-elites were tied together by kinship, trade relations, religion, or on other structural or ideological bases into what Charles Tilly (2005) calls "trust networks." Tilly argues that trust networks weaken and lose efficacy as members are drawn out of tight communities by proletarianization. Proletarians face risks that the old networks are unable to address, and the sheer number of landless migrants cannot be accommodated in locally based trust networks. This provides the basis for an accommodation between the state and its subjects. As subjects offer their resources and lives to the state, they come to see themselves as citizens, and states needing those resources offer ever greater inducements, most importantly social welfare benefits and political rights, including the democratic franchise, to win subjects' acquiescence to taxes and conscription. We will examine citizens' struggles for benefits and rights in the next chapter.

The relationship between elites and subjects is dynamic. Where elites combine in states and their own conflicts decrease, subjects become more vulnerable to state demands, even when they have not yet been proletarianized. As states become more capable at extracting resources from subjects, multiple elites have an ever greater interest in insinuating themselves into the state to share in those revenues. Elite unity and subjects' vulnerability combined to produce dramatic increases in governmental revenues in the nineteenth and twentieth centuries in centralized nation-states.

Britain established an income tax during the Napoleonic Wars as an emergency measure, as did both the United States and the Confederacy during their Civil War. Britain reinstituted the income tax in 1842, supposedly as a temporary measure to raise revenues for war, but the tax was never repealed (Sabine 1966); other European nations established it in the 1890s, and most of the rest during World War I to help finance their military costs. The United States' income tax became permanent in 1913. Income taxes, along with corporate income taxes, value added or national sales taxes, and dedicated payroll taxes for old-age pensions and health care led to a dramatic increase in government revenues in the twentieth century. Before World War I, the revenues of all European states totaled below 10 percent of Gross Domestic Product, except for brief spikes during wartime. After World War I, the average settled around 15–20 percent, and then after World War II climbed to over 25 percent (Flora et al. 1983: 262–80). The percentage, in the thirty OECD[2] countries, has increased gradually in recent decades from 25.6 percent in 1965 to 29.7 percent in 1975, 32.9 percent in 1985, and 35.1 percent in 1995, before flattening at the turn of the twenty-first century. In 2004, those governments took in 35.9 percent of GDP in tax revenues. This ranged from 19 percent in Mexico to 50.4 percent in Sweden. The United States, at 25.5 percent, was closer to Mexico than to the European average of 38.3 percent, having barely risen since the late 1940s (OECD 2006: 19, 70).

Governments are able to collect taxes from the millions of citizens and corporations under their jurisdiction because they have developed the capacity to track income and assets. Again, this has been a matter of political power and will far more than of bureaucratic technique or technological innovation. Britain and the United States achieved a high level of compliance and accuracy with paper returns audited by clerks recruited during the Napoleonic and Civil Wars. With the creation of permanent tax regimes, revenue bureaucracies became professionalized and developed ongoing records of incomes that could be checked for irregularities. While computerization obviously speeds governments' capacity to check tax returns against income reports filed by employers and corporations, such cross-checking was accomplished with paper records in earlier decades.

Political opposition to taxes can affect the honesty, efficiency, and comprehensiveness of collection, as well as the rates levied by governments. The waves of tax cuts enacted during the Reagan and Bush administrations in the United States in the 1980s and 2000s were matched with simultaneous cuts in the budget of the Internal Revenue Service. Those cuts, along with legal restrictions on audits enacted by a Republican-controlled Congress in the 1990s, made it easier for wealthy individual and corporate taxpayers to file fraudulent returns that hide income. European governments, especially that of Britain, have joined the Americans in their indulgence of off-shore banking and tax havens, allowing their citizens and corporations to maintain accounts there and making little effort to compel taxpayers or the tax havens to disclose the income funneled through off-shore accounts. States could compel disclosure and they could exclude polities that function as havens from participation in transnational currency flows. The continued, and expanding, diversion of wealth to tax havens is not a failure of governments to adapt to globalization, but rather a deliberate political decision to allow favored categories of taxpayers to escape their obligations in their home countries.

At the same time as central governments dramatically increased their powers to appropriate resources from civil society, they also created another method for generating revenues: the creation of a national currency. Through most of human history, gold and silver (and occasionally other rare and precious substances) were used as means of exchange. The amount of each state's currency thus was limited by the supply of gold and silver within their territory. To some extent, governments could increase their budgets by debasing coins, reducing the amount of gold and silver in them. But that tactic always backfired. Subjects quickly figured out that the coins were light and prices rose to compensate. Both economic exchange and government budgets, were constrained by the limited supply of gold and silver in Europe. As a result, states sought, with little success, to increase the flow of gold and silver into their territory and block its outflow. We will discuss the consequences of such mercantilist policies in chapter 5 when we look at the history of state efforts to foster economic development.

The limits of metal-based currencies ultimately were overcome by the creation of paper notes. Private banks issued paper currencies, and their value varied depending on whether those banks held, or were believed to hold, gold, silver, or other assets that could back those notes. Governments issued bonds in return for loans and those bonds were traded and became a de facto paper currency. When governments issued too many bonds their value could crash, as happened numerous times in ancient China, where paper currency was invented, and later in Europe. The thirteen American colonies issued currency to pay the costs of their War of Independence. Their value steadily dropped as more were issued. The speculators who bought them were bailed out by the new United States government, which pledged to buy and redeem the "Continentals" (Chown 1994; Timberlake 1993).

States, beginning with Amsterdam in 1609 and then Britain in 1694, chartered central banks that were allowed to issue currency backed by gold and silver on deposit, and then by government bonds (Carruthers 1996; Neal 2004). These banks coexisted for centuries with private authorities and local governments that issued their own notes and printed paper money. Britain and then other governments in the nineteenth century, and the United States in the early twentieth century, banned private issuance of money, as the state exerted control over private banks and the central government limited the autonomy of local and provincial authorities.

Once national currencies had been created, and competing private and local currencies abolished, states could determine the amount of money in circulation and add to it at will. As with the debasement of metal coins in previous centuries, this created the danger of inflation as governments printed money to cover deficits. In a few cases, governments printed money so rapidly that hyperinflation quickly wiped out the value of the currency, most notably in the Confederate States during the Civil War, in Weimar Germany from 1921 to 1923, in Greece and Hungary at the end of World War II, in Yugoslavia after the collapse of the Soviet Union, and in Zimbabwe in the first decade of the twenty-first century when the Mugabe regime attempted to pay salaries to its retainers as the economy entered a depression.

When governments are restrained in issuing notes, the value of a currency can be sustained over long periods and governments can supplement their revenues by slowly expanding the supply of notes. The greatest beneficiary of this is, of course, the United States, which by 2008 had $700 billion in paper currency in circulation, much of it in use outside the country, functioning as a permanent interest-free loan to that government.

National currencies also make the national governments that issue them a daily presence in their citizens' lives. Every time someone uses currency they are reminded of their national identity and of their government's power to confer value on pieces of paper bearing that government's name and symbols. Nationality is further reinforced when citizens go abroad and need to convert their home currency into the local monetary unit.

Governments then became capable of taxing subjects' income to the extent that they achieved political control over rival elites and broke apart local trust networks. Tax collection was primarily a political rather than administrative achievement, as was the creation of single national currencies. Some national governments have ceded the political power they derive from their currencies to other states, such as the Latin American countries that make the US dollar their official currency, or to supranational authorities, most notably the countries that use the euro and hence defer monetary policy to the European Central Bank. As yet, national governments have not allowed international bodies to collect significant taxes on their own. That would constitute a fundamental transfer of authority to supranational entities.

Men

Armed forces, until the end of the eighteenth century, were conglomerations of mercenaries, whose numbers, loyalty, and fighting spirit rose and fell with the amount of cash rulers had to pay them, and of military companies recruited, equipped, and trained by provincial aristocrats, who often devised their own battle plans and could and did go home with their soldiers if they decided they no longer agreed with their rulers' objectives or were unwilling to assume the financial or human costs of war. Only with rare exceptions did rulers command cohesive forces that were capable of conquering and controlling large territories. Most often, such conquerors were charismatic leaders who elicited strong loyalty from followers who shared a single tribal or ethnic background. Almost always, when those leaders died their empires shattered or became highly decentralized because their less charismatic heirs were unable to maintain an armed force large enough and loyal enough to ensure control over provincial elites. As we saw in chapter 1, the Roman and Chinese Empires stood out for their capacities to recruit loyal armed forces over centuries.[3]

Rulers had three methods for enlarging the forces under their control. First, they could hire more mercenaries, but only to the extent that they could increase and gain control over their subjects' resources, and we saw in the previous section how difficult that was, and how it was only in the eighteenth century that France and Britain, alone among the nations of the world, realized enough revenues to field armies or navies large enough to fight across Europe and beyond.

Second, rulers could try to take direct command over the troops fielded by aristocrats and towns. Monarchs accomplished this when elites agreed or were compelled to incorporate themselves within states, bringing the armed men under their control into the army, although usually in return for the right to serve as their commanding officer. As elites lost their autonomy, it became easier for the state to shift officers around, shuffling some to less responsible positions and giving command over "their" men to other, more capable, officers, some of whom were no longer aristocrats but men promoted through the ranks on the basis of ability. Soldiers were amalgamated into national armies earlier in Eastern Europe than in the West, although Eastern aristocrats retained a monopoly on access to the officer corps, albeit under unified commands and without venal control over particular positions. In the West, Britain and the Netherlands, especially in their navies, were the first to allow non-aristocrats to become officers, even as other commands remained venal. Russian and Ottoman rulers recruited both commoners and nobles into their armies, granting lands with serfs and tenants in return for long years of military service. As the Russian and Ottoman armies gained strength, the rulers could use them to conquer new lands, which could then be awarded to additional fighters, allowing for the further expansion of their empires (Barkey 2008). Armies in Japan, France, and the Habsburg dominions remained decentralized and under hereditary noble officers until the nineteenth century.

Finally, rulers could attempt to convince or force their own subjects to serve in their nations' military. Many polities had local, part-time militias which, under noble command, would serve in the agricultural off-season or when threatened with foreign invasion. Such forces were not suited for offensive fighting far from home or for extended campaigns. Impoverished farmers and unemployed townspeople were hired as mercenaries by their own governments, but such soldiers were even less motivated than foreign mercenaries and far less skilled, and many deserted. The small size and low morale of all these armies made "Old Regime warfare profoundly indecisive. At the strategic level, limited aims – a few colonies or provinces – did not warrant great risks" (Knox 2001: 61), since if a significant portion of a ruler's army were killed or captured he could not recruit new men and would be defenseless before his enemies.

The slow and uneven growth of national armies was transformed fundamentally by the first genuine draft in world history, which occurred in the United States in 1778 during the Revolutionary War. This was a world historical development. For the first time a state was able to enlist armed men beyond its fiscal capacity and without appealing to local elites. The American Continental Congress, faced with defeat and the likely execution of its leaders at the hands of the far more powerful British, shattered the parameters of national politics and international warfare by fostering "the emergence of the national citizen as an organizing principle in politics," which provided an ideological justification for state policies to conscript those national citizens, and allowed the "initial mobilization of the wide swath of 'the people' for war by the state" (Kestnbaum 2002: 119). The revolutionary French government, facing extinction at the hands of foreign invaders and aristocratic exiles, copied the American innovation. The 1793 *Levée en masse* brought in more than a million men and allowed France to defeat its enemies. Later drafts supplied the men for Napoleon's armies.

"Citizen conscription . . . help[ed] consolidate a politically mass-mobilizing regime . . . by rendering all citizens formally equal . . . by integrating them and their state into a single polity . . . by politicizing them, their relations to one another, and to the state" (Kestnbaum 2002: 131). Such a radical innovation, which was so destabilizing of existing elite power and privilege, was possible only in revolutionary polities, like those of the United States and France, where old elites were under attack and revolutionary leaders saw the draft as the most powerful way to elicit loyalty by giving the masses a stake in the state's survival, making them citizens with individual and uniform political rights as well as military obligations.

The draft gave a huge advantage in military manpower and motivation to governments that were willing to grant citizenship to its subjects. This eventually forced rivals to attempt their own drafts. Prussia instituted a draft, in 1814, in response to Napoleon. No other country followed this example until both the Confederacy and United States drafted soldiers during the Civil War. By the late nineteenth century, almost all European countries had instituted the draft, as did Japan in 1872, providing the basis for its twentieth-century imperial expansion (Jansen 2000). Britain was the last major power to adopt conscription, which it did only in 1916. Earlier, Britain took advantage of its wealth to pay its large pool of impoverished proletarians to serve in the military.

Conscription allowed drastic increases in the size of armed forces. Before conscription, the largest armies in Europe were those of the Habsburgs in the 1630s, at 300,000 men, and France in the 1690s, at 400,000 soldiers. France under Napoleon was the first army with over a million men, but by the late nineteenth century the peacetime, conscripted armies of Russia and France approached that size, and in World War I all the major combatants fielded multiple millions of troops, and continued fighting even after suffering hundreds of thousands of war dead (Kennedy

1987: 56, 99, 154, 203). Casualties and war deaths were even higher in World War II. The availability of mass armies that could be compelled to fight for years without interruption and that could be replenished through conscription also altered military strategy. War changed from sieges of strategic targets and flanking maneuvers to capture territory, into efforts to kill as many enemy soldiers as possible. Militaries used the machinery of the Industrial Revolution to develop and mass produce new weapons such as machine guns, poison gas, bombers, missiles, and more, all designed to kill large numbers of the enemy (Knox and Murray 2001; Ellis 1975). Universal conscription made civilians into military targets since they were potential soldiers (Kestnbaum 2009: 242–6). Governments bombed cities, and in World War II sought to exterminate entire populations. "Civilians accounted for less than 10 percent of deaths in World War I . . . rocketed to over half in World War II and to somewhat over 80 percent in wars fought in the 1990s" (Mann 2005b: 2). Nuclear weapons are designed to target civilians and are the ultimate assertion that an entire nation's mobilized population is the enemy.

Nations and Citizens

Conscription, more than any other governmental action, turned subjects into citizens. Citizen-soldiers, and their wives, parents, children, and neighbors, came to see themselves as part of a nation. National identity, in turn, deepened soldiers' willingness to kill and die. Subjects' understanding of their nation, and of their citizenship in it, became so all-encompassing that it came to transcend the specific actions of paying taxes and military service, which we've just discussed, and voting and receiving social benefits, which are the topics of the next chapter. Citizens felt themselves members of a collectivity that extended far beyond the lineages, occupational groups, religious communities, and localities that were the limits of almost all humans' feelings of solidarity until the American and French Revolutions. The remainder of this chapter is concerned with how citizens' notions of national identity were fostered and deepened, and how ideas of nationalism and national culture have spread beyond the American and European sites where they originated to encompass the globe.

Citizens identify not just with their state but also with each other. Citizens see themselves as part of a nation, and they come to regard their nationality as so valuable, so much a part of their essence that they are willing to "mutually pledge to each other our Lives, our Fortunes and our sacred Honor," as the authors of the US Declaration of Independence wrote in 1776. The men who signed that Declaration gathered in a single room, but the white men on whose behalf they issued the Declaration were scattered across thousands of miles of territory and before 1776 were subjects of thirteen distinct colonies. Only because many of those unseen men came to believe themselves to be citizens of a new nation was it feasible to challenge British rule. On what basis did those men commit themselves to an as yet unrecognized state? Why do men and women in so many countries around the world risk their lives for unseen fellow citizens and cherish their national identity? Such a powerful and historically unprecedented bond had its origins in various social realms and was manufactured through the efforts of state officials, intellectuals, revolutionaries, and ordinary citizens who often worked at cross-purposes with one another.

Citizens need to communicate with one another and with their government. Benedict Anderson convincingly argues that nations and languages formed in tandem. Anderson describes nations as "imagined communities . . . because the members of even the smallest nation will never know most of their fellow-members . . . [and] because, regardless of the actual inequality and exploitation that may prevail in each, the nation is always conceived as a deep, horizontal comradeship" ([1983] 1991: 6–7). Anderson locates the origins of these imagined communities in the development of what he calls "print-capitalism." The first commercial printers quickly saturated the tiny market of Latin readers and then translated and published books, beginning with the Bible but rapidly expanding to works on agriculture, science, fiction, and pornography, which then as now was the "killer app" of the new technology.

How did publishers select a vernacular into which those works would be translated or written and then printed? They usually picked the "administrative vernacular," the language in which kings communicated with local elites who were not literate in Latin. As both published books and administrative documents became more common the "varied" oral languages in which people communicated were "assembled . . . into print-languages far fewer in number" (p. 43).

> These print-languages laid the bases for national consciousness . . . they created unified fields of exchange and communication below Latin and above the spoken vernaculars. Speakers of the huge variety of Frenches, Englishes, or Spanishes, who might find it difficult or even impossible to understand one another in conversation, became capable of comprehending one another via print and paper. In the process, they gradually became aware of the . . . millions of people in their particular language-field . . . These fellow-readers, to whom they were connected through print, formed, in their secular, particular, visible invisibility, the embryo of the nationally imagined community. (Anderson [1983] 1991: 44)

Written languages created their own territorial maps as oral languages close to written vernaculars gradually adapted to the emerging national language. This is different from the effects of Latin and Chinese in the pre-modern eras. Those written languages tied together the elites, but had no influence on the oral vernaculars of the mass of subjects who remained illiterate and had no need to interact with the government through written documents. Oral languages that were too distant to assimilate into an existing written language then were relegated to the status of "sub-nationalities [unless and until they could] change their subordinate status by breaking firmly into print" (p. 45).

Print languages, in addition to fostering national identity, "helped to build that image of antiquity so central to the subjective idea of the nation" (Anderson [1983] 1991: 44). National languages become the medium for national literatures (as we will discuss in the next section), and the existence of a literary tradition, championed by "a long-established cultural elite . . . was the basis of the Italian and German claims to nationhood, although the respective 'peoples' had no single state with which they could identify" (Hobsbawm 1990: 37).

Once a state had an official written language it became the language of instruction in government schools, for training soldiers, and what every subject had to know to fill out government forms. As schooling – at least at the primary level – became universal, all citizens became literate in the national language and use of exclusively oral languages declined. The world currently is undergoing a massive extinction of oral languages. Probably half of the 6,000–7,000 languages in use in the world today will be dead (meaning there will not be a single living speaker) by the end of the twenty-first century (US National Science Foundation 2008).

Subjects showed themselves eager and deserving of citizenship by learning the national language. After the 1789 Revolution, "acquiring French was one of the conditions of full French citizenship (and therefore nationality) as acquiring English became for American citizenship" (Hobsbawm 1990: 21), and it has become a requirement in ever more countries of the world. Linguistic minorities have used their shared language to assert nationality and demand an independent state, as did most of the non-German speakers in the former Austro-Hungarian Empire after World War I. French speakers in Quebec were unsuccessful in their quest for independence, but did secure linguistic recognition from the now officially bilingual Canadian state. Similarly, linguistic minorities in India have won official recognition for their languages even as Hindi and English remain the governing languages of the state. As of this writing, the most intense linguistic conflict is in Belgium, but it remains uncertain whether that polity will be split apart by Flemish speakers' demands for an independent state. Linguistic minorities have been most likely to achieve independence if they occupy a distinct portion of the larger nation's territory and also if they make their demands at a moment when the central state has been weakened by defeat in war and/or the collapse of the imperial power that dominates their territory.

The correspondence between linguistic and state borders is not exact and, of course, many polities existed long before they were associated with a single national language. Eric Hobsbawm argues that the mere longevity of a state or monarchy is a basis for national legitimacy. "Hence there was little dispute about the existence of an English or French nation-people, a (Great) Russian people or the Poles, and little dispute outside Spain about a Spanish nation with well-understood national characteristics" (1990: 37). Similarly, the unbroken line of imperial succession, which stretches back 1,800 or perhaps 2,600 years, was and is a central prop of the Japanese state's legitimacy and a touchstone of Japanese nationalism, as an ancient imperial history is for China even under communism.

Monarchs and states can derive legitimacy and tie themselves to long histories by presenting themselves as protectors of churches, although that linkage has been of varying efficacy in sustaining nation-states. This sort of claim pre-dated the modern era of nation-states. When the Ottoman Empire expanded eastward in the sixteenth century, it "found itself in a different demographic, institutional, and cultural framework that changed its main constitutive identity, causing it to model itself more clearly as an Islamic empire" (Barkey 2008: 70–1). Ireland and Poland successfully defined themselves as Catholic against conquering neighbors (Hobsbawm 1990: 67). Russian Czars presented themselves as protectors of the Orthodox Church, a stance revived by the post-communist leaders of Russia. In both eras, other Orthodox nationalities did not see their common faith as a reason to submit to Russian rule. Similarly, Pakistan's self-proclaimed Muslim identity and *raison d être* did not prevent the successful separatist movement of Muslim Bangladesh, or the de facto separatism of various provinces and tribal areas. India's officially secular state policy has been more successful at quieting ethnic and religious schisms than either Pakistan's increasingly fundamentalist state religion or the militant Hinduism of the proto-fascist BJP (Mann 2004: 371–3).

Nationalism also can be grounded in "a proven capacity for conquest. There is nothing like being an imperial people to make a population conscious of its collective existence" (Hobsbawm 1990: 38). Krishan Kumar argues that it is not conquest per se that confers nationalism but rather those few "empire-builders . . . [who] saw themselves as engaged in the development and diffusion of civilization projects of world-historic importance . . . [derived] 'missionary' or 'imperial' nationalism and national identity" from their success (2003: x). Kumar's list of imperial nationalists is short: the ancient Romans, Russians, Austrians, Ottomans, and, above all, the English. But, as we saw in previous chapters and as Kumar's list reveals, many of the conquerors were empires rather than nations.

In fact, war and conquest in empires and monarchies created solidarity and attachment to the polity almost exclusively among the elite, and elite interests and divisions shaped colonial policy. Steinmetz (2007) explains the very different colonial policies in the German colonies of Samoa, Southwest Africa, and Qingdao as artifacts of the struggles among military officers from aristocratic families, colonial settlers and entrepreneurs with bourgeois back-grounds, and university-educated middle class whose political and cultural capital rested on claims of expert knowledge about the conquered natives in German colonies. German national interests and even German, as opposed to a broadly conceived Western or European culture, played only secondary parts in colonial officials' self-conceptions of their missions. There is virtually no evidence that the mass of subjects in Germany, Britain, or France felt that the victories of the empire or kingdom in which they lived had anything to do with them or brought them honor. Kumar's book addresses only Britain, the one empire from his list that was formed in the era of nations. The causality between conquest and British nationalism flows both ways, was built up unevenly and contingently over centuries, and reached the mass of citizens only as the empire began to collapse, leaving the central question that Kumar poses in his book: what happens to imperial nation-alism when the empire is gone? However, that question cannot be answered without recognizing that Britain, like other nations, today derives institutional and cultural legitimacy from a variety of sources so that its former empire is no longer, if it ever was, the crucial base of its legitimacy.[4]

War fosters nationalism mainly when it gives rise to conscription, which in turn transforms the ways in which military veterans are honored and war dead are commemorated. De Gaulle's "certain idea" defined the French nation mainly in terms of military sacrifice. The United States, which invented conscription, and whose Civil War was the first conflict in human history fought between two conscripted armies, also pioneered a new method of commemorating war. Empires, most notably Rome, had built war monuments to commemorate their victories, a pattern followed by later empires and monarchies. When wars came to be fought by citizens, especially mass armies of conscripts, "the meaning of the war had come to inhere in its cost. The nation's value and importance were both derived from and proved by the human price paid for its survival" (Faust 2008: 268). The United States, beginning with the 1867 National Cemeteries Act, became the first state to assume responsibility for identifying and burying all war dead (ibid.: 211–49). Other states, many beginning during and after World War I, have followed this model, creating national cemeteries, Tombs of the Unknown Soldier, and holidays and monuments to commemorate the war dead.

Soldiers defend the integrity of their nation's borders from internal schism as well as from external invasion. Over time, borders, regardless of their origins, give historical legitimacy to nations. Newer states use borders, often drawn by colonial powers, to manufacture a national history. The rapid emergence of independent nations around the world, beginning in the nineteenth century, and especially after 1945, was made possible by the boundaries and administrative structures that had earlier been created by colonial powers. "Each of the new South American republics had been an administrative unit from the sixteenth to the eighteenth century" (Anderson [1983] 1991: 52). Indeed, very few of the post-colonial states have altered their boundaries in any way or split apart since achieving independence. Nation-states defend their borders in civil wars, often at far greater cost in lives than from repulsing foreign invasions. The Taiping Rebellion and US Civil War were the bloodiest conflicts in the world from the end of the Napoleonic Wars until World War I. Similarly, the most violent conflicts since 1945 (aside from the wars fought by the United States and Soviet

Union in Korea, Vietnam, Afghanistan, and Iraq), have been civil wars in which the governments of Nigeria, Angola, Mozambique, Pakistan, the Philippines, and others endured and inflicted massive death tolls to preserve the territorial integrity of their nations. New nations not only fight to preserve the borders inherited from colonial rulers, but many of them also continue to use English, French, Spanish, or Portuguese as their official languages since those "official vernaculars" link together local elites and ethnic groups that continue to speak other languages but increasingly need to write and communicate across regions in the single national language.

Only rarely have already formed nation-states split apart along ethnic lines (as opposed to empires which fragment all the time, as the Soviet Union did most recently), and those instances all followed military defeats inflicted by other nations and/or the withdrawal of imperial powers. India's army fought Pakistan to ensure Bangladesh's independence in 1971. The end of Soviet hegemony in Eastern Europe and the collapse of communist regimes made possible the peaceful split of Czechoslovakia and the fragmentation of Yugoslavia into ever smaller and more ethnically homogenous states. The Kurds won de facto independence in Iraq after Saddam Hussein's defeat in the 1991 Gulf War. Conversely, ethnic and linguistic minorities in still powerful states, such as China, Spain, and Britain, have been unable to win independence. The Kurds in Turkey, Iran, and Syria, and the Hungarians in Romania, have won neither independence nor autonomy from their powerful states.

The temporal relationship between nationhood and language, then, is variable and provides ideological justification for both of what Rogers Brubaker (1992) presents as two logics of citizenship: The French model opens citizenship to anyone who is willing to acquire the linguistic and cultural requisites, while the German conception is that of a people united by a common language, who then strive to achieve political unity in a single state. The German model depends on "the existence of a long-established cultural elite, possessing a written national literary and administrative vernacular. This was the basis of the Italian and German claims to nationhood, although the respective 'peoples' had no single state with which they could identify" (Hobsbawm 1990: 37). Nationalism as a cultural project has enjoyed varying success. Multiple German-speaking kingdoms combined into Germany in the nineteenth century, as the various Italian-speaking polities were unified into Italy, but many German speakers were consigned to the Austrian state, while others were relegated to minority status in the other states that emerged from the Austro-Hungarian Empire. The desire to bring all German speakers into Germany was an ideological foundation of Nazism which also sought to withdraw citizenship from those who were not "pure" Germans, which the Nazis defined in racial rather than linguistic or cultural terms (Somers 2008; see also Hobsbawm 1990).

Mann (2005b) shows that nations are most likely to define themselves in ethnic and exclusionary terms when they are "newly embarked upon [or in recent retreat from] democratization" than are stable authoritarian regimes which "tend to govern by divide-and-rule" (p. 4). For this reason, Mann sees ethnic cleansing as modern, a pathological yet sociologically predictable result of efforts by regimes to define and control territories that once were kingdoms or parts of empires by identifying and mobilizing distinct ethnicities. A state's ability to mobilize "ethnonationalism is strongest where it can capture other senses of exploitation" (p. 5), that is, where one ethnic group believes itself economically exploited by another. Mann argues that ethnic antagonisms turn murderous only where rival ethnic groups both are organized and "where the state exercising sovereignty over the contested territory has been factionalized and radicalized amid an unstable geopolitical environment that usually leads to war" (p. 7). Thus, murderous ethnic violence is absent from places where stable democratic or authoritarian states rule. The recent upsurge of ethnic cleansing follows the destabilization of states due to the decline of state socialism, neoliberal policies that sap state capacities, and the rise of religious fundamentalism in some of those weakened states that evokes religious-ethnic identities that are turned on minority sects (pp. 509–14).

The United States and other immigrant nations follow the "French" model; indeed, around the world that model is more often associated with the United States than with France. Newly independent nations invite or coerce the many ethnic groups and indigenous peoples living in their territory to assimilate into a nation defined in cultural and linguistic terms. The German model has only rarely been a program for uniting multiple polities into a single state. Instead, linguistic, religious, and ethnic claims mainly have been used since the nineteenth century to demand independence from polyglot empires and states. The non-German speakers of the Austro-Hungarian Empire claimed nationhood for Hungary, Czechoslovakia, and Yugoslavia largely on linguistic terms, as did the Greeks from the Ottoman Empire (Barkey 2008: ch. 8). The Arabs in the Ottoman Empire sought to create a single nation at the end of World War I, based on their common language and religion. The multiple states of the Middle East lack legitimacy in the eyes of some of their citizens because they were drawn by Britain and France, and their borders are an affront to notions of Arab and Muslim unity, yet more citizens of those states identify with their nations and are willing to fight to preserve those borders. Zionism was grounded in religious identity, but its successful revival of Hebrew as a modern language was crucial in melding Jewish immigrants into an Israeli nation.

Nationalism, National Cultures, and a World of Nations

So far, state officials have been presented as the main agents of nationalism. For such state actors, the fact of nationalism is more important than its content.[5] States benefit, above all in military fervor, from nationalism regardless of its basis. The different ways in which state elites frame nationalism derive, as we saw in the previous section, mainly from the exigencies of historical circumstance: the old regime's age and claim to legitimacy, the degree of linguistic, religious, or ethnic homogeneity within its borders, and whether the state already was independent or was trying to win independence from an empire.

State elites did not act alone in fostering nationalism. Intellectuals and ordinary citizens have been decisive in molding the national identities and cultures for which states elicit loyalty. Indeed, both the French and German models of citizenship discussed above are ideal types; their specific and varied realizations around the world emerged out of interactions between intellectuals who created the historical myths that asserted the existence of nations, and governments that selected among and then implemented intellectuals' cultural programs of nationalism.[6] Intellectuals, as we will see in the remainder of this chapter, are the crucial carriers of nationalism from its sites of invention in Europe and the United States to the rest of the globe in the twentieth century.

Where did intellectuals and others first develop their notions of national identity and envision national cultures that differed from one another? Norbert Elias ([1939] 1978, [1939] 1982, [1969] 1983) locates the early emergence of national cultures in the efforts of rulers and court elites to incorporate provincial notables and then the emerging bourgeoisies in court culture. To the extent that each court culture was distinct, so too were the national cultures that formed as the civility of courtly life was imposed and adopted in the social and geographic peripheries of kingdoms. In that way, provincials, bourgeois, and finally commoners derived their ideas of national identity from state elites, but they also were active agents themselves in forming a national culture and became invested in making those cultures distinct from one another. Since most provincials, not to mention bourgeois and commoners, never made it to the royal court, their ideas about national civilization came from books, written in the new literary vernaculars.

Elias focuses on books of manners as the carriers of national cultures, while Kuzmics and Axtmann (2007) examine works of literature and show how the very different ideas of English and Austrian "national habitus" were developed and conveyed through novels. Mennell (2007) identifies a diffuse array of political, class, religious, and literary influences in molding the American character. These recent authors build on Elias's approach by showing how the "civilizing process" continues in the modern world as other social forces supplement and then supplant (or in America substitute for) the role of courtly society in creating and deepening national character. Their analyses also complement, although they fail to cite, Benedict Anderson, since the national literatures they present as evidence for national cultures are each published in a common written vernacular. The difficulty with carrying Elias's analysis into modern times is that Kuzmics and Axtmann, and Mennell, fail to identify the motives which propelled novelists, preachers, and indeed any non-state actor to take up the role that kings and courtiers play in Elias's work. Nationalism may be a project of intellectuals; but we still need to explain why intellectuals have made nationalism their project.

National projects are embedded in global systems of nations. National culture gains meaning through its differences with other cultures as much as through the commonalities it asserts among the citizens of a single country. The best analysis yet written of how national cultures emerge comes from Pascale Casanova in *The World Republic of Letters* ([1999] 2004). Casanova goes beyond Anderson and Hobsbawm's insight that print languages shape as well as reflect national borders, to examine how writers actually conceive their relationship and that of the books they write to national and world literature.

National literatures need their own language, but in Casanova's analysis they borrow from as much as they shape the oral vernacular. She notes that Renaissance writers quickly moved from translating Greek and Latin classics as well as the Bible into their vernacular to composing original works. Italian was the first language in which significant new literature was written. Yet, despite an auspicious fourteenth-century debut, led by Dante, Petrarch, and Boccaccio, Italian literature did not remain in the forefront, with later authors imitating the increasingly archaic forms of the three Tuscan immortals. Casanova argues that the absence of a national state and the continued strength of the Catholic Church retarded Italian literature, especially in comparison with French, English, and to a lesser extent Spanish literature, all of which developed distinct national trajectories.

The first contributions to those literatures were written in the Latin-influenced language and style of the royal court and high clergy. French became the first modern literary language when

Rabelais introduced words and expressions (including sexual and scatological vocabulary) from everyday oral speech into his writing (Bakhtin [1965] 1968). These popular vernaculars, even more than the distinctive manners and rhetoric of royal courts emphasized by Elias, "served as 'difference markers'" (Casanova ([1999] 2004: 104) that gave a singular character to each national culture and literature.

Key authors, above all Shakespeare for English, gave shape to their national literatures. Among other contributions, Shakespeare invented numerous words, and his commanding presence in world literature made English the rival of French as the leading literary language of Europe, even though France continued to outclass England as a political and military power for two more centuries. Cervantes did the same for Spanish thanks to the immense influence of *Don Quixote*.

The establishment of English and French, and to a lesser extent Italian and Spanish, literary traditions, which were equal in linguistic and stylistic depth and world prestige to classical Greek and Latin, made it possible for Herder, an eighteenth-century German literary critic, to claim that each nation and age can aspire to create its own authentic literature. Casanova traces how authors in countries outside the established literary centers created literatures for their nations and in so doing built their careers. Writers gained the most visibility by positioning themselves within emerging national literatures rather than imitating the high prestige styles of established nations. Nationalism was a font for writers' language, style, and themes, and organized their audiences. Writers and other artists and intellectuals became active agents of nationalism, key creators of national cultures.

The individual and collective choices made by writers molded their nations' literature and, in turn, the decisions and careers of their successors because:

nationalization had tangible consequences for literary practice. Acquaintance with the texts of a particular national pantheon and knowledge of the major dates of a country's nationalized literary history had the effect of transforming an artificial construction into an object of shared learning and belief. Within the closed environment of the nation, the process of differentiation and essentialization created familiar and analyzable cultural distinctions: national peculiarities were insisted upon and cultivated, chiefly through the schools [that is the main reason why Casanova sees a national state as necessary for a national literature], with the result that references, citations, and allusions to the national literary past became the private property of native speakers [but also potentially of immigrants willing to learn the literary tropes of their adopted nation]. National peculiarities thus acquired a reality of their own, and helped in turn to produce a literature that was consistent with accepted national categories. (Casanova [1999] 2004: 106)

This is the approach that most authors in most countries adopted in the nineteenth and subsequent centuries, as they sought to challenge or adapt to French and English domination. It produced literatures that are stylistically conservative and often directly engaged with domestic politics. Such literature, though, has little influence beyond its borders because it is not innovative.

Innovation is not necessarily produced in the nations whose literatures enjoy the highest prestige. Rather, Casanova shows that the most influential authors of the twentieth century came from nations or minorities that were literary backwaters (most notably, Joyce and Beckett of Ireland, Kafka, a Jew in Austro-Hungarian Prague, Faulkner of the US South, the magical realists of Latin America), yet who either at home or in exile developed formal innovations that allowed them "to transform the signs of cultural, literary, and often economic destitution into literary resources and thus to gain access to the highest modernity" ([1999] 2004: 328). This modernity of the marginal catapulted those authors to the forefront of world literature. "The great literary revolutionaries . . . find themselves at odds with the norms of their native literary space" (ibid.: 110), which remain stylistically conservative. Ironically, the innovators become sources of inspiration for writers from other backward places more often than in their homelands; Faulkner's novels set in a rural and racially segregated US South inspired García Márquez of Colombia, Rachid Boudjedra of Algeria, and Juan Benet of Spain among others, all of whom wrote of, if not from, their own backward, rural homelands (ibid.: 336–45). Such channels of influence explain how authors amass cultural capital from beyond their national literature and use it to catapult themselves and their nations to the forefront of world culture, jumping ahead in literary time to become the most modern and, by inspiring authors in other countries, becoming centers of international networks of literary innovation.

Casanova's model of world literature shows how individual writers can shape their national cultures. It also traces a very different sequence of cross-national influence from Meyer's crude theory of a world culture created by institutional isomorphism. Instead, Casanova shows that each nation's literary and cultural development depends on how writers and other intellectuals understand their nation's position in a world system of literature. Those varying understandings produce literary programs that range from highly conservative to innovative, from nationalist to internationalist, and from politically engaged to aesthetic formalism.

Artists who work in cultural peripheries can create innovations that advance their nation to a central position, even when their own goal is to unmoor themselves from their home country so that they can experiment while still advancing their careers. In other instances artists' careers rise along with their nation's cultural identity. The patterns Casanova found in literature, in careers from Dante on, appear in other cultural forms as well. Guilbaut traces how Abstract Expressionist painters and their champions moved the United States from the periphery to the center of world art. Up through World War II, American art was Hollywood, "New York and its skyscrapers . . . industrial art that was said to be representative of this modern civilization, oppressive and brutal of course and yet endlessly fascinating" in the eyes of the Parisian critics who "by shaping critical discourse . . . kept a firm grip on Western culture, as everyone was aware. To move up a rung on the scale of cultural values was no mean feat. These values were as clearly delineated and as jealously guarded as colonial possessions" (1983: 43–4).

The Abstract Expressionists propelled themselves to the apex of the post-1945 art world with the assistance of critics who sought to redefine the criteria for great art. In so doing, those critics elevated their own intellectual standing as they advanced the position of the US in the cultural hierarchy. At the end of World War II, artists grappled with the question of how to depict the Holocaust and the specter of nuclear annihilation. Both Soviet realism and Cubism were seen, in Europe as well as America, as unequal to the challenge. Abstract Expressionism was both "the logical culmination of a long-standing and inexorable tendency toward abstraction" and a way of projecting "American 'force' and 'violence' as universal cultural values" (ibid.: 177). Jackson Pollock and the other American Abstract Expressionists, like Joyce and Beckett in literature, were radical innovators, yet unlike the peripheral writers they were located in the nation that, after 1945, was at the center of world power and wealth. Those painters, and even more the critics who championed their work, redefined American national character, at least as it could be expressed in art, and in so doing elevated US prestige and influence in world art. American artists' prestige among leading critics was soon reflected in newspaper coverage in the US and Europe. France, which still dominated journalists' coverage of the arts immediately after World War II, lost primacy to the United States, which became dominant, and remains so at the outset of the twenty-first century, in most high and popular art forms (Janssen et al. 2008).

National culture matters not only for how it affects artists' and nations' capacity to situate themselves in a world hierarchy of literature, painting, music, or other arts. It also, as we saw earlier, influences how citizens understand their nation and it shapes the process by which children and immigrants are trained to become citizens. Let me close with two exemplary illustrations from the two revolutionary nations that created the idea of national citizenship that this chapter traced as it developed and spread around the world.

French citizens see their national identity as an amalgamation of language, culture, and the land itself. Food has been elevated into a symbol of that unity, and France in inventing the notion of food as a creative enterprise has made itself into the world center of culinary arts. French authors, most notably Marie-Antoine

Carême in the early nineteenth century and Georges Auguste Escoffier at the beginning of the twentieth century, codified recipes that they asserted conveyed the proper way to prepare dishes and also styles of presentation. They elevated chefs from servants into professionals, and linked their skill to the nation by claiming that the recipes required authentic ingredients whose quality and flavor could not be reproduced outside of France. This cultural claim was codified by the French national government with the creation in 1919 of *Appellation d'origine contrôlée*, a specific geographic zone that was given exclusive right to make a certain wine, cheese, or other product. The concept of *terroir* served brilliantly to make the distinctive character of a locality, which even in the early twentieth century was the primary identity of many citizens (Robb 2007), constitutive of the national essence. This French claim to the authenticity of ingredients and the artistry of their creators was duplicated by Italy, Spain, and Germany, which quickly created their own *appellations*, and have been followed by other countries since and by the European Union, which, in 1992, began granting Protected Geographical Status to foods. Other nations have codified their cuisines, and see it as part of their national culture. European nations have yet to include questions about cooking in the "citizenship tests" they give to immigrants, but cuisine has been enshrined as a regular section in most newspapers, is the subject of shows and even entire channels on television, and its national basis is reinforced in the way in which restaurants around the world are classified in terms of whether they serve the national or a foreign cuisine. Conversely, countries demonstrate their openness to immigrants by elevating fusion cooking to haute cuisine as the United States and Canada have done.

The United States is a nation of immigrants, although the rate of immigration has ebbed and flowed through its history. One peak of immigration occurred in the period between the Civil War and the Great Depression. US citizens whose families had been in America for generations, and were mainly Protestants of Northwestern European origin, debated what to do about the new immigrants, who for the most part came from Southern and Eastern Europe and were Catholic, Orthodox, or Jewish. One faction argued for segregating themselves from the new immigrants, retreating to the countryside or to the nineteenth-century equivalent of gated communities. Nativists later argued for, and in the 1920s were able to impose, immigration restrictions that lasted until the 1960s. Nativists also pressed to ban substances that they believed made immigrants unmanageable. Thus, a Constitutional Amendment prohibiting alcohol was in force from 1920 to 1933. Various drugs were made illegal in response to waves of fear about Chinese immigrants (opium), Mexicans (marijuana), and African American internal migrants to northern cities (heroin and cocaine).

The other side of the debate asserted that immigrants, or at least their children, could be educated to be Americans in culture and behavior as well as legal citizenship. That education took various forms, from civics classes in schools to the creation of public parks. New York's Central Park opened in 1859. Frederick Law Olmsted, its designer, "was convinced that he had created 'a distinctly harmonizing and refining influence upon the most unfortunate and most lawless classes of the city – an influence favorable to courtesy, self-control, and temperance'" (Levine 1988: 202). Central Park and its imitators in other US cities were American versions of the public gardens of London and Paris, adapted to the task of acculturating immigrants as well as providing a refuge for established citizens.

A different sort of park, unprecedented in world history, was created by the US Congress in 1872 at Yellowstone. In contrast to the royal and private parks of Europe, Yellowstone, though inaccessible then in fact to most Americans, was established to be free and open to all as a symbol of the nation's democratic character. That park symbolized and preserved as an open-air museum what was and still is portrayed as the distinctive natural beauty of America. Just as many nations have imitated the French in codifying their own cuisines and registering the "terroirs" of their foods, so too have many countries followed the US in creating parks to preserve the natural beauty that is seen as distinctive and constitutive of the nation.

Central Park and Yellowstone are expressions and shapers of

the two sides of national culture and of citizenship. Yellowstone expresses an essentialist view of nation, rooted in land, unique, enduring and unchanging. Citizens of essentialist nations are born to that status, see themselves as coming "from the land," and are bound together by a common language, culture, or race. This is Brubaker's German notion of citizenship. Central Park speaks to the aspirational nation, engineered and designed even as it appears natural, and planned to transform any and all arrivals willing to learn the customs, language, and culture of their adopted nation. This is Brubaker's French model and it becomes ever more dominant in the growing number of nations that receive substantial numbers of immigrants. Immigrant nations combine a core national culture, to which all immigrants must assimilate, and a redefinition of nationalism that invites in the bodies and practices of immigrants that augment and compliment the core identity.

Yellowstone and Central Park are ideals. The living citizens of actual states combine elements of both in their understandings of their national cultures, and there is of course variation within nations among citizens in how they understand their own identities and evaluate those of their fellow citizens. Notions of citizenship continually are reinforced, modified, and tested against the concrete obligations imposed by government, the heaviest of which are the military service and fiscal payments we examined at the outset of this chapter, and by the rights that states grant to citizens, above all the voting and social benefits that are the subject of chapter 5. Immigration, like military victories and defeats, alliances with other nations, and fundamental economic changes (and perhaps in the future environmental catastrophe) all have the potential to transform national culture to the extent that they cannot be subsumed within the categories of belief and experience that have developed around citizenship in the past history of each nation.

National cultures, like everything else about nations, exist in a world of multiple and competing states. We have seen that intellectuals are part of a world cultural system that is subject to dynamics that are different than, and partly autonomous from, those of the international system of states. Intellectuals vary in how closely they align themselves with a national cultural project, and often their intentions toward their birth or adopted nation are at odds with their effect. Yet, most often, intellectuals and artists, as they attempt to create a presence and reputation for themselves in a world cultural system, are also contributing to a collective project that distinguishes their national culture from that of others and in so doing specifies and conveys a certain idea of the nation to other citizens. Culture thus joins an array of other actions and obligations that make the nation real, and animates individual citizens' understanding of their part in a community of often unseen fellow nationals both living and dead.

4

States and Capitalist Development

States and capitalism have come to dominate the world simultaneously. This chapter examines how states set their economic policies in a capitalist world. My goal is not to re-evaluate the debate over the relationship between state formation and the origins of capitalism. To do so would require a book in itself.[1] Rather, this chapter begins at the point when capitalism already is the dominant mode of production in Europe and through colonialism and imperialism is extending its reach to the entire globe.

To what extent are economic policies made by state elites on their own, and when do state managers respond to the needs or expressed desires of capitalists, or some faction of capitalists, within their polity? Why do states vary in how effective they are in spurring economic development? Why have some states elevated themselves from peripheral positions in the world capitalist economy, while most others have failed at that task? How did states that sought to exclude themselves from the capitalist world economy fare in their efforts at socialist economic development? Why, in recent decades, since the demise of the Soviet Union and state socialism, did so many states abandon the developmental policies of the previous era, while a few managed to resist and insulate themselves from neoliberalism? I am concerned in this chapter with how neoliberalism affects economic relations among nations and development within countries. We will address neoliberal social welfare policies in chapter 5 and will save a discussion of the prospects for future governmental interventions in the

101

economy, and of state responses to the economic crisis that began in 2008, for the concluding chapter.

Economic Development Before States

We take for granted today that governments have an interest in, and indeed an obligation to formulate, measures to ensure economic growth and to prevent or counteract economic contractions. Yet, until the advent of capitalism, neither rulers nor subjects believed that economic expansion was regular and normal or that it could be fostered through conscious policies. Rulers, through most of human history, made little effort to affect economic production. The hallmark of all pre-capitalist social formations, as Marx ([1867] 1967) rightly emphasizes, is that the dominant class used its power to extract a surplus after production was completed. Slaves and peasants for the most part managed production on their own, provided for their subsistence, and then under threat of force turned over a surplus to masters, feudal lords, and other rulers.

There really were only three ways for a member of a pre-capitalist ruling class to increase his income. One was to seize land and subjects from other members of the ruling class. The second was to subordinate lesser rulers within a larger polity, allowing them to keep part of what they extracted directly from subjects and compelling them to send the rest up the ruling hierarchy. The third was to squeeze non-elites to extract more of what they produced. All three methods relied upon force ultimately, and all were zero-sum games during the long eras of economic stagnation.

While Marx presents his insight in terms of classes and modes of production, we saw in earlier chapters that elite organizations regulated production to extract revenue and that their conflicts stymied rather than fostered economic development in empires, feudal polities, and city-states. Irrigation works, roads, and rulers' purchases of military provisions did stimulate economic growth, and fostered embryonic metallurgy industries and long-distance trade. Yet we need to be careful not to exaggerate rulers' influence on economies in the ancient and medieval worlds. Farmers' productivity increased little in the millennia between the development of agriculture and the advent of capitalism (Allen 1992: 131–3). The technological stagnation and lack of improvement in humans' standard of living that we noted in ancient empires in chapter 1 continued in the millennium from the fall of the Roman Empire to Columbus's voyages. Nor was there more economic growth elsewhere in the world (Goldstone 2008). Mann (2005a) may be correct that indigenous Americans' plant-breeding and ecological alterations resulted in a more rapid advance from hunter-gathering to agricultural societies that supported a substantial urban sector in the western hemisphere than had occurred on other continents. However, there is no evidence that the scale of urbanization or the level of trade and non-agricultural production in the Americas approached that of the empires we examined in chapter 1.

Almost everything left after the producing classes' subsistence needs were met was taken in tribute and taxation and spent on conspicuous consumption by elites and on the military forces needed to sustain those in power. Little or nothing was left for investment. Where rulers intervened it was to prevent the establishment of rival power centers and to funnel existing resources to the center, as the Egyptian Empire did with Nile trade and the Romans did when constructing roads and giving legal protection to private property. China's elaborate system for stockpiling grain and transporting it to locales where crops failed, and which prevented famines in ways that the British Empire later failed to emulate (Davis 2001), was designed as a political mechanism to prevent rebellion, not to revive economies weakened by natural disaster.

Pre-capitalist ruling classes had little interest in or leverage over how the exploited class went about creating their means of subsistence and the surplus that the rulers appropriated. The most dynamic economies in pre-modern Europe were located in city-states where innovative merchants and producers thrived, as we saw at the end of chapter 1, in the interstices of feudal power, just as Asian merchants prospered mainly by transporting the spoils of empire and catering to rulers' demands for luxuries and military goods. Merchants built trade networks and developed new lines of production where central power was absent. As political control solidified in city-states, merchants refeudalized their enterprises, offices, landholdings, and investments, and the city-state economies declined (see Lachmann 2000: ch. 3, for an extended treatment and for further references), just as cities, trade, and manufacture rose and fell along with Asian and Middle Eastern empires. As we saw in our discussion of feudalism in chapter 2, elites affected production mainly indirectly through their efforts to guard their organizational means of extraction from rival elites. The consolidation of elites within centralized polities was the essential dynamic of state formation, and it transformed the ways in which newly unified elites exploited non-elites, creating capitalist relations of production, first in England (Lachmann 2000: chs 4 and 6), and eventually across the entire globe (Wallerstein, 1974–89; Arrighi, 1994).

Marx, and later Marxists, as we noted in chapter 2, take an instrumentalist view of the relationship between capitalists and the state; they argue that states develop whatever capacities are needed to allow capitalism to reproduce itself. Thus, states guard property rights, expand markets, increase the supply of proletarian labor, and overcome the contradictions of capitalism, which periodically create falling profits and insufficient demand. How states do that, and why state managers (who for the most part are not capitalists themselves) serve capitalists' interests is not adequately explained by any Marxist or non-Marxist instrumentalist. Occasionally, most famously in Marx's *Eighteenth Brumaire*, the potential for rulers to pursue their own interests is acknowledged.[2] However, self-interested state managers in turn are limited by capitalists' ability to withhold investment and weaken the economy. This forces state managers to conform to capitalists' demands because economic decline reduces the resources rulers need to fund wars and their administrations, and can provoke popular discontent (Lo 1982 provides the best concise review of the debate over whether capitalists can exercise a business veto over state policies). The problem with this view of state managers, as passive observers of capitalists' investment decisions, is that it loses sight of how governments under capitalism differ from those in all previous eras.

In fact, state managers were initiators of, as well as reactors to, economic developments. If pre-capitalist rulers' relationship to the economy was simple, because it was simply exploitative, it has become complex in cause and effect as capitalism has come to dominate the world economy over the past five centuries. We cannot deduce the variable and contingent pathways of that relationship from Marxist or any other general theory. Instead, we need to trace the ways in which states have intervened in the economy and interacted with capitalists and others. As we specify change over time and variation across states, then we will be in a position to draw theoretical conclusions.

Mercantilism

Rulers' relationship to the economy began to change in the sixteenth century. Mercantilism was the name given to a set of state policies that were aimed at drawing gold and silver into the country by encouraging domestic production and exports, taxing imports, and chartering companies that would engage in trade and establish colonies and other territorial presences abroad. Mercantilism had a vital military element, as states deployed armies and navies and fought wars to control trade networks and capture colonies. While rulers had always used armed force to capture territory and treasure, before mercantilism they did so on their own behalf. Mercantilist states, like some Italian city-states, also deployed armed forces on behalf of their subjects' economic interests. Why did states adopt these policies, and were they effective?[3]

The Marxist answer is best summarized, surprisingly, by Max Weber ([1927] 1981: 347):

The essence of mercantilism consists in carrying the point of view of capitalist industry into politics; the state is handled as if it consisted exclusively of capitalistic entrepreneurs. External economic policy rests on the principle of taking every advantage of [other countries]

. . . importing at the lowest price and selling much higher. The purpose is to strengthen the hand of the government in its external relations. Hence mercantilism signifies the development of the state as a political power, which is to be done directly by increasing the tax paying power of the population.

In other words, state rulers served the interests of their domestic capitalists because as capitalists got rich, the economy, and hence the tax base, would expand.[4]

Rational choice theorists (Ekelund and Tollison 1981) qualify Marx and Weber's analyses by noting that not all capitalists benefited from mercantilism, just those granted government monopolies and shares of cartels. From this point of view, which builds on Heckscher's [1931] 1955 classic history of mercantilism, newly centralized European states sold monopoly rights to raise revenues for self-aggrandizement and for military competition with rival states. Any benefit to capitalists as a class was inadvert. Indeed, Ekelund and Tollison argue that mercantilism generally retarded capitalism by diverting capital and entrepreneurial efforts into "rent-seeking," that is, political competition for monopolies.

The difficulty with all these approaches is that they are unable to explain why so few European states adopted most of these policies, and why those that did varied so much in their success. Spain, which created the first and (until the nineteenth century) largest colonial empire, failed to establish any chartered colonial companies; France's colonial companies were stillborn. The Dutch chartered companies brought most independent merchants within a single organization, while British merchants excluded from royal firms came to dominate Britain's Atlantic trade and play a growing role in commerce with Asia. Only Britain and the Netherlands became commercial and manufacturing centers, and the Dutch state never adopted mercantilist policies to control imports and exports. France, the most avid mercantile state, remained a second-rate economic power, and Spain never developed a significant domestic industry (Deyon 1969).

We can make sense of the variety of state commercial and colonial policies by abandoning a priori claims about the interests of capitalists and state managers. We saw in chapter 2 that European state formation drew various elites into states. Those elites continued to jostle for privileges and power once inside the state. Their relative power determined which families and which elites were granted monopolies or shares in chartered companies, how those companies operated, and how trade was regulated.

The Habsburgs' strategy of favoring single, mainly aristocratic elites, in each province, eliminated town autonomy and left few merchants who could have launched colonial ventures. Instead, the Habsburgs commissioned conquistadors and rewarded them for financing and manning American voyages and conquests with *encomiendas* – permanent rights to the forced labor of Indians within a conquered territory, as well as to any gold and silver already held by the natives or which the natives could be compelled to mine for their overlord. The *encomienda* system served to consolidate power in each American colony in the hands of a single aristocratic elite. As a result, the Crown was forced to accept a steadily declining share of mine revenues from an ever more independent elite in the Americas. Its share fell from 30 percent in the early sixteenth century to 1.2 percent in the 1650s (Flynn 1982: 142; Lynch 1992: 283).

The paucity of autonomous merchants, either in the Americas or back in Spain, created an opening for other Europeans to capture most of the business of supplying Spanish-American settlers. The Habsburgs themselves recognized the need to strengthen merchants both in America to challenge the *encomienda* holders, and at home to counterbalance the provincial aristocracies. The Crown, in their one attempt to establish a mercantilist policy, granted the merchants of Seville a monopoly on trade with the Americas in hopes of generating a new revenue stream that could be taxed. This mercantilist initiative failed in the face of aristocratic power. Neither Seville nor any other Spanish city became a commercial center. The Genoese with immediately available capital, not the Seville merchants with only the potential of future wealth, became the prime beneficiaries of trade with the Americas and of servicing Habsburg debt (Muto 1995). The infusion of American treasure sparked inflation, which benefited only those landlords able to raise rents and which undercut Spanish manufacturers competing against established industries in the relatively low inflation economies of France, the Low Countries, and Britain. The lack of a privileged and therefore loyal merchant elite left the Habsburgs with no room for maneuvering against any provincial aristocratic oligarchy within Spain or in the Americas, making it impossible to sustain any mercantilist policy.

French monarchs adapted their strategy of vertical absolutism to colonial ventures, creating various chartered companies. The companies attracted little investment since venal offices and government loans at home remained far more lucrative. As a result, lesser merchants, who lacked the capital and political connections to participate in venal enterprises, fostered most French colonial settlement and commerce. The success of independent planters and merchants in creating lucrative slave colonies attracted the Crown's attention. The Crown realized that "the metropolis could gain most from colonial development by controlling trade in their plantation exports, thus making Bordeaux and Nantes into leading suppliers of sugar and coffee" (Blackburn 1997: 298). The Crown's focus on trade also was shaped by French settlers' success in resisting official control over their plantations, and settlers' eagerness for French naval protection for their vulnerable ships.

Mercantilism within France was hobbled by the Crown's inability to do without revenues from internal tariffs and by venal officials' power to prevent reforms that would have reduced their authority or capacity to collect revenues from taxes, tariffs, and monopolies. As in the colonies, French commerce grew mainly in the limited gaps between state and venal elite authority, and was propelled by small-scale capitalists. The state fostered economic growth to some degree through transportation improvements, and more dramatically in the Paris region, as spending by court elites supported luxury industries and military procurement spurred some manufacture. By the time royal controls on the economy were swept away in the French Revolution, Britain had become hegemonic in world trade, making new mercantilist efforts futile.

The state that emerged in the Dutch struggle for independence was collectively controlled by elites, above all the Amsterdam merchants, who used Contracts of Correspondence to specify the rotation of offices among families and their share of revenues. Those contracts became the template for the charters of the Dutch East and West Indies Companies, which specified how colonial offices, trade routes, and colonial estates would be divided among the same families that controlled power at home. The Dutch state's only mercantilist action was in enshrining those agreements in company charters, which then prevented any further state action to modify Dutch colonial ventures. Similarly, the contracts precluded any state regulation of the economy in the Netherlands.

While the Dutch were conquering trade routes, markets, and American and Asian colonies (which were relatively empty of European competitors in the sixteenth and early seventeenth centuries), the self-serving autonomy of each family and town did not impede Dutch commercial hegemony. Rather, the same locally based alliances and privileges that protected each family's interests also allowed elites to mobilize resources rapidly to realize their congruent goals, and allowed Amsterdam to dominate European commodity markets, to form the first stock market, and to become the financial capital of Europe. However, once Britain sought to vie for opportunities the Dutch had previously monopolized, the Dutch, despite their greater wealth, were hampered by each province and town's right to veto tax increases and to withhold their separate navies from battles that did not further their particular interests. This allowed Britain to use its more cohesive and better-funded military to take colonies and trade routes from the Dutch. Similarly, in the colonies, officials and merchants, protected by their patrimonial shares of company enterprises, engaged in self-dealing, often through the British East India Company.

Britain, from the 1660s until the 1780s, achieved economic dominance, at the expense of the Dutch, in one sector after another. Britain's dominance is notable for its two-century duration and because Britain was able to sustain and strengthen its advantage, even as its economy and those of its rivals made the transition to the exploitation of carbon fuels for energy and the resulting mass production of industrial goods. Britain also is notable because its state adopted few mercantilist policies, even as its rivals sought to shield their markets and sponsor trading companies. The British state did little to regulate or subsidize manufacture or finance. Except for the Corn Laws of 1815–46, tariffs were low.

Britain's first great leap forward came in agriculture during the seventeenth century, when yields per acre and agricultural labor productivity increased more rapidly than anywhere else in the world and outstripped the levels achieved in the Netherlands and Belgium, the previous leaders (Allen 1992). Most of the surplus generated by agricultural improvement was kept by landlords and either reinvested in land improvements or spent on luxury consumption. Agriculture's main contribution to the wider British economy was in freeing labor that could be employed in industry, thereby suppressing wages and allowing British manufacturers to undercut their Dutch competitors who were unable to reduce their labor costs (Allen 1992: 235–80; Arrighi and Silver 1999: 51–6). Britain's agricultural revolution was propelled by gentry and yeoman who gained private property in land, and the ability to dispossess tenants, through the series of elite conflicts that began with the Henrician Reformation and culminated in the Civil War and Glorious Revolution. The state did not transform land tenure in England; rather, as we saw in chapter 2, the state itself was formed out of those conflicts after land already had become private property.

The political system that was forged by the victorious elites in the Civil War and institutionalized after the Glorious Revolution of 1688 provided a mechanism for the ever more powerful industrialists and the ever more numerous petty bourgeois and skilled workers to influence government policy without the risk of destabilizing or provoking violent challenges. The gentry and London merchants controlled parliament, gained access through patronage to the royal administration, and governed their home counties and boroughs through a two-party system. The parties needed to appeal to the growing numbers of wealthy and voting manufacturers and merchants to hold power in parliament and at court, and they were forced to give "virtual representation" to non-voting petty bourgeois and artisans (because they lacked the property qualifications) to maintain order in the counties. Ties of political and economic patronage linked landowners, manufacturers, and lesser strata into county and urban party blocs. Those blocs provided the mechanism for joining the investors from various classes who capitalized railroads, with landowners' leverage within parliament to win parliamentary private Acts authorizing rights-of-way (Mann 1993: 127–8). Each party pressed for national reforms to keep their local supporters from joining the other party, which offered similar concessions. Thus, laissez-faire was institutionalized from 1760 to 1820, with the abolition of regulations over waged apprenticeships and unions, and the end of trade monopolies. These steps were taken by an unreformed parliament, "whose members were merchants or bankers, or landowners and professionals with merchant or banking interests. There were virtually no industrialists" (Mann 1993: 101). The policies of the nineteenth century that facilitated continued British economic dominance – free trade, reform of the domestic and colonial civil service, the abolition of patronage – were enacted by a government controlled by the old elites that had forged the British structure of politics and government during the conflicts of the seventeenth century. Britain's capacity to reform held off challenges to its economic dominance by the United States until the twentieth century and forced rapidly industrializing Germany into an ultimately catastrophic strategy of trying to build hegemony in Central Europe.

British imperialism was neither laissez-faire nor patrimonial. Britain, like France, was unable to prevent "colonial-interloper" merchants from encroaching on the monopolies granted to chartered companies. The interloper merchants supported parliament in the Civil War and, once the Crown was defeated, those merchants and allied manufacturers enjoyed open entry into foreign trade (Brenner 1993). The victory of the parliamentary forces and their allies also prevented the creation of patrimonial offices and privileges in India and the other British colonies. As a result, the East India Company, unlike its Dutch counterpart, was able to discipline its agents. This allowed it to control the Indian economy and to extract wealth from the subcontinent. "This drive for political control did not happen without considerable debate within the framework of the Company . . . [T]he [EIC] Court of Directors and the British government . . . came to feel that the British government had really only one choice, which was to take over the operation more directly" (Wallerstein 1989: 180–2). The British government's takeover of the Indian colonies, and the resulting expansion of the colonial civil service, set the political and institutional pattern for centralized control over its vast empire and ensured that colonial profits would continue to be funneled back to London and that the government could raise enough tax revenues in the colonies to finance the military and administrative costs of empire.

Imperialism and Capitalism

The four main powers of early modern Europe faced mainly internal political constraints on economic development. Where provincial and colonial oligarchies endured, and elites sustained the capacity to embed their interests in patrimonial offices, resources were encumbered, productive investment was limited, and states were unable to meet geopolitical challenges. Nevertheless, those states' only economic rivals were each other. The dynamics were different for all the other states in the world, a majority of which was colonized by those European states.

The central debate between Marxist and non-Marxist authors has been over how to characterize and explain the economic backwardness of non-core countries. Marx spanned the debate in his own work. In his first writings on India, published in 1853 in the *New York Daily Tribune*, Marx touted British imperialism as a progressive force, which dragged traditional Indian society into capitalist social relations. Marx later saw colonialism as retarding development in the periphery and argued that only when colonies became independent could national bourgeoisies develop and be protected by their state with tariffs (Larrain 1989: 45–62), but Marx didn't explain how class and state formation would occur after independence.[5]

Lenin ([1917] 1996) viewed imperialism as a combination of military-political and financial domination. As such, imperialism could be as exploitative when exercised over nominally independent countries as in formal colonies. Indeed, as capitalists in core countries faced ever more severe crises they intensified their exploitation of peripheral countries.[6] Lenin argued that genuine economic development could occur only after revolution had eliminated both foreign exploiters and their domestic bourgeois allies. As a result, Lenin focused his attention on how to build revolutionary movements, not on how to spur development within imperialist constraints. In so doing, Lenin minimized differences in the state forms and economic development of peripheral countries.

The most sophisticated Marxist analyses of imperialism are those of Wallerstein and Arrighi. They show how the world system shapes class relations and determines state forms in peripheral countries. Imperial powers recast land tenure and labor relations in their colonies, forcing their subjects into commodity production and mining to supply industries in the metropolis. Unlike previous empires and the Habsburgs, capitalist European powers did not simply loot their colonies. Rather, they enlisted local elites to manage sustained production. Complex relations developed between core capitalists, colonial administrators, and local elites. Yet, for world systems authors, those relations varied only by location in the world system. The class structure in the core countries differed from that in the periphery, and social relations in semi-peripheral countries took yet another form. Arrighi (1994) devotes extended analysis to the hegemon of each era, and argues that it differed from other core countries and that the state form needed to achieve and sustain hegemony varied in each era, as Britain succeeded the Netherlands, and then the USA achieved supremacy.

The problem with world system analyses is that they have no way to account for the rise of some countries from periphery to semi-periphery and others from semi-periphery to core. This model is all about how the world system is maintained and how crises reorder relations among core countries. The model acknowledges that crises create openings in the world system, and that in such moments countries lower in the system can rise, but how or why some do is not explained.

Modernization theory, the dominant non-Marxist theory in the decades following World War II during which almost all former colonies achieved independence, studiously avoids most mention of imperialism except as a force that "shocked traditional society and began or hastened its undoing, but . . . also set in motion ideas and sentiments which initiated the process by which a modern alternative to the traditional society was constructed out of the old culture" (Rostow 1960: 6). Whether this shock produced a "take-off" depended on "the emergence to political power of a group prepared to regard the modernization of the economy as serious, high-order political business" (ibid.: 8). Where world system theory has trouble explaining successful development, modernization theory can't account for failure. Why, when the global norm has become modernization, have some nations not created modernizing elites? Indeed, modernization theorists assume that all countries eventually will achieve modernization; the only question is the speed of the transformation (Larrain 1989: 98–102).

Raul Prebisch, the founder of the United Nations Economic Commission for Latin America and later of the United Nations Conference on Trade and Development, made the most influential, and theoretically sophisticated, effort to bridge Marxist and modernization theory. Prebisch argued, contrary to classical economic theory of relative advantage, that technological progress over time reduced the relative prices of raw goods and raised those of industrial products. As a result, peripheral regions that concentrated in agriculture and mining would fall ever further behind core industrial regions. This would happen even in the absence of imperial or other forms of exploitation. The solution, in Prebisch's view, was for peripheral states to adopt policies of import substitution, using domestic resources and foreign aid to develop domestic industries.[7]

Prebisch's policy advice was directed first at Latin American governments in the 1950s, and then followed on other continents as well. His contention that legacies of underdevelopment and imperial exploitation could be overcome with well-designed development strategies seemed credible in the post-war period. The United States, through massive foreign aid, which exceeded a tenth of the Federal budget from 1947 to 1950 (Amsden 2007: 57), spurred the rapid reindustrialization of Western Europe and Japan. It seemed plausible that similar strategies would work in non-core countries as well. Peripheral countries became sites of Cold War competition with the Soviet Union and the United States, and the International Monetary Fund and World Bank, which the US then controlled, "became amenable to heterodox ideas" (ibid.: 39), including a heavy state role in development.

Import substitution and most other aspects of the "development project" failed to spark sustained economic growth in most countries (McMichael 2004; Amsden 2007). For world systems theorists, and for non-Marxist structuralists such as Pinto, Sunkel, and Furtado, development remained constrained by the continuing capacity of the US and other core countries to exploit the periphery. Hinkelammert, Cardoso (who became the president of Brazil in 1995), and Faletto focus instead on class relations within dependent countries. While they acknowledge that the dominant classes of those countries are shaped in part by external powers, they argue that internal class struggles and economic development have their own dynamics. Unfortunately, those authors' important insight is not followed by detailed case studies or comparisons that could trace the actual political struggles that determine state economic policies.

Dependent Development

Master processes of imperialism, capitalism, the world system, and modernization are theoretical instruments that are too blunt to explain the divergent economic fates of peripheral states. We need to apply the same close analysis to understand development in the last two centuries as we did at the outset of this chapter to the original core countries of the capitalist world economy that emerged in the sixteenth century.

If we want to understand how and why some colonies and states dominated by imperial powers managed to escape economic exploitation and rise to core positions in the world economy, we must begin by acknowledging that such achievements were rare, and that in some cases development has been reversed. We need to examine the internal political dynamics of each country, even as we acknowledge that elites, classes, and states are both embedded in a world capitalist system and are vulnerable to formal colonial and indirect imperial control.

The few independent countries of the nineteenth century were the first states that adopted policies to imitate and challenge Britain's economic hegemony. Indeed, if we look at the past 200 years of economic development, political independence clearly is a necessary but not sufficient cause for success. No colonial government, or nominally independent government that was indirectly controlled by a foreign power, was able to institute an economic development policy. However, if we look at the set of independent countries, we find a clear divergence in nineteenth-century policies and achievements.

The independent states in Scandinavia, Belgium, the Netherlands, France, Switzerland, newly unified Germany, plus the United States all began their rise to wealth during the nineteenth century. All of them adopted protectionist policies: high tariffs and/or state subsidies, and guaranteed purchases for a few sheltered industries (Chang 2002). Japan subsidized industries, since it was prevented from imposing tariffs higher than 5 percent by unequal treaties that had been imposed by Western powers. Once those treaties expired in 1911, Japan also raised tariffs (ibid.: 46), as did Ireland as soon as it had achieved independence from Britain (O'Hearn 1998: 36).

All these states shared several characteristics. First, they had central governments that never had been, or no longer were, dominated by foreign powers. Second, all these polities had elite structures which resembled that of seventeenth-century Britain. There were multiple elites, cross-cut by economic sector and/or locality yet linked together in the state through mechanisms that ensured their interests would be represented, even as they were blocked from vetoing state policies and were unable to shelter resources from the overall economy or from the national government. Patrimonial offices had been largely eliminated. These elite structures were created through various pathways. Napoleon's invasion of the Low Countries finally destroyed the patrimonial offices and Contracts of Correspondence (and similar structures in Belgium) that blocked state initiatives. The Meiji Restoration (discussed in chapter 2) and the US Civil War crushed the regional autonomy of landed elites.

The great contrast is to be found in Latin America, the other region of the world in which most countries gained independence in the nineteenth century. For a time, the three countries of the southern cone, Argentina, Chile, and Uruguay, were among the richest countries in the world, profiting from the export of grain, meat, and, in the case of Chile, minerals. Yet none of those countries industrialized. For world systems theorists, the reason is clear; they all remained dependent for capital on Britain and later the United States. However, as Maurice Zeitlin (1984) shows, Chile had a path to becoming an industrialized core economy thanks to its large reserves of key minerals. The state could have built infrastructure, above all rail lines, and offered other subsidies to allow Chilean firms to develop independently of British mining interests. A domestic mining industry then would have created enough demand to stimulate a manufacturing sector in Chile. Owners of the large Central Valley estates managed to block such policies, in part because they would have been taxed to support industrial development and a growing industrial sector would have drawn workers away from agriculture, raising labor costs. Chile's fate was sealed in two Civil Wars in the 1850s and 1890s, which the faction headed by large landlords won, partly because the mining elite was divided on regional and familial lines. Ironically, in the second Civil War, the mining bourgeoisie was allied with an authoritarian president, so the agrarian elite's victory also fortified electoral democracy even as it ensured Chile's dependent economic position. Zeitlin concludes, "class relations within nations shape the global relations between them" (p. 234).

Even among the small and export-dependent countries of Central America, there was variation in state capacities to sustain development schemes. Where the coffee estate-owning elite was linked, by kin ties and political faction, to the industrialists who processed coffee, the agrarian elite dominated and prevented state investment in mechanized agriculture or processing techniques that added value to coffee. Only when and where the two elites split, was there any degree of development. Thus, Costa Rica stands out because many small producers there counterbalanced the large estate owners, allowing the industrial elite to shape state policy. In the rest of Central America, estate owners remained dominant and blocked developmental projects, at least until they were weakened in the successful Sandinista Revolution of 1979 in Nicaragua and the ultimately failed El Salvador revolution (Paige 1997).

The next great wave of independence occurred after World War II. In the following quarter-century almost every colony in the world became independent. Sustained economic development occurred in only a few countries. A number of recent studies are exemplary in showing what factors matter and how they vary among countries, giving empirical and analytic substance to Cardoso and Faletto's theoretical insights. The crucial factor in all these states is the structure of domestic elites, their relation to the state, and to foreign capitalists. Domestic elite structure, in turn, was decisively shaped during the era of foreign colonization and domination. Colonization transformed the ruling elites of societies around the world as Europeans enlisted local allies to do most of the work of managing empires. European colonialism differed from previous empires, as we discussed earlier, in its move to replace or at least augment looting and tribute with sustained enterprises and a focus on extracting resources crucial for industries in the metropole. This created local elites of commercial landlords and merchants, as well as state bureaucrats.[8] Few Europeans, with the exception of the British settler colonies (the United States, Canada, Australia, New Zealand, and South Africa) and the French in Algeria, actually lived outside the metropole. Britain had 2,700 employees in its Colonial Office in 1890, and an additional 2,200 in the India Office. There were 100–150,000 personnel in the army and navy in the second half of the nineteenth century (Porter 2004: 26), but they were not administrators. They were on call to suppress rebellions.

After independence, local elites took command of the state

and, though often still subordinate to foreign capital, of the economy. Elite interests did not necessarily favor development. As McMichael rightly argues, developmental and other universalistic theories suffer from an "inability to acknowledge that states are first and foremost instruments of rule: Whether they can successfully 'develop' their societies depends on their social structures and historical circumstances, rather than the predictions of development theory and/or natural processes of development" (2004: 29).

Which social structures and historical circumstances matter in determining each state's development policies and successes? Theorists distinguish themselves by their answers to that question. Most begin by examining the colonial legacy, the structure of elite and class relations, and governmental forms created in the colonial era. Where landed and locally autonomous elites survived, or were fortified by colonialism, the successor independent states were predatory. Kohli (2004) shows how Nigeria's local elites were empowered under British rule. The few British administrators in colonial Nigeria sought merely to exclude other European powers and to extract resources and revenues. They accomplished that by dealing with local elites, forging personalistic rule within ethnic regions. After independence, ethnic conflict undermined electoral politics, leaving power in the hands of the military. A strong bureaucracy capable of implementing development projects, or even collecting significant taxes, never formed, so the military state remained dependent on fluctuating oil revenues. Money, when available, was lost to a corrupt military or on prestige projects that depended on foreign supervision. That is why Nigeria became one of the great economic disasters of the previous half-century.

Belgian rule in the Congo similarly left a legacy of autonomous regional elites, and a weak central government that used what power it had after independence to act in a purely predatory manner as individual officeholders enriched themselves. Zaire's rulers intervene in civil society only to disorganize opponents and extract resources (Evans 1995), and their low capacity makes other interventions designed to foster development impossible, even if they were in state officials' interests. Large areas of Africa,

Central Asia (including Pakistan), and the Philippines have highly decentralized elite structures with weak, patrimonial predatory states, often organized along chains of manufactured ethnic identity and loyalty, and hence with little development (Castells 2000: 95–114).

Korea, in contrast, was bequeathed a strong and authoritarian state by its Japanese occupiers. That state was further strengthened under the subsequent US occupation. The US also turned over the industries created under Japan to Korean entrepreneurs, forming a capitalist class. Meanwhile, to blunt communist support, the US pushed radical land reform while crushing trade unions. The Park Chung Hee regime, which took power in 1961, inherited an ideal social structure for a developmental policy: weak landlords and a free peasantry, a small but cohesive capitalist class, and a highly bureaucratic state. The South Korean state offered subsidies and imposed discipline as Korean capitalists used Japanese firms' capital and market connections to build export-led industry. Kohli (2004) and Amsden (1989) emphasize the Korean state's capacity to impose discipline and far-sighted planning, although the initiative for the opening to Japan came from business (Chibber 2003). The Park administration turned away from its predecessor's corrupt allocation of subsidies, under pressure from student demonstrations (Amsden 1989), and also because its military officials were linked to the few giant firms (*chaebols*) that benefited from the new policies at the expense of smaller capitalists. Evans (1995) rightly sees Korea as the outstanding example of "embedded autonomy," a system in which close ties between business and the state prevent officials from adopting self-serving and predatory policies, while allowing officials to gather the information and perform the supervision needed to ensure that firms actually use state benefits for long-term national economic goals, yet leaving those firms free from state claims on their profits. Such embeddedness is possible only when the capitalist class is relatively small and cohesive, and when the state is unified at the national level so that local elites can't appropriate resources and authority.

Evans (1995) argues that a similarly autonomous bureaucratic state developed in Taiwan when Kuomintang officials, who had been predatory when they ruled mainland China, reformed agriculture and turned over enterprises seized from Japanese collaborators to allied businessmen. Wade (1990) argues that the Taiwanese government was able to discipline capitalists because it maintained ownership or close control over the financial sector and used the allocation of capital, along with tariffs and targeted aid, to force domestic firms to invest in export-oriented production. The state also limited foreign investment to the export sector. Taiwan's export push was much more a government initiative than in Korea (perhaps because Taiwan was entering the world market later and was forced to maneuver around the markets already controlled by Japanese-Korean combines). However, both states were capable of developing embedded autonomy because they had shaped a political landscape in which non-elites were satisfied (peasants) or suppressed (workers), local elites were disempowered, and capitalists were cohesive.

The colonial legacy was more ambiguous and the state less centralized in most developing nations. Scholars have focused, rightly, on India and Brazil, two of the largest non-OECD economies in the world, and ones that fall in their development trajectories between the East Asian tigers and the failed and predatory African states.

Brazil emerged from Portuguese rule with a weak central state. Landowners remained in control of their tenants and of local government, and the national government continually jockeyed for power and resources with highly autonomous state governments beholden to their own local elites. Only under the Vargas presidency (1930–45) was the state centralized. Kohli (2004) doesn't explain how that centralization occurred. Indeed, he sees the state as still weak and fragmented, and therefore vulnerable to demands from mass constituencies for increased consumption that caused inflation and uneven development. Evans (1979, 1995) explains the strength and limitation of the Brazilian state in terms of the process of elite and class formation. He shows how foreign investment in Brazil spurred the creation of a domestic bourgeoisie and also a cohort of Brazilian managers of foreign firms. Evans traces a convergence in personnel and interests of Brazilian capitalists, managers, and state officials who combined to weaken landed interests and patrimonial local governments. Yet, because Brazilian firms remained tied to foreign suppliers of capital, technology, and markets, those firms remained ambiguous in the policies they demanded from the state, focusing more on subsidies and protection for domestic markets rather than export-led development. The state's protection of the large domestic Brazilian market made that nation an attractive site for foreign joint ventures, so some Brazilian industries did manage to develop. However, the state's capacity to foster and discipline domestic industry continued to suffer from political divisions and the ability of state officials to create competing agencies and lard them with clients.

India's national government was weakened by its initial decision after independence to offer autonomy to states and patronage to local elites (it is probable that national political leaders didn't have the power to decide differently), and later by Indira Gandhi's packing of the bureaucracy with political allies (Kohli 2004). However, Chibber (2003) convincingly documents that India's development was retarded mainly because Indian capitalists were able to block effective import-substitution planning. Indian industrialists allied with Congress Party leaders to undermine labor unions that could have served as a counterweight to capitalists in the immediate post-independence years when planning legislation was passed. In the absence of effective working-class opposition, Indian industrialists were able to ensure that government planners never received the power to impose discipline on capitalists who diverged from the investment plans that justified their subsidies. India was left with a weak planning bureaucracy, which was further undermined by challenges from other government ministries. Facing challenges from rival ministries, and lacking political support from the top of the government or the Congress Party, Indian planning officials never could make credible threats to withdraw licenses or to take back allocations of foreign exchange or other resources.

Chibber compares India with a variety of cases to explain why India became "locked in place" and was unable to adopt a different developmental plan when the problems with Indian import substitution became apparent. Chibber convincingly argues that India never could have switched to a successful export-oriented strategy. Such opportunities were rare and, as with Korea, largely dependent on outside help never available to India. More realistically, India could have adopted a better-crafted policy of fostering domestically oriented industrialization. Key to such a strategy would have been the strengthening of the labor movement, as happened in the communist-led Kerala State, which enjoyed the highest rate of growth and the healthiest social indicators in India.

Chibber provides the most nuanced and historically grounded analysis we yet have of how developmental policies are determined and why Korea's success was so rare and hard to follow. India's divided and pro-capitalist state created an opening for the personalistic and corrupt regime of the Indira Gandhi years, which led business to demand internal deregulation combined with continuing protection from more efficient foreign competitors. Chibber's model thus explains not only the lack of reform during the crucial decades when East Asian rivals grabbed the available international opportunities, but also the limited nature of recent reforms.

While Chibber doesn't directly address state socialist economies, his analysis of export-led development and Evans's discussion of embedded autonomy can be combined to account for the poor performance of state socialist development in the post-1945 era. Only the Soviet Union, as the first socialist state, benefited from ending the control of foreign capital over its economy. All the others were pressed into subordinate positions in a smaller, far less well-capitalized world system dominated by the USSR. China's rapid growth came only after its escape from the Soviet economic bloc and after it established itself at the crossroads of overlapping trade and financial networks with the US, EU, and, most vitally, its Asian neighbors (Arrighi 2007). All the other socialist countries were doubly constrained: pressed into a Soviet-controlled economic system, they were ruled by a single elite that commanded both the state and firms.

State socialist development plans mirrored existing bureaucratic power, reproducing in production the increasingly autarkic control of firms and state agencies by party officials. As parties became more rigid, economic growth stagnated in the 1970s (Castells 2000: 6–19). Castells attributes Soviet technological stagnation to the diversion of resources to the military and to the top-down command structure of the economy, but the Soviet Union's high military budget was more than made up by low allocations for consumer products, while the top leadership repeatedly saw the need for innovation and created institutions and mechanisms to promote scientific and technological research. The problem, as became apparent in the rapid appropriation of almost all firms by party insiders after 1991 (Burawoy and Krotov 1992; Walder 2003), was that local party officials and firm managers had gained autonomous control over industrial plants, distribution networks, and raw materials. Those resources could not be effectively marshaled for centrally planned innovations. After Stalin, party officials were determined never again to allow themselves to be left at the mercy of arbitrary central power. Their political success ended the possibility of any form of embedded autonomy and productive innovation in the Soviet Union.

James Scott (1998) offers a different, and highly influential, explanation for the failure of so much state-led development. He argues that large-scale development plans can be imposed only when "a prostate civil society lacks the capacity to resist those plans. War, revolution, and economic collapse often radically weaken civil society as well as make the populace more receptive to a new dispensation. Late colonial rule . . . occasionally met this last condition" (p. 5). Scott's analysis partly parallels our discussion above: both see the weakening of local groups (elites in the above discussion, communities in Scott's) as necessary to empower state managers to appropriate and deploy resources. However, Scott sees state officials alone, rather than allied with capitalists, as the engineers of development. State officials, in Scott's view, are motivated by the desire to see and control their subjects, to make them "legible" and then to reorder society according to "high-modernist ideology . . . a strong . . . version of the self-confidence about scientific and technical progress, the expansion of production, the growing satisfaction of human needs, the mastery of nature (including human nature), and, above all, the rational design of social order commensurate with scientific understanding of natural laws" (p.4). Officials pursued high modernist schemes, such as the planned cities of Brasilia and Chandigarh, India, Soviet-forced collectivization and Tanzanian "compulsory villagization," and mono-crop forests and farms "because these forms fit into a high-modernist view and also answered their political interests as state officials" (p. 5) to control their subjects.

High modernist schemes are doomed to failure, in Scott's view, because central planning cannot anticipate the complexities of human relations and natural environments. Collective agriculture fails to boost production, mono-crops succumb to disease, and planned cities are lifeless and crime-ridden. Scott's critique of state planning echoes (probably unconsciously) Hayek's argument in *The Road to Serfdom* that state planning and redistribution inevitably destroy freedom. Scott's causality is the opposite of Hayek's. For Scott, only after political autonomy is destroyed can high modernist planning proceed.

> Like Hayek, Scott exaggerates and he focuses on extreme, worst-case scenarios of state planning (yes, Brasilia, but what about Saint Petersburg and Haussmann's Paris? What about the New Deal, Scandinavian social democracy, the US interstate highway system, public health successes such as the eradication of yellow fever, cholera and polio?). Yet he suggests (and certainly his title suggests) that all states are disposed to "seeing like a state" and thereby threaten the indicated harms to human well-being. (Lukes 2006: 10)

Neoliberalism

Scott's book, though written from an avowedly "anarchist" perspective, is testament to the intellectual as well as political reach of the recent wave of neoliberalism. Most studies on the rise of neoliberalism present it as an unstoppable ideological force and attribute the decline of developmentalism to the irresistible dictates of the United States and global institutions such as the World Bank, International Monetary Fund, and World Trade Organization.

In this view, third world governments, especially those countries that defaulted on debt in Latin America in 1982 and in East Asia in 1997, have no choice but to reduce tariffs and subsidies to home industries, embrace "free trade," cut social programs, and link their currencies and financial markets to financial institutions headquartered in the United States and Western Europe. (Brenner 2003 and McMichael 2004 offer the best descriptions of neoliberalism, even as they critique it.) States not only face international diplomatic and financial demands, but intellectual pressure as well. Economists trained in the United States in neoclassical economics return home and delegitimize developmental and Marxist theories that once provided a basis for formulating alternative policies (Babb 2004).

In fact, states have varied in whether and how they have adopted or resisted neoliberal policies. The richest and most powerful countries, especially the United States, have been able to demand exceptions and special privileges in international agreements that allow them to protect domestic industries and to manipulate their currencies and interest rates. Most notoriously, the US and the EU maintain agricultural subsidies that allow their farmers to undercut third world producers. The US, European nations, and Japan have sought to manipulate their currencies to benefit domestic producers (Brenner 2003 traces such efforts and their effects on the economies of the US, Japan, and Germany). Usually, the hegemon prevails, as Britain did in the nineteenth century, and the US since 1945. China currently is trying to use its huge dollar holdings and trade surplus to undermine US control over the global terms of trade, but China's interests in protecting its domestic manufacturers and guarding its massive investments in the US, both of which rely on a strong dollar, limit China's freedom of maneuver, as do the interests of other states.

Countries with strong domestic capitalists and large, horizontally or vertically integrated firms have been better able to resist the demands of external powers to deregulate and to merger home firms with multinationals. Amsden (2001 ch: 9) finds a clear and widening gap in the 1980s and 1990s between Argentina, Brazil, Chile, Mexico, and Turkey on the one hand, and Korea, Taiwan,

China, and India on the other. In the former, local firms were bought out by or linked with foreign investors, reducing domestic investment in research and development by firms and in science and education by the state. The Asian states all found ways around the new WTO rules and continued to subsidize domestic firms, providing the capital those firms needed to avoid having to merge with foreign enterprises. Where consolidation was needed to achieve the scale necessary to compete internationally, those states fostered mergers among domestic firms.

Ireland, Taiwan, Israel, and, to a lesser extent, Singapore have, since the 1980s, pioneered a different strategy to become "developmental network states." These states have forged a "social partnership between business, unions, and government" which makes possible agreements on wage restraints and tax cuts, along with government investment in education and industrial development, such as innovation centers and university-industry collaborations (Ó Riain 2004: 10). These policies are neoliberal but with targeted state investment and regulation, designed to take advantage of each country's particular advantages, thus allowing an unusual degree of embeddedness in international networks of high-tech firms. Ireland and Singapore did this by encouraging foreign investment, which Ireland leveraged with subsidies and other assistance derived from its membership in the European Union. However, while Singapore deliberately sought investment from various core countries and sectors, and "diversified very early on into financial services," Ireland remained heavily dependent on US electronics and pharmaceutical firms, and its strategy generated fewer jobs and less income growth than did Singapore's or the efforts of the other Asian Tigers to develop their domestic firms (O'Hearn 1998: 153 and passim). "In Israel and Taiwan, this strategy is built around early ties to the diaspora and to transnational technical communities" (Ó Riain 2004: 196). Israeli high-tech firms benefited from an extra layer of subsidies provided by the state's large investment in military research, much done in universities. Taiwan's network of small firms was better suited to this model than Korean *chaebols*. Taiwan's "flexible state-sponsored institutions [are] a critical supporting and guiding force, connecting the relatively small Taiwanese firms with their myriad international networks" (p. 201). Those institutions, lodged in "a strong central state . . . can act 'flexibly' because they are rarely constrained by worries at the center regarding political competition" (pp. 208–9), just as Singapore's highly centralized and autonomous state can invest in local firms and cut deals with foreign investors. In all four of these countries, neoliberalism exposes ordinary citizens, but not high-tech firms selected for growth, to unfettered market forces.

Neoliberalism promises the end of a development project that began in early modern Europe and was taken up in varying forms by each newly independent country. Neoliberalism, on an ideological level, rejects the nationalistic goals of all previous development projects. Instead, neoliberalism claims that economic growth comes only from dismantling barriers between the domestic and world economies. Of course, capitalists in many countries in past centuries found their own opportunities for amassing wealth, as individuals, families, and classes, through links to foreign capital. As we have seen in this chapter, the greater the extent to which domestic capital was subordinated to foreign investors, the narrower the opportunities for the state to pursue mercantilist, protectionist, or developmental policies. The most constricted states were colonies or newly independent states still dominated by foreign powers. World systems, and other models of capitalism as a global system, are useful in identifying the moments when capitalists in peripheral countries come under the greatest pressure to accept investment, trade relationships, and other organizational links from abroad. Yet peripheral capitalists and their states varied in each of those eras in the degree to which they were compelled to submit to foreign control. Economic autonomy and robust development concentrated in countries with bureaucratized states and a capitalist class that was linked together and represented in the state. Isolated elites, above all agrarian landlords, capable of withholding resources from the national polity, undermined economic development in all eras. The state in unified polities was able to aid capitalists who were not yet subordinated to foreign capital, and that aid was effective when states had disciplinary mechanisms to prevent capitalists from converting state assistance into patrimonial or corrupt entitlements. The sort of state and relationship to capitalists that is most compatible with economic development has been constant, even as the strategies needed to move a country toward the core has varied as the world capitalist economy and the forms of production within it have been repeatedly transformed.

5

Democracy, Civil Rights, and Social Benefits

So far the history of states I've presented in this book has focused on elites: rulers, capitalists, state officials, and even intellectuals. All the other inhabitants of states have been presented as taxpayers, soldiers, nationalists, or other objects of elite initiatives. In fact, non-elites also were active agents in the making of states. This chapter brings those subjects into that history.

Citizens are different from subjects. Citizens have individual rights and collectively they elect the legislators and (at least indirectly) the executives of their government. This chapter explains how citizens came to have those rights and how democratic control over government was achieved in some places, beginning in the eighteenth century. We will identify the factors that account for why particular countries participated in the waves of democratization and de-democratization that have swept the world over the past 200 years.

Democracy is more than voting. To be meaningful it also must include the right to participate in politics beyond elections. Citizens can only exercise a meaningful vote if they are secure from arbitrary government pressures and threats, and have the means and freedom to organize and to discuss issues with fellow citizens.[1] Thus, we need to examine whether and how civil liberties developed in tandem with electoral rights.

Citizens throughout the world have parlayed mass democracy into claims for social benefits. Yet the relationship between voting and social welfare provisions is highly variable and not automatic.

130

We will explore why voters have won extensive social benefits in some polities while far less in others. Specifically, we will examine why the United States, once a leader in social benefits, has lagged behind European and some other societies in those provisions since the end of World War II, and why a few third world and non-democratic states countries created substantial welfare states while most have not. (We will save for the concluding chapter a discussion of the future prospects for social welfare benefits in both rich and poor nations.)

Finally, as we trace the decline of social benefits under neo-liberal regimes, we must ask whether citizenship and democracy can be sustained when and where social rights decline. Margaret Somers describes citizenship as "the right to have rights . . . political membership must include the de facto right to social inclusion in civil society" (2008: 5–6). At issue is what degree and nature of political inclusion is possible where social benefits are too narrow to ensure participation in civic life. In other words, how much economic and social inequality is compatible with electoral democracy and civil rights? What benefits are necessary to ensure social inclusion? The answers to these questions are not absolute; indeed, our task is to trace and explain why the menu of social benefits seen as necessary to full citizenship has expanded drastically in some polities, while it remains more constricted in other nations that have elections as well.

Elite and Pre-State Democracies

For most of human history leaders have come to power through inheritance or by force. Max Weber's ([1922] 1978: 901–1157) typology of authority is also a lineage of regime change. Leaders who came to power through violence were, at first, illegitimate unless and until they established themselves as patrimonial officials who had an orderly procedure for passing on their leadership to an heir. Until the eighteenth century, few leaders came to office through bureaucratic procedures. Most notably, Catholic popes, who (with rare and illegitimate exceptions) did not have heirs, headed the longest-lived bureaucratic organization in the world. The Catholic and other churches created a model for elites to collectively select a leader, a pattern followed by the nobilities of Poland, Hungary, and Bohemia, which, as we saw in chapter 2, elected a king for life who could not pass his crown to an heir.

Participation by less exclusive groups in selecting a leader was rare and confined to small polities. Most famously, Athens created a General Assembly in which all male citizens, who were perhaps a tenth of the total population, had an equal right to speak and to vote. Other Greek cities in the fifth and fourth centuries BC had similar democratic assemblies. This model was imitated two millennia later for limited periods in some of the small city-states of medieval and Renaissance Italy. Peasant villages in parts of Europe had assemblies or courts in which all heads of families with land had an equal vote. In parts of what would become Switzerland, village assemblies amalgamated to form cantonal bodies. Similarly, the Iroquois of North America often elected their sachems (chiefs) and the sachems in turn served on a council of tribes. Some Protestant churches, especially in Scandinavia and England, were governed democratically by male congregants. Examples of village democracy can be found in India, parts of Africa, and no doubt elsewhere in the world. However, all these bodies were small in scale, ranging from villages of a few hundred to city-states or cantons of tens of thousands. Ancient Athens, the Roman Republic, and Renaissance Florence and Venice are the only polities of more than 100,000 inhabitants with democratic bodies until the establishment of the United States, and of course only a minority of men voted in those city-states, and an even smaller minority in the Roman Republic, while all or most men voted in the much smaller tribal, village, and congregational polities (Tilly 2007: 25–31 offers the best summary of this history).

The Origins of Democracy

States, as we saw in chapter 2, came into existence when elites and their organizational capacities were combined into a single institution. Non-elites also were incorporated within states as subjects, and became vulnerable to new demands (in addition or in place of their old obligations to landlords, clerics, and other elites) as states increased their capacity to draft subjects and tax their resources. State demands elicited continued resistance but they also fostered a growing sense of nationalism, turning subjects into citizens, a process which we traced in chapter 3.

At the same time as states became the sites of elite consolidation and objects of nationalist loyalty, they also became increasingly subject to democratic controls. The academic debate over the causes and process of democratization can be condensed into a single question:

> Was democracy a gift by states to their citizens in return for taxes paid and military service rendered (and perhaps as a sop to deflect workers' economic demands) or was it a right won through struggle by popular forces against elites that sought to retain their monopoly on state power?[2]

Marx championed the view that democracy is created in struggle and that it is done so by the working class. Marx's *The Eighteenth Brumaire of Louis Bonaparte* ([1852] 1963) examined an unprecedented and radical extension of democracy: the Second French Republic of 1848–51. That Republic's Constitution was the first in world history that granted all males the right to vote for a national government without a property qualification, and provided for direct election of the president of the Republic. It also was the first republic overthrown in a coup. How does Marx explain the democratization and de-democratization of France?

Marx sees the proletariat as the only class with a genuine commitment to democracy. France got a radically democratic Constitution because the relatively small French working class was concentrated in Paris, which also was the seat of government. Workers overthrew the monarchy and wrote the Constitution before the rest of France could mobilize. Yet, because workers were a minority of the nation beyond Paris, democracy and the Republic were doomed in Marx's view. The peasant majority, by contrast, did not understand its interests in class terms, or at least was unable to express its interests through electoral politics (on this point Marx did not do enough research to specify the causes of peasants' political passivity). As a result, peasants were swayed by bogus issues and voted mainly for parties that were financed and controlled by capitalists, landlords, and the Catholic Church, and which did not have a commitment to the Republic. In the presidential election they supported Louis Bonaparte, nephew of Napoleon, who was a symbol of patriotism and national regeneration rather than the proponent of a specific program.

Capitalists occupy a contradictory position in Marx's analysis. On the one hand, they prefer a constitutional order to either monarchy or dictatorship since the rule of law protects their property rights from arbitrary demands, while their unparalleled capacity to finance candidates and their campaigns gives them leverage over elected politicians. At the same time, capitalists understand that electoral democracy creates the danger that the oppressed classes, which constitute the majority, could elect parties that represent the majority's material interests and thereby challenge capitalist relations of production and private property. That was the dilemma the French bourgeoisie faced in the Second Republic. As workers gained strength, capitalists sought to weaken French democracy by imposing residence requirements that would have eliminated many workers' voting rights. Capitalists got captive politicians in the National Assembly to support their interests, which de-legitimized the Republic and created mass acquiescence in Louis Bonaparte's coup. Democracy, in Marx's analysis, is always threatened by self-aggrandizing public officials like Louis Bonaparte. However, Bonapartism can't overthrow a constitutional republic unless capitalists either align with the putative dictator or inadvertently undermine electoral democracy through their efforts to compel the state to support their interests.

Abraham (1981) reaches a similar conclusion in his analysis of the downfall of the Weimar Republic. Abraham finds that most German capitalists did not support the Nazis. However, their maneuvers to undermine the powerful working-class movement, represented by the Communist and Social Democratic Parties, disrupted electoral democracy, which served to weaken the mainstream parties of the right, opening the way for the Nazis to seize control of the government in a constitutional coup.

Mann (2004) in his study of the five countries where fascists took power – Germany, Italy, Austria, Hungary, and Romania – identifies agrarian landlords, army commanders, and the Church as the elites that felt most threatened by the emerging democratic states and "turned toward more repressive regimes, believing these could protect themselves against the twin threats of social disorder and the political left" (pp. 24–5). Those five countries differed from Spain and other authoritarian polities in the presence of violent paramilitaries, outside the control of the elites. The paramilitaries were a genuine source of fascist electoral popularity and symbols of the fascist movement's commitment to cleansing the state of enemies and transcending the conflicts between left and right. As such, fascists ultimately threatened the old elites that made their bids for power possible, just as Louis Bonaparte eventually was able to turn on his ruling-class sponsors.

The fate of democracy, for Marx, depends on the balance of class forces. He believed democracy could develop where the working class is dominant. If capitalists are stronger, then a limited democracy in which capitalists control elected officials remains possible. Dictatorship occurs when workers and capitalists are stalemated or when pre-capitalist classes (most notably landlords and peasants) remain dominant.

Marx's complex analysis of electoral politics under capitalism was greatly simplified by later Marxists. Indeed, today, many understand Marx, not through a first-hand reading of works such as *The Eighteenth Brumaire*, but in terms of what Lenin told us Marx means. Lenin's central argument is that "the state is an organization of violence for the suppression of some class" (([1917] 1976: 30). All states, in Lenin's view, are designed to serve only the class that created it. A capitalist state, then, is only a false democracy. Lenin derides parliaments as "talking shops," designed to divert attention from the true decisions of the state, which are made by unelected bureaucrats operating in secrecy. For that reason, proletarian revolution was necessary to overthrow the capitalist state and create a state that would serve working-class interests and be truly democratic. How such a revolution would be realized, and whether and how the resulting "dictatorship of the proletariat" would evolve into democracy became the central points of debate among Lenin and other Marxist intellectuals in the decades leading up to World War II.[3] These authors (most notably Leon Trotsky, György Lukács, Karl Kautsky, Rosa Luxemburg, and Antonio Gramsci, as well as Lenin), despite their differences, all reject both Marx's claim that the state has the potential for (Bonapartist) autonomy under capitalism and the social democratic view that elections provide an avenue for the gradual achievement of worker interests within a state that would evolve from servant of capitalism to neutral to subversive of capitalism.[4]

Gramsci ([1929–35] 1971) advanced the Marxist understanding of politics by arguing that capitalist power was grounded not only in the force wielded by the state, but also in ideological hegemony that encompassed civil society as well as the state. As a result, revolutionary movements, in Gramsci's view, must engage in a "war of position" against capitalist hegemony in both realms. Gramsci's vagueness on how that could be done does not detract from his sharp analysis of how the task of forming working-class consciousness grounded in a counter, anti-capitalist hegemony must precede both the overthrow of the capitalist state and the creation of proletarian democracy.

Marx and Gramsci have had influence on the study of democracy, among non-Marxists as well as Marxists. Gramsci's concept of hegemony has given rise to a large literature on civil society, which we will examine later in this chapter. Marx's view of the state as an expression of the balance of class forces was taken up by Barrington Moore, in his *Social Origins of Dictatorship and Democracy* (1966). Moore directly addresses the problem of this chapter in his effort to explain why electoral democracies developed in Britain, France, and the United States, while Germany and Japan ended up with fascist regimes, and Russia and China underwent communist revolutions. He identifies the agrarian classes – landlords and peasants – as the key actors.

Where agriculture remained labor-repressive rather than commercial, landlords were the dominant political class. The outcome then depended on the revolutionary potential of the peasantry. Where peasant communities remained intact, communist revolutions occurred. Where landlord-controlled states instituted limited development from above, the peasantry was weakened as a class, making possible fascist regimes. Only where commercialization weakened landlords did the bourgeoisie become the dominant class with the capacity to create democratic regimes that served its interests. Thus, Moore explains democracy as the result of a particular balance of class forces among capitalists, landlords, and peasants. Unlike Marx, Moore has little to say about the working class, which in his view enters politics only after the character of the regime has been determined.

Moore's final chapter addresses India, which sustains a democratic regime in the absence of commercialized agriculture. Moore's discussion of India is unsystematic and unconvincing, and suggests that a different sort of analysis may be needed for understanding regimes established in the aftermath of colonial rule. Most work on new democracies comes from outside the Marxist tradition and will be addressed later in this chapter. Recent Marxist work on democracy is of two sorts. One, exemplified by Paige (1997) and Zeitlin (1984), offers precise analyses of class coalitions and their effects on regime types, while world systems theory seeks to explain democratic and authoritarian regimes in terms of their states' position in the world system.

Wallerstein notes that "the world-economy . . . had various kinds of workers [slaves, sharecroppers, wage laborers, skilled craftsmen, etc.] . . . each mode of labor control is best suited for particular types of production . . . the modes of labor control greatly affect the political system (in particular the strength of the state apparatus) and the possibilities for an indigenous bourgeoisie to thrive" (1974: 86–7). Only where indigenous bourgeoisies dominated strong states could they implement a "liberal agenda" of "universal (male) suffrage, the beginning of a welfare state, and national identity" to quiet the revolutionary stirrings of the working class (Wallerstein 2000: 421). Outside the core, indigenous ruling classes relied on authoritarian regimes to suppress the "dangerous classes." Arrighi (1994, 2007; Arrighi and Silver 1999) makes a significant addition to world systems theory by showing that voting rights and social welfare benefits expanded when competition among core capitalist countries for hegemony peaked, most notably right before, and especially in the aftermath of, World Wars I and II. In Arrighi's view, competition among capitalists weakens them vis-à-vis workers.

Working-class electoral gains, however, varied in the core, and peasant political mobilization was uneven in the periphery. Neither Wallerstein nor Arrighi are able to account for variations within zones of the world system. Nor do their models provide the specificity to account for regime change within single polities. Zeitlin (1984) addresses that problem in his analysis of alliances and schisms among class fractions, which, as we saw in the previous chapter, he used to explain Chile's stymied economic development. Zeitlin's case study shows that position in the world system doesn't automatically determine political regime. Rather, class fractions in Chile achieved control over the state through alliances that could be preserved only through electoral democracy and a liberal constitution, even at the cost of granting suffrage and slowly growing political leverage to workers and peasants.

Geopolitical pressures are contingent and changing, as Paige shows in the emergence of neoliberal democracy. Paige examines the coffee-producing countries of Central America, which appear to fit Moore's typology, with El Salvador as authoritarian, Nicaragua as revolutionary socialism, and Costa Rica as democratic. However, in none of those countries was there a clear split between landed aristocracy and industrial bourgeoisie because those two classes were linked by familial and business ties. El Salvador and Nicaragua established electoral democracies in the 1990s. Paige follows Moore in identifying the end of labor-repressive agriculture as a necessary condition for that transformation, but adds that the move away from reactionary forms of agrarian production and regimes required a break between the agro-industrial and agrarian class fractions. That split occurred only under the pressure of armed leftist insurgencies. US political and military interference, by halting leftist insurgencies short of victory, ensured that Central America did not follow the Russian and Chinese paths. However, because the insurgencies weakened agrarian landlords, democracy developed, albeit with elections producing governments that followed US-favored neo-liberal policies.

Zeitlin and Paige give agency to class actors and give cross-class alliances causal power. Yet all the works reviewed in this section, with the exception of Marx's *The Eighteenth Brumaire*, present state officials as passive servants of the dominant class or of cross-class alliances. Authors who see state actors as independent agents, and the grantors of democratic rights, come mainly from a non-Marxist tradition.

States and Democracy

Charles Tilly (2007), in attributing autonomous interests and agency to state actors, allows for the possibility that state officials can alter social relations in civil society in ways that foster various classes' participation in public politics. Rulers, in Tilly's analysis, offer voting rights, civil liberties, and social welfare benefits as a way to bind subjects to the state as citizens. Subjects demand those rights, not as part of a Marxist class struggle, or even as a way to check arbitrary state power, but because two master processes – capitalism and state formation – undermine the "local trust networks" that provide a measure of protection against economic and security risks.[5] States, through police, national laws, and social welfare provisions, create a new system of risk protection, binding subjects to the national polity. At the same time, states sought to weaken "autonomous power centers," partly by attacking them and partly by offering their members "binding consultation." This meant that voting rights first were offered to privileged minorities and only later were extended to a majority of the adult, male, population. As more and more citizens won electoral rights, legal protections, and social welfare benefits, "categorical ine-qualities," the institutionalized privileges of elites, were reduced.

"[E]xpanding state activity drew more citizens into state-coordinated efforts, which enlarged public politics" (p. 194). This virtuous cycle leads to a growing electorate of citizens who are dependent on and committed to the national state. Conversely, "if rich states dismantle the redistributive and equalizing arrangements that have grown up within democratic capitalism and rich people disconnect their trust networks from public politics by such means as gated communities and private schooling, we should expect those measures to de-democratize their regimes" (p. 204). This seems to be a comment on contemporary neoliberalism rather than the basis for a systematic analysis of the factors that lead the rich in some countries to try, and succeed in, withdrawing from public trust networks.

Tilly, like Marx but unlike most Marxists, acknowledges state officials' self-interest, but goes beyond Marx in showing how state officials' actions transform as well as dominate classes and elites in civil society. States, in alliance with subordinate groups, make democracy, while privileged elites have the potential to undermine democracy. Tilly's causal models are presented at a high degree of abstraction, and his brief accounts of particular national trajectories of democratization are merely descriptive. Fortunately, other scholars have identified factors that account for variation in democratization across time and space.

Stein Rokkan (1970) identifies representative bodies, such as aristocratic assemblies and estates, as the sources of democracy. The earlier such bodies win recognition by the ruler, and the stronger those bodies' powers, the earlier opposition parties will be legitimized and contested elections will become institutionalized, as happened in Britain. However, such precocious representative systems also served to slow the expansion of the franchise, in Britain, most of Scandinavia, the Netherlands, and Belgium. Conversely, the sudden creation of electoral democracy was quickly reversed in France, Germany, and Greece in the 1840s "when new regimes temporarily installed both representative legislatures and general male suffrage, but authoritarian regimes then took over, sapping legislative power without eliminating elections" (Tilly 2007: 63).

Higley and Burton (2006) contend that liberal democracy is possible only in the rare event that "warring elites" reach agreements to abide by elections. Such elite "settlements . . . are deliberate and sudden and depend upon highly contingent elite circumstances and choices" (p. 4). Elite settlements also were possible in settler colonies with long traditions of self-rule. Today, democracy is most likely to be institutionalized when and where prosperity unites elites and makes electorates "adverse to drastic alternations of the status quo" (p.4), undermining support for radical parties of the left and right that threaten constitutional governments. Higley and Burton's work suffers from an inability to explain why settlements happen when they do, or how elites and, in recent decades, entire electorates become risk adverse.

Garrard (2002) finds that British democracy expanded because non-voters were linked to enfranchised elites through local patronage chains. Elites, rather than state officials, pushed to extend voting as a way to reward lower-class allies, partly because those elites – confident that their subordinates would follow their lead in voting – saw an expanded franchise as a way to strengthen their political power locally and nationally. Democratization in Britain was not a result of class conflict but of the expansion of regionally based cross-class alliances.

Garrard and Rokkan's histories give temporal and causal priority to "contestation," the right and ability of opposition parties to "form a sovereign government upon winning a free and fair election," over "participation," the formal right to vote (Mann 1993: 83). Mann notes that kings, such as those of Germany, granted the right to vote as a way to pacify the masses, even though that right had little meaning since the monarch continued to control the government. Kings played to the masses as a way to undercut regional elites, which sought to sustain their power by fostering "confederalism" instead of centralization (p. 84). Protestant clerics and the transnational Catholic Church often sided with local elites with whom they had long-standing alliances.

Democratization, at least in Northwestern Europe, emerged out of a centuries-long series of dialogues and confrontations between rulers and elites. However, Tilly, like the Marxists, makes the

141

mistake of differentiating too sharply between rulers within the state and elites outside the state. In fact, as Mann highlights in his focus on local power bases, non-state elites controlled political, economic, and ideological institutions that remained state-like in their powers and functions, and that also exerted control over organs within the consolidating national state. Democratization occurred in different sequences and with varying timing because the structure of relations among elites varied, and as a result so did the ways in which those elites made concessions to non-elites as they sought to enlist or demobilize them in the course of elite conflicts.

Markoff (1996b) offers the most illuminating portrayal of the ways in which elite conflicts determined the content of concessions to mobilized masses. He shows how the French National Assembly reacted to peasant uprisings, regardless of their actual motives and targets, by passing legislation to abolish feudal privileges. That decision was, in part, a misreading of popular desires, but it also was smart strategy by a rising set of rulers seeking to undercut elite rivals' institutional bases. Similarly, the leaders of the American Revolution harnessed popular rebellions to eliminate rival local elites, who lost their properties and were forced into exile, as well as to attack the British. The US Constitution reflected that twin objective in creating institutions that protected "individual [capitalist] property rights and freedoms" and also legitimized the mechanism through which a growing array of Americans won voting and civil, though never . . . much social citizenship" (Mann 1993: 158; ch. 5 passim).

Markoff (1996a) generalizes that democratization is a collaboration between reforming, often secondary, elites and mobilized masses. The vote in this analysis is not a concession to popular forces by "the state" as Tilly claims, or by capitalists, as Marxists argue, but rather the outcome of a cross-class alliance animated by the ultimately successful elites' need to reach across class lines for allies. Unfortunately, there are few systematic studies that link the contours of elite and class conflicts to the specific ways in which democratization was first institutionalized. Collier (1999) offers the most comprehensive study of the actors who propelled democratization in Europe and South America, but has little to say about the states that emerged from those chains of contention. Conversely, Przeworski et al. (2000) "find it difficult to explain why dictatorships die and democracies emerge" (p. 137), but they are precise in specifying the consequences of each type of regime on state policies. They find that democracies and dictatorships have similar records of economic growth, but they achieve it in quite different ways. Dictatorships rapidly expand the labor force (in part by subordinating women who then have more children), and "rely on force to repress labor . . . pay lower wages, with high returns to capital" (p. 179). Workers earn better wages in democracies, which result in more efficient use of labor and lower returns to capital. Political instability (resulting from strikes, changes of government) is more frequent under democracies than dictatorships. Instability has no effect on economic growth in democracies, but greatly retards growth in dictatorships. "The prospective demise of a dictatorship causes investors to flee, but its advent makes them flock" (p. 212). Democratic regimes foster policies that develop classes and institutional arrangements that preserve democracy, while dictatorships manage, at least for a time, to suppress the social forces that can overthrow them.

Decolonization, Waves of Democracy, and the Undemocratic Past and Present

After the slow and uneven development of contested elections and universal suffrage in Western Europe and North America, democracy came to vast swaths of the rest of the world in three great twentieth-century waves. One occurred in the years surrounding World War I, the next accompanied decolonization after World War II, and the most recent one came with the end of the Cold War. World systems theory is unable to predict the mix of core, semi-peripheral, and peripheral countries that achieved democracy in each wave. However, the combination of economic crises and military defeat (and in the victorious nations the high casualties of World War I and the heavy economic sacrifices of both World

Wars) go far in explaining the scope of popular protest that marked each wave, states' reduced capacities to suppress those protests, and, most significantly, divisions among elites in how to respond to popular demands.

Those elite divisions lead to disjunctures, such as the one described by Markoff (1996b) regarding the French Revolution, between protesters' demands and what state elites end up offering as concessions. After World War I, protests were led by mutinous soldiers, striking industrial workers, women demanding suffrage, and, in the defeated Ottoman and Austro-Hungarian Empires, ethnic nationalists. Those protesters made many demands, but suffrage was the one most commonly conceded to them. In part, state rulers calculated, often correctly, that a majority of the new voters would be more conservative than the protesters. Women especially were extended the franchise after World War I because they were seen as more conservative than male voters (Markoff 1996a), and so they have proven to be in all countries but the United States.

Moments of crisis offer an opportunity for elites to cement a place for themselves within the state and/or to undercut rival elites by widening the electorate, with lower-class allies linked to them by patronage or common economic or regional interests. In Britain, as we saw above, each party sponsored voting rights for lower-class clients who were linked to them through the system of "virtual representation." Whites who supported black voting rights in the US after the Civil War, and again in the civil rights struggles of the 1950s and 1960s, were motivated by deep moral claims but also by the opportunity to destroy nineteenth-century "slave power" and twentieth-century oligarchies based in legal segregation. India's long-lived democracy, which remained a mystery for Moore, empowers local elites that sit atop chains of caste-derived patronage fueled by state government budgets, while the national government supports the big bourgeois who monopolized government licenses subsidies, as we saw in Chibber's analysis in the previous chapter.

Democracy came in waves, not only because military and economic crises provided fuel for popular mobilization and openings for lesser elites to challenge the dominant state elites, but because the end of foreign rule – in Eastern and Southern Europe after 1917, in the third world after 1945, and in the Soviet bloc after 1989 – created scrambles for power in every newly independent nation. Silver (2003: 4) similarly finds that labor unrest worldwide peaked in the years following the two world wars as "national hegemonic compacts" that had been forged in the wars were disrupted. In the vacuums left by military demobilization in the core, and decolonization in the periphery, leaders of popular movements, colonial stooges who assumed positions in newly independent governments and armed forces, and capitalists, both indigenous and those still tied to firms and markets in the metropolis, all vied for power and resources, while workers sought leverage over capitalists and states through strikes. Even the weakest and most embryonic state was a font of military, institutional, and economic resources that had the potential to turn those who grabbed possession into the new nation's rulers.

Durable democracy with contested elections was most likely in countries such as India, where multiple elites, which each enlisted supporters on the basis of appeals to class, ethnic, geographic, or patronage ties, were strong enough to vie for power but not strong enough to eliminate rivals. Most of Africa lacked multiple national elites, mainly because European rulers had succeeded in isolating indigenous elites at the local level. As a result, even though departing colonial rulers, with the aid of the United Nations in the post-1945 era, supervised the first elections upon the new nations' independence, power passed to a single elite, based in the military or civilian state. In some cases that elite was placed in power as a proxy for the departing imperial power. African capitalists were too few and too weak to act as a counterweight, while European firms cultivated links to the new rulers in return for continued favorable concessions. The combination of single, weak national elites and autarkic local elites blocked democracy in much of Africa and, as we saw in the previous chapter, created predatory dictatorships rather than developmental states.

The Democratic Republic of the Congo is an extreme version of this pattern and stands as the polar opposite to India's democracy. Belgium systematically eliminated indigenous hierarchies and political networks, eventually killing and starving 4–8 million Congolese (Hochschild 1999). At independence, there were two Congolese elites: local-level ethnic leaders and the embryonic state which itself was divided between a leftist faction, led by Patrice Lumumba, and the military, commanded by Joseph Mobutu. Mobutu, with support from Belgium, and probably the US as well, killed Lumumba and eliminated his faction. Mobutu (who renamed himself Mobutu Sese Seko, and renamed Congo as Zaire) looted the state, limited only by his need to buy off local elites, while foreign firms extracted resources as they had done in the colonial era. By the 1990s, Mobutu's support from Europe and the US was overwhelmed by provincial elites' support from Rwanda and Uganda. Congo, like many other African countries with no national elites outside of the state, and hobbled by extensive foreign interference, oscillates between periods of dictatorial central power and civil war among provincial elites. Congo's civil conflict is unusual in that seven neighboring countries became involved in what became Africa's "World War" of 1998–2003.

Even where multiple national elites provided the structural bases for electoral democracy, foreign intervention often gave military or, in the Soviet bloc, party elites the leverage to assume dictatorial power. The United States repeatedly fostered military coups in Latin America and Asia, usually through covert means, but occasionally with direct military intervention. US political and military leverage over states in its sphere of influence were compounded by its economic control, which stunted the formation of indigenous capitalists who could form the core of an opposition party.

The Soviet Union after World War II suppressed multiple elites and mass organizations in Eastern Europe, fostering the development of single-party elites whose cadres staffed the state administrations, industrial firms, and other institutions, blocking the emergence of rival elites or popular forces. Those single elites were integrated with the ruling elite of the Soviet Union, which provided the military muscle and formulated the legitimating ideology. Those elites demonstrated their internal unity and their indivisibility from their Soviet sponsors at moments of mass rebellion. Even when individual members of the ruling elites defected

146

to the rebels' side, they did not carry with them an organizational sector capable of sustaining a new elite.

Two key changes occurred in the structure of the ruling Eastern European elites in the 1980s. First, the Soviet Union under Gorbachev abandoned its military defense of Eastern European communist parties, leaving the elites of each nation in control of autonomous organizations of extraction and domination. Second, partly in response to their abandonment by the Soviet Union and partly in reaction to economic crises, the unified elite of each country divided. Those members of the ruling party most directly in control of organizations of production sought to convert their political positions into private capital capable of surviving the transformation or demise of communism.

The shattering of monolithic party elites created a structure of multiple competing elites capable of sustaining electoral democracy. Conversely, in most of the successor states of the Soviet Union, including Russia, a distinct capitalist class never emerged. Firm owners remained linked to the state elite, and the new states either had elections that were shams, or limited by restrictions on speech and organizing as in Russia under Putin, or became outright dictatorships as in most of the Central Asian republics.

To sum up: electoral democracy develops where multiple national elites are forced to recruit non-elite allies in their competition for state power. Although popular forces often demand the vote as a price for their support, democracy is usually just one in an array of demands. Elites offer voting rights, along with or instead of civil liberties and social benefits, to meet the exigencies of political conflict. Those exigencies are determined by the structure of elite relations within the country and also by the intervention of external forces: imperial powers and foreign capital.

Capitalism and economic development do not automatically foster democracy, contrary to the claims of neoliberal ideologues or various iterations of modernization theory. Rather, capitalism created capitalists who, when they challenge older, aristocratic and state elites, create an opening for non-elites to embed their demands in cross-class coalitions. Once multiple coalitions are invested in and empowered by electoral access to state power, democracy endures. Przeworski's finding of a strong relationship between per capita income and democracy is not a causal link. Rather, structures of multiple elites foster forms of economic development (as we saw in the previous chapter) and democracy, while single autarkic elites block economic growth and democracy.

The democratic waves that followed World Wars I and II were not due primarily to the prestige of the democratic states that won those wars, as Markoff (1996a) argues. Rather, the wars mattered because the winners disrupted elite and class relations in the losing countries through occupation, redrawing borders, expropriating the land and firms of enemy elites, forcing demilitarization, and imposing constitutions.

Not all post-war interventions were so benign in intent or effect. The British and French consolidated monarchies in the new states they created in the Middle East, after the dissolution of the Ottoman Empire, as well as in their colonies in Muslim North Africa. A century later, some remain monarchies, while the others are dictatorships, with Syria (and perhaps in the future Egypt and Libya as well) having developed a hereditary dictatorship. Those rulers strengthened their "sultanistic regimes" (Brachet-Marques 2005) when they turned on their former colonial patrons and nationalized their oil industries. Control over such vast resources, which in many oil states are a majority of GDP and provide all the state's revenues, allows existing royal rulers to maintain, and military rulers to assert, patrimonial control over the state itself. Non-state elites remain dependent on the ruler for resources and have no leverage, since the ruler needs neither their wealth nor their services as administrators, and even soldiers can be contracted from abroad.

Foreign interventions also come in waves as geopolitical balances are disrupted. During the Cold War, both the US and the Soviet Union undermined, or blocked, the emergence of democracies in their satellites. This is seen most starkly in Latin America where the US encouraged or directly fomented a wave of military coups in the 1960s and 1970s, and then with the end of the Cold War acquiesced while elites in coalition with popular forces demanded the restoration of elections. The growing ability of international financial agencies such as the World Bank and IMF to impose austerity on third world countries undermines state capacities and disrupts electoral coalitions, and narrows the scope of democracy even if elections still are contested.

Civil Society

So far our focus has been on the presence or absence of contested elections rather than the content or quality of democracy. Voters have the potential to select policies as well as elect officials. Our goal in this section is to explain when and how citizens do that. In so doing, we will provide the analytic basis to explain variations in social welfare benefits in the final section of this chapter.

Marxists, because of their contention that bourgeois democracy is a sham that can never represent working-class interests, are of little help in explaining how voting affects policy. Gramsci, who was decisive in shaping Marxist research on civil society, was concerned with how workers outside the state could prepare themselves for a war of position, a revolutionary assault on the state. He identified civil society as the site where workers' notions of their identity, interests, and allies were formed, not where they selected candidates to stand for office or formulated demands for policy reforms.

Later Marxists (Williams 1977: 108–14 is the clearest formulation), who developed Gramsci's vague concept of counter-hegemony envisioned it as a totalistic challenge to capitalist social relations and the state. Reformism and voting were part of capitalist hegemony, not challenges to it. Laclau and Mouffe (1985) contend that revolutionary challenges cannot be predicted from existing social structure because solidarity can be based on non-class identities. They argue that class conflict has largely given way since the 1960s to New Social Movements whose participants are drawn together by their shared gender, racial, ethnic, sexual, or generational identity, or by their shared concern for non-class issues such as the environment and human rights. Laclau and Mouffe and other scholars[6] laud New Social Movements for

149

raising consciousness, envisioning a new social order, and winning concessions by forsaking electoral politics and acting outside of recognized state institutions and mechanisms.

Piven and Cloward (1971) attribute all the major social welfare gains in the US to demonstrations and riots on the part of poor people. The government then responds by offering just enough welfare benefits to end the disorder. Piven and Cloward's historical account is like Markoff's analysis of the French Revolution, in that they find little direct interaction between protesters and government officials. However, Piven and Cloward, unlike Markoff, make little effort to figure out what the protesters actually demanded in each era. Nor do they explain why the government settled on the specific concessions they offered. This weakness in Piven and Cloward's work is even more pronounced in most scholarship on social movements. Such scholarship is concerned with how individuals come together into movements, and at times attempts to explain why protesters make certain demands and not others, but doesn't usually integrate the movement into a dynamic model of policy formation that includes state actors and citizens outside the social movements. Unfortunately, this scholarship examines social movements in isolation from the larger civil society, and has little to say about how the health of civil society contributes to or retards social movements. Nor does it explain how, or if, social movements refresh or disrupt civil society.[7]

Alexander offers a way to situate social movements in the broad dynamics of civil society. He describes the "civil sphere, a world of values and institutions that generates the capacity for social criticism and democratic integration at the same time. Such a sphere relies on solidarity, on feelings for others whom we do not know but whom we respect out of principle, not experience, because of our putative commitment to a common secular faith" (2006: 4). Alexander's definition of the civil sphere invites a research agenda that examines how social movements speak to both state officials and the larger civil society. He examines the US civil rights movement in those terms and shows how demonstrations were structured to dramatize the moral issues of segregation and to offer a way for whites to join in the work of civil repair. Alexander specifies how the civil rights movement shaped its strategy and calibrated its tactics to elicit regulatory and legislative action by government officials, by provoking reactions from racists that would transform the sympathies of the broad publics to whom state officials were attentive.

A separate strand of civil society scholarship begins with Tocqueville's *Democracy in America* ([1835–40] 2000). Unlike Gramsci and the Marxists, Tocqueville and his followers are agnostic about the interests of non-state actors. How members of the public come together and what demands they make upon the state are open and variable, and shaped by the institutions that they construct in civil society.

Tocqueville portrays the United States as unique in the richness and efficacy of its civil society. "Americans . . . constantly unite" in "associations . . . religious, moral, grave, futile, very general and very particular . . . Everywhere . . . you see the government in France and a great lord in England, count on it that you will perceive an association in the United States" (p. 489). Associations seek to "discover the most appropriate arguments with which to make an impression on the majority" and then convey those arguments in newspapers that are independent of state control or censorship (p. 185). Those associations that succeeded in convincing the majority of voters took office, implemented their ideas, and then were themselves vulnerable to new challengers with new ideas.

Tocqueville attributes the openness and flux of American civic life to the "great equality among emigrants" (p. 46) which, in turn, was due to the richness of the new continent, the availability of new lands for settlement (pp. 265–74), and estate laws that required equal partition among children and prevented the accumulation of wealth over generations (p. 47). Such economic and social equality in fact created "a passion for equality" in sentiment (p. 52), which led to progressive elimination of property qualifications for voting, especially during and after the Revolutionary War. Tocqueville suggests, but doesn't explain how, equality and mobility reduce the intensity and range of political differences. Instead, he asserts that in the US "opinions differ only by nuances"

(p. 185) and therefore citizens are more open to new ideas and to joining new associations than they are in Europe. In any case, Tocqueville believed that the centralization of power and limited franchise in Europe rendered local civic groups impotent (pp. 651–61). Power could change hands in Europe only by violent attacks on the national government.

Tocqueville's analysis of European politics is dynamic, with kings acting to undermine local political institutions and once-independent estates and judicial bodies, thereby making national politics more violent and rulers more tyrannical. His analysis of America is static: an Edenic society of equality and harmony is present from the first settlement and sustains a rich civic life. The content of political debates is hardly mentioned.

Tocqueville's claim that autonomous local government, economic and social equality, and, above all, voluntary organizations prevent the emergence of elites and sustain democracy has given rise to a long literature that extols the importance of civil society. Robert Putnam (2000) is the most prominent recent exponent on this approach. He defines "social capital" as the sum of all social ties, from involvement in political parties, social movements, churches, and veterans' organizations, to having dinner with neighbors and drinking beer in a bowling league. He argues that a variety of social changes, from geographic mobility and women entering the workforce to the ever increasing amount of time spent watching television, have reduced Americans' commitment to voluntary organizations and social interactions. As a result, political action has declined. Putnam (1993) contrasts the dismal civic life of late twentieth-century America to the more vibrant political world of Italy where he correlates social capital with civic involvement.

Unfortunately, the strand of civil society research begun by Tocqueville and exemplified by Putnam is largely self-referential. They describe the culture and institutions of civil society in loving detail, but their accounts become vague and amorphous when it comes time to explain exactly how a rich civil society actually affects state policies. Putnam fails to identify any mechanism that could explain why some citizens use their social capital to host potluck suppers or coach swim teams, while others campaign for office. Putnam certainly has no explanation at all for how the politically active decide on which issues to engage with or what position to take.

Skocpol (2003) follows a more fruitful path by focusing on the actual organizations within which citizens join and act. She finds that, prior to World War II, the largest US membership organizations were cross-class in membership and had local chapters from which leaders were elected and could rise in a national hierarchy. At the local level, the organizations "combined social or ritual activities with community service, mutual aid, and involvement in national affairs. National patriotism was a leitmotif" (1999: 465).

Such organizations were highly effective at mobilizing members across the nation to lobby for government programs that addressed concerns that members raised at the local level. A prime example is the Servicemen's Readjustment Act of 1944, or GI Bill, which provided subsidized home mortgages, unemployment benefits, and free university educations for returning veterans. This Bill was the first significant piece of social legislation since 1937 and came long after the New Deal coalition lost control of Congress. It was pushed primarily by the American Legion, a veterans' group that became notorious during the Vietnam War for the ultra-reactionary political positions of its members. The plans that Congress proposed to address the millions of soldiers who would be demobilized, and thrown onto the housing and job markets with the end of the war, were regarded as inadequate by the veterans who had suffered the consequences of a similarly weak program at the end of World War I. Those veterans, who met at American Legion halls to socialize, discussed the issues and formulated a stronger program. Veterans' organized presence in every Congressional district allowed them to pressure Congress to approve the Bill. This was legislation from the bottom-up.

The mass membership organizations lost potency in the second half of the twentieth century as women went to work, sex-segregated social activities lost favor, and the number of veterans declined. They were supplanted by new sorts of organizations, staffed by professionals and reliant upon contributions solicited through the mail (and today on the Internet). Those organizations do not call on members for anything but money and so their proposals have little resonance with their members. Since the members are not mobilized, elected officials feel free to ignore them and instead cater to the desires of their largest financial contributors who, in the US, are mainly investors and officers of large corporations.

Skocpol's mode of analysis is far better able to explain why citizens mobilize, and what motivates the topics of their activism, than Tocqueville or Putnam. She shows that veterans' political demands emerged from their identities and were enacted into law because of the American Legion's strategic structural location in the American polity.

Somers (1993) undertakes a similar analysis for Britain from the seventeenth to twentieth centuries to show how citizenship and its civil, political, and social rights were an "instituted process" that developed out of "networks of memberships and relationally." "There is no firm relationship between social classes as categorical entities and patterns of citizenship formation. To the extent that any *essential* properties, interests, or capacities can be attributed to the capitalist economy, the state, or social classes, these attributes clearly were *outrun* by the contingencies of the relational and institutional environment in which they operated" (p. 611). Somers contrasts arable and pastoral regions of England. In the pastoral areas, village governments structured dense networks of farmers as political actors well before citizens had any significant influence over the national government, and laborers were linked through apprenticeship networks. In arable regions, the lack of popular participation in gentry-controlled government and primogeniture, which forced migration, left non-elites atomized.

Somers's sophisticated analysis shows how citizenship rights, civil society, political participation, and state forms developed together through a complex and interacting sequence of contingent historical events. Citizens, their rights, and the civil society in which they live are artifacts of local social networks that operate in relation to the developing states that are the objects of their

154

demands and struggles. States and their policies are creations of political actors located in both the state and civil society. The national policies that developed from the content of those policies are historical outcomes that cannot be derived from essentialist logics.

Social Benefits

Social benefits vary widely in their generosity, the portion of the population covered by them, and in "their capacity for 'decommodification' . . . the degree to which they permit people to make their living standards independent of pure market forces. It is in that sense that social rights diminish citizens' status as 'commodities'" (Esping-Andersen 1990: 3). Variations cannot be explained by the level of capitalist development or overall economic prosperity since some countries, most notably the United States today and Britain in the nineteenth century, had social welfare systems that were significantly meager in comparison with less wealthy nations. Further, spending levels mask the variety of forms that benefit programs take, with different degrees of universality, criteria for coverage, level and form of benefits, and whether the programs are administered directly by the state or by churches, non-profit organizations, mutual societies, or capitalist firms with state regulation and subsidy.[8]

Until the twentieth century, no country had social programs that covered all its citizens with old-age pensions, disability or unemployment insurance, or health care. Government workers were the first in most European and American countries to receive such benefits, beginning in Britain in 1834. In Latin America, they remain far better covered than the rest of the population. In the United States, in 2008, government employees were five times more likely to be union members than those in the private sector and are far more likely to have fixed-benefit old-age pensions than other workers.

Governments always have an interest in ensuring the loyalty of their soldiers and veterans, and of "workers in factories supplying the front." Such loyalty was bought through the "expansion of both workers' rights [to unionize and strike] and broad democratic rights" during and after the two world wars (Silver 2003: 174), as well as with social benefits, which often were first directed toward veterans, as we saw with the home loan and education benefits for US veterans after 1945. The US created a system of old-age pensions for Civil War veterans that, by the early twentieth century, covered a majority of Northern white males and their widows. Repeated efforts to use the veterans' system as a platform to create a universal program were rejected by Congress, in part because many pensioners had won benefits through political patronage rather than military service, giving the system, and indeed government programs in general, an aura of corruption. Britain's civil service, by contrast, had banished most opportunities for corruption in government programs by 1900, giving both major parties confidence that schemes to win working-class support with new benefits would actually be implemented (Orloff and Skocpol 1984).

Orloff and Skocpol's analysis highlights the importance of states' capacities in determining the timing and scope of social programs. Capacity encompasses both a bureaucratic apparatus (a civil service capable of collecting personal data and allocating funds or administering agencies) and a system of mechanisms to minimize corruption. Yet those capacities themselves are produced by political processes that yield not just state agencies, but also political coalitions that favor certain programs and particular mechanisms to implement those programs. If we want to understand the variety and timing of social benefits across countries over time we need to trace those political developments.

Esping-Andersen, in surveying all eighteen of the wealthiest industrialized nations, finds three patterns of politics that produced three distinct "social welfare-state regimes." Germany was the prototype of what Esping-Andersen labels the conservative regime. Powerful states, which often began as absolutist monarchies and are linked to dominant Catholic Churches, offered a growing list of benefits in an effort to neutralize developing working-class parties and labor unions. The integration of elites within the state facilitated strategic responses to the left and "accentuated the centrality of the state," although the strong Catholic, and after 1945 Christian Democratic, Parties were powerful enough to demand "that private organizations (mainly the Church) be prominent in social services" (Esping-Andersen 1990: 134). Churches also were crucial in maintaining farmers' support for conservative parties, blocking the sort of worker-farmer alliance that produces socialist welfare regimes. Workers in these countries were, and continue to be, mobilized through neocorporatist organizations (occupational groups that developed out of guilds, the Church, ethnic, and language groups), and welfare programs were tailored to the needs and demands of each group, producing systems with varying levels of benefits even today.

The conservative welfare regime also dominated in Latin America. Benefits in most of those countries were offered only to civil servants, until the mid-twentieth century, and then were granted only to those workers who were mobilized through corporatist groups allied with authoritarian regimes. Centralized states plus a civil society largely organized through churches and status groups led to the creation of a welfare system that offered varying benefits to different social sectors, while excluding the poor and most rural workers who remained disorganized and repressed throughout most of Latin America.

Argentina was exceptional in its expansion of social benefits and also in the rapid redistribution of income under Peron in the 1940s and 1950s. Peron's alliance with unions, and the massive return to workers from that alliance in government benefits, cannot be explained entirely by the strength of worker mobilization, which was not greater than in other Latin American or European countries that provided far more meager benefits. Rather, union leverage was magnified by Peron's conflicts with capitalists, landlords, and old-style conservative parties. Those elites split, and Peron's efforts to consolidate control over the state deepened his dependence on unions and also encouraged him to expand social programs as a way of increasing a corps of officials loyal to him in the civilian sector of the state. Similar considerations fostered the creation, unique in Central America, of a social welfare sector in Costa Rica. The split between agro and industrial elites that was noted in chapter 4 (Paige 1997) created an opening for leftist military officers to ally with workers and small farmers, and then to reward those allies and cement control over the newly demilitarized state by constructing a social welfare sector.

Esping-Andersen sees rural classes as decisive in determining political coalitions and welfare state forms, just as Barrington Moore did for the presence or absence of democracy. This is because "the traditional working class has hardly ever constituted an electoral majority . . . It is a historical fact that welfare-state construction has depended on political coalition building . . . Where the rural economy was dominated by small, capital-intensive farmers . . . [rather] than where it rested on large pools of cheap labor" social democracies, epitomized by Sweden, developed. Such "red-green" alliances developed "where farmers were politically articulate and well-organized (as in Scandinavia)" (p. 30).

Eastern Europe followed a different pattern to achieve socialist welfare. There, farmers were not decisive and, before World War II, social democratic parties were largely ineffective at widening the limited benefits that conservative coalitions offered to urban workers. After communist parties took power, benefits were provided first to urban workers. Only when farmers were brought under party control through collectivization in the 1950s were benefits extended to rural workers.

Liberal regimes are Esping-Andersen's third type. They are characterized by limited and means-tested social programs combined with private pension plans and health insurance subsidized by state tax breaks. Politically, this is a residual category, with neither a strong central state nor an effective farmer-worker alliance. These states have the least well-developed welfare system. Esping-Andersen attributes the burst of social welfare legislation in the New Deal to a temporary farmer-worker alliance, which was later undermined by the lack of independent farmers in the South.

Esping-Andersen classifies Japan as liberal, and the more recently developed East Asian states fall into that category as well. Singapore and Malaysia, which inherited public health systems from their time as British colonies, are defined-contribution in form. Korea and Taiwan are developing similar models, and none of these countries have national old-age pensions. The Philippines and Thailand have even less.

Esping-Andersen's model is path dependent. Once political alliances are set, and a welfare state is formed, classes come to have an interest in sustaining programs that provide their benefits. The growing middle classes of the post-1945 period were incorporated into politics and received benefits through the templates of their countries' existing social welfare regimes. Conservative welfare systems were "best equipped to manage the new and loftier welfare-state expectations [of the middle classes] simply by moving from contribution to earnings-graduated benefits without altering the framework of status-distinctiveness" (p. 25). In that way, those with the highest earnings got the largest benefits. Liberal states maintained "an essentially modest universalism in the state, and allow the market to reign for the growing social strata demanding superior welfare" (p. 26), as in the expanding private health insurance sector in Britain and the purchase of private disability or nursing care insurance in the United States. Socialist states "incorporate the new middle classes within a luxurious second-tier, universally inclusive earnings-related insurance scheme on top of the flat-rate egalitarian one . . . this solution reintroduces benefit inequalities, but effectively blocks off the market. It thus succeeds in retaining universalism and also, therefore, the degree of political consensus required to preserve broad and solidaristic support for the high taxes that such a welfare-state model demands" (p. 26).

We need to meld Esping-Andersen's analysis of class alliances with a focus on state structures, if we want to explain variations within each regime and moments when particular states enact policies at variance with the trajectory of their regime type. Such seeming anomalies, most notably Argentina and Costa Rica, can best be understood as consequences of the ways in which elites, class fractions, and state officials themselves embed their interests within state institutions and political regimes. I will outline the parameters of such a broad analysis as I conclude this chapter by looking at: (1) the United States' unique trajectory of rapid reform during the New Deal and almost total lack of social benefit expansion since 1937; and (2) the variable implementation of neoliberal "reforms" of social welfare programs.

Why is there No Socialism in the United States?

Werner Sombart's 1906 [1976] question blurred two quite distinct issues. One concerns the reason why there is no socialist party in the United States. That broad and vague question yields broad and vague answers, such as those of Lipset and Marks (2001). They point to the lack of a feudal past against which socialists can organize (although Esping-Andersen shows feudalism led to conservative systems rather than socialist welfare), powerful ideological support for notions of liberty that are at odds with collectivist programs (despite unassailable support for the comprehensive and redistributive programs that were enacted), geographic and occupational mobility that blur class lines to make workers prosperous by world standards, and ethnic – and especially racial – divisions that undermine class solidarity, all of which they cite as the principal reasons for socialism's political failings. However, if we focus on policies rather than party labels we get a more complex picture. After lagging behind Britain in the early twentieth century, as we saw in Orloff and Skocpol's (1984) analysis above, US benefits advanced well beyond most of those in Europe during the New Deal. In 1938, the US spent a higher percentage of GDP on social programs than any nation in the world, and twice as much as Sweden (Amenta 1998: 5). As we noted earlier, the US pioneered government-subsidized education in the 1944 GI Bill, producing levels of university enrollment that no European nation has yet matched. The Democratic Party served, in the 1930s and 1940s, as well as any European socialist party, as the home of labor unions and independent small farmers and as implementer of new social programs. The real questions, then, are: why was the US diverted from a socialist to a liberal welfare regime after World War II, and why, despite its position throughout the twentieth century as the richest capitalist nation in the world, have US social benefits lagged behind those of most of Europe since the 1950s?

Class coalitions – as we have seen in our analyses of how governments formulate economic development policies (chapter 4) and social benefits (this chapter) – mobilize within the structures of the state where other elites and classes also seek to sway policy. States do not necessarily assume a coherent character once they are captured by a particular coalition, as Esping-Andersen assumes. Lack of bureaucratic capacity may preclude states from adopting certain policies, as Skocpol and her colleagues demonstrate, but capacity can be left unused or employed to enact a range of policies. The US state has always been divided among various agencies which in some cases, most notably the Federal Reserve and other agencies whose officers hold terms longer than the presidents who appoint them, enjoy a high level of autonomy and are closely linked to elites with narrow industrial and sectional interests. Members of Congress pass, rewrite, or block legislation to protect the interests of the capitalists and mass groups from their states who elect them. Once programs exist, groups come to understand their interests in relation to those programs. That applies to mass groups as well as elites.

Social programs were enacted in the US when mass groups were able to form national organizations and formulate demands that spanned regional divides. That happened during the New Deal, as the Townsend Movement for old-age pensions, leftist Democratic senator Huey Long's Share the Wealth Club, and rapidly expanding labor unions all pressured President Roosevelt and an overwhelmingly Democratic Congress. Yet those demands were enacted into laws by a Congress that under the American Federal system represented states (the Senate) and districts (the House of Representatives) where class fractions, elites, corrupt political machines, and ethnic blocks often determined elections. New Deal legislation was tailored by Congress to meet the interests of many of those groups. Most notoriously, many New Deal programs excluded Southern blacks at the behest of Congressmen from that region.

Once enacted, New Deal and 1960s Great Society programs restructured American politics. Voters were categorized and their interests and identities shaped by their status in government social programs. Mainly elderly beneficiaries of the relatively generous universal Social Security and Medicare programs were separated from the poor and disproportionately non-white recipients of demeaning and poorly funded means-tested welfare programs. The progressive coalitions of the 1930s and 1960s were shattered as the white working class became ever more resentful of funding welfare programs through taxes. The programs themselves, more than the pre-existing racism or individualistic ideology emphasized by Lipset and Marks, prevented the formation of broad coalitions that were necessary for enacting new social benefits.

Capitalists were divided in their response to reform proposals. Quadagno (1984), Skocpol and Amenta (1985), Jenkins and Brents (1989), and Amenta (1998) are the central contributors to the sociological debate over the role that elites played in limiting or molding legislation. While they differ on the particulars, they agree that capitalists were not unified in the 1930s and therefore were unable to totally block reforms and had to settle for legislative and administrative provisions that shielded them from having to pay the full cost, either financially or in loss of their ability to commodify labor.

Those capitalists who supported the New Deal most strongly saw the reforms as an opportunity to break the power of banking oligarchs that blocked new firms from expanding and regional banks from attracting capital. Similarly, the other great era of social legislation, the 1965–6 Great Society under Lyndon Johnson, attracted support from business sectors eager to shatter the hold of regional capitalists over the segregated South, politicians who sought Federal funds controlled by the Johnson administration to bypass and disrupt urban and regional political machines, and firms that saw an opportunity to profit from the contracts that flowed from the new Federal health programs.

Social reforms in the United States require an extraordinary level of popular protest and heavy Congressional majorities to overcome regional elites' ability to block legislation in Congress. The United States also is unusual among advanced capitalist societies in the high degree to which the state regulates firms (Prasad 2006). Those regulations, while loathsome in principle to business, also provide opportunities for specific blocs of capitalists and regional elites with leverage over legislators and administrators to gain advantage over rivals, lock in control over markets, and siphon government subsidies and contracts. Those firms then come to have an interest in existing government programs and regulatory structures, and exercise power through their links to Congress and "captured" Federal agencies. All these interest groups thus control sites within the American state, the structure of which affords them numerous "veto points" to block new social legislation. Moller et al. (2003) find that the greater the number of such veto points, the less are advanced capitalist democracies able to execute policies that reduce inequality.

President Clinton's 1993–4 effort to enact a National Health Insurance program was blocked, as were previous proposals, by insurance companies, pharmaceutical firms, physicians, and other medical enterprises that profit from the existing fragmented system and were able to find numerous veto points to block reform. The lack of mass organizations of the type that existed in the first half of the twentieth century prevented Clinton from mobilizing countervailing popular support, while large firms that face international competition lack the leverage over smaller firms – through banking or trade relationships, corporatist organizations, or political parties – to compel them to agree to plans that would force them to pay the health costs of their employees (Skocpol 1996; Quadagno 2004). US government domestic initiatives, since the 1970s, have been limited to areas in which those capitalists whose interests were at stake agreed on legislation. Thus only "neoliberal" reforms have been enacted, yet in the US as elsewhere the nature and extent of those policies depend on capitalists' and other actors' capacities to mobilize within the particular political and state structures of their nations.

Neoliberalism

David Harvey (2005) offers a straightforward definition of neoliberalism as "a theory of political economic practices that proposes that human well-being can best be advanced by liberating individual entrepreneurial freedom and skills within an institutional framework characterized by strong private property rights, free markets, and free trade" (p. 2). This belief leads to a desire for "a state apparatus whose fundamental mission was to facilitate conditions for profitable capital accumulation on the part of both domestic and foreign capital" (p. 7), and which "is necessarily hostile to all forms of social solidarity that put restraints on capital accumulation" (p. 75). Although proponents of neoliberalism presented it as a cure for the economic stagnation of the 1970s, in fact, states that adopted neoliberal policies experienced lower growth than those that did not. Nor have neoliberalism and globalization spurred growth on a world scale. "Aggregate global growth rates stood at 3.5 percent in the 1960s and even during the troubled 1970s fell only to 2.4 percent," while declining to 1.4 percent and 1.1 percent for the 1980s and 1990s, respectively (p. 154; for indepth analysis of economic growth, see Brenner 2003).

Neoliberal policies have been far more effective at redistributing wealth and income than at generating growth (p. 159). Neoliberal states and international agencies accomplish this with what Harvey terms "accumulation by dispossession" which, like Marx's "primitive accumulation," is the appropriation of other people's wealth through political power, force, and fraud. Harvey (pp. 160–5) identified four types of methods used by to accomplish that redistribution.

1. *Privatization and commodification*: State-owned firms, utilities, schools, lands and other assets are privatized, and often (as in the Soviet Union and Eastern Europe after 1989 and in China over the past thirty years) sold to favored capitalists at absurdly low prices. Intellectual knowledge, including DNA codes and seeds that are the product of centuries or millennia of cross-breeding, are turned over to private firms to own as "intellectual property."
2. *Financialization*: Banks and other financial firms have been deregulated and allowed to engage in speculative behavior that concentrated profits from industrial firms in the financial

sector This process is highly unstable and produced the 1997 East Asian financial crisis, the collapse of the high tech bubble in 2000–01, and the real estate and financial collapse that began in 2008.

3. *Crises are manipulated* to compel governments to abolish protections for domestic firms, privatize government agencies, and abolish social benefits, often as part of "structural adjustment programs" mandated by the IMF or World Bank in return for loans that will mitigate the effects of crises that were made possible in the first place by deregulation and financialization. Naomi Klein (2007) argues that some of these crises are deliberately induced to shock citizens and their governments into acquiescing to policies they never would have accepted before the crisis dulled their capacities for analysis and resistance.

4. *States redistribute* wealth by making taxes more regressive and through outright subsidies to capitalist firms. Evans points out that "politically protected monopoly rents [especially from pharmaceutical patents and copyrights on software] are at the heart of profitability in the most advanced sectors of the global neo-liberal economy" and "has the same kind of anti-developmental effects that politically maintained monopoly control over land did in an agrarian economy" (2008: 278).

Harvey is vague on how capitalists were able to make states adopt neoliberal policies. He suggests that capitalists always had that power, but were willing to put up with a more egalitarian distribution as long as there was "an increasing pie . . . But when growth collapsed in the 1970s . . . the upper classes had to move decisively if they were to protect themselves from political and economic annihilation" (p. 15). They then concentrated campaign contributions on neoliberal parties and candidates (Republicans in the US and Conservatives in Britain) and created think tanks that spread neoliberal ideas. Harvey recognizes, but does not explain, the uneven implementation of neoliberal policies in advanced capitalist countries. He believes that neoliberalism is imposed comprehensively and with virtually no resistance in the third world. All that varies is the nature of the tools that US and capitalist firms use to impose their will. In most cases, the IMF and World Bank do the dirty work. In a few cases – Chile in 1973 and Iraq in 2003 – the US used force to overthrow resistant governments and replace them with compliant ones.

Harvey's analysis is relatively nuanced in comparison to Hardt and Negri (2000), or Klein (2007), in that he acknowledges how incomplete the implementation of neoliberal policies has been in the richest countries, even if he is unable to see similar variation in the rest of the world. Our task is to account for those differences, which we can do by first acknowledging that neoliberal policies, like any other initiative by a class, elite, or popular group in civil society, are implemented within existing political regimes.

Prasad (2006) cautions us to focus on "policy episodes," specific changes in government rather than long-term quantitative shifts in income distribution, state spending, poverty rates, or amount of foreign trade and investment which can have a variety of causes. The US, British, French, and German governments differed in the neoliberal policies they actually were able to implement. Firms were privatized in France under Chirac and in Britain under Thatcher, as were the government-owned council houses where 30 percent of Britons lived, but there was virtually no privatization in Germany or the US. The main neoliberal policy in the US consisted of tax cuts, of which there were some in Britain but almost none in Germany and France. Social benefits were cut for the poor in the US under Reagan but not for the middle class, while social programs remained largely intact in the other three. Deregulation was confined mainly to the US and to the financial sector in Britain. How does Prasad explain the incompleteness and particular foci of neoliberal policies in the four countries?

Privatization happened only in those countries and for those firms whose managers and workers had not embedded themselves in political parties and government agencies. Germany's state firms had allies in both main parties and, most crucially, in state governments. They were able to block any privatization. France's state-owned firms also had tentacles deep in the main political parties and in government agencies, but those alliances were disrupted by a new wave of nationalizations under Mitterrand's socialist government in 1981. State firms became isolated from the right-wing parties and were denationalized after the Socialists lost power. Thatcher's denationalizations initially were motivated by a desire to plug budget deficits without raising taxes. Council houses were sold to tenants and British Telecom shares were sold directly to the public. Only after both sales were highly popular and lucrative did privatization become a centerpiece of British policy.

This pattern in core countries held elsewhere in the world. Firms were sold where managers and workers were isolated from parties and lacked links to local governments and elites, as with the Mexican telephone company, but were impossible where dense patronage chains embedded the firms in the state and unions, as with Pemex, the Mexican national oil monopoly. The widespread and rapid privatizations in Latin America during the 1980s and 1990s (Aguiar de Medeiros 2009) followed the end of military dictatorships that had embedded retired officers in state firms. The new civilian regimes were linked instead to rising financial capitalists who, in turn, had ties to European and US investors. The US government did not press for an end to military rule to open up investment opportunities; the military juntas were unnecessary after the weakening of popular movements and the end of the Cold War. However, the militaries' loss of function certainly made it easier for the new governments and their backers, in the US and in international agencies, to press for policies that undercut the economic interests of the military and of capitalists tied to them.

Eastern European and Soviet firms could be privatized only after the fall from power of communist parties, and the sale had to be lubricated politically by distributing shares to the public. Of course, those shares rapidly were bought up, often through fraudulent means, by a few oligarchs, many of whom relied on foreign partners for capital. However, the combined power and desire of neoliberal officials, domestic capitalists, and foreign investors were not enough to dislodge those firms that retained broad and deep links to parties, localities, and workers.

Even in Chile and Iraq, two cases Harvey and Klein present as the most violent impositions of neoliberalism, political ties protected some state firms from privatization. Chile's mass privatizations, after the 1973 coup that removed the democratically elected Socialist President Salvador Allende from office, did not include copper – the largest and most lucrative industry – even though the state's holding had been expanded by Allende's nationalization of US-owned copper mines. The Pinochet dictatorship resisted the political demands of the US and the ideological assertions of neoliberals because the Chilean military was entitled by statute to 10 percent of the revenues from all state-owned copper holdings. Allende had agreed to continue that provision and extended it to the newly nationalized holdings, in an unsuccessful effort to win the military's loyalty. Pinochet and all his civilian successors have maintained national ownership of the copper industry. The military, which still retains a constitutional right to its 10 percent, has been the political anchor for maintaining the copper sector in state hands, regardless of regime type or international forces.

The United States embarked on a program of extreme neoliberalism in Iraq immediately after its invasion, refusing to allow state-owned firms to reopen unless they had been privatized. Schwartz (2008) traces how the US succeeded in destroying indigenous Iraqi industries and making Iraq dependent on foreign, mainly American, companies for the import and servicing of goods and infrastructure. Schwartz sees the mass unemployment and destitution created by the destruction of the state sector as the principal cause of the insurgency. Only the oil sector remains nationalized, and US effort to compel the Iraqi parliament to approve a US-drafted Bill that would have granted foreign firms long-term access to Iraqi oil fields, on terms amounting to de facto privatization, was never approved. The Iraqi national oil company had links to labor unions and regional elites that transcended its links to the Baath Party that was destroyed in the invasion. Other firms were smaller, localized, and lacked the political networks that gave the oil industry the capacity to mount resistance to US demands in parliament, at the workplace, and throughout the country. Even under the most extreme conditions of foreign occupation, intact political networks of great coherence and breadth can resist neoliberal demands.

Neoliberal policies in the other realms identified by Harvey also

have been widely resisted, and implemented only in some countries and often incompletely. Prasad argues that taxes in Europe
(and she could have added East Asia, as well) are regressive, targeted at consumption rather than income or wealth, and directly
linked to social programs. Any tax cuts would immediately trigger
benefit cuts, and would not significantly redistribute resources
from workers to capitalists. Where programs and tax revenues are
administered by local governments, as in Germany or Britain, or
where local governments have control over national revenues, as
in France where officials simultaneously hold both departmental
and national offices (Ashford 1982), national officials have little
leeway to cut or restructure taxes.

The US stands alone among wealthy capitalist countries in its
devotion to tax cuts (Martin 2008). Tax cuts in the US have been
far larger than in any other OECD country. Federal revenues as
a percentage of GDP declined from 20.9 percent in 2000 to 16.3
percent in 2004, a greater decline than the drop (2.2 percent of
GDP) from 1981 to 1984 (Congressional Budget Office 2006). The
2004 level was the lowest since 1959. Except for Social Security,
whose dedicated tax was increased under Reagan, social and other
spending are not linked to any particular stream of revenue. Taxes
can be cut with no consequence but overall Federal deficits, which
so far have been easily financed because the US dollar still is the
reserve currency of the world. State and local governments finance
their programs with their own highly regressive taxes.

Social benefits, the bullseye of neoliberalism's ideological offensive, have survived largely intact in France, Germany, and Britain
(Prasad 2006), and even expanded modestly in Eastern Europe
since the end of communism, and in East Asia, as well, while
holding mostly steady in Latin America (Haggard and Kaufman
2008: ch. 5). The severe cuts in means-tested welfare programs
under Reagan, Clinton, and Bush were highly unusual among
wealthy and even newly industrializing countries. It is a mistake
to see US politics as paradigmatic or predictive of the world as a
whole.

The realm where neoliberalism has been most successful is the
financial sector. Regulations were progressively dismantled in the

US from the 1970s onwards, and Britain underwent a Big Bang of financial deregulation in 1986. Most crucially, the US has been able to use its control over the World Bank and IMF, and to leverage its (now disappearing) hegemonic position to force trade and financial liberalization through bilateral trade treaties and the WTO. Yet some countries, especially in East Asia, have been able to resist opening their banks and markets to free trade, as we saw in the previous chapter. Where banks were under the control of national governments (most notably in China and Singapore), or were themselves the central nodes of cohesive national capitalist classes that are held together by links of loans, investments, and shared directors (as in Japan, Korea, and Germany), banking liberalization could be successfully resisted, and the worst practices of financialization and the bubble of speculation were avoided.

Even in the United States, financial deregulation was a long and contentious process. Proposals for deregulation, similar to those enacted under Clinton, were rejected by Congress in the 1970s and 1980s. National firms, linked together by director interlocks centered on the biggest commercial banks, coexisted with regional and local banks and firms that were shielded from competition with bigger rivals, thanks to Federal and state regulations that local elites had the political muscle to sustain through influence on their Congressional delegations and in their state governments (Davis and Mizruchi 1999; Prechel 2000). Mergers of banks and firms, which began to be more widely allowed under the Nixon administration in the 1970s, weakened those regional and local political alliances, reducing pressure on Federal officials to block regulatory changes, which in turn made further waves of mergers and acquisitions possible. In the banking sector, mergers created new regional behemoths that could compete with national banks. Mergers reduced intra-industry differences over government policy, creating unified voices that pushed legislative changes to enactment in the 1990s. A weakened state, combined with the decline of labor unions, undermined "two of the key forces that had disciplined the business community" (Mizruchi 2004: 607; see also Davis and Mizruchi 1999; Prechel 2000). This unified business interest, combined with the end of the Cold War that had

170

forced the US government to support developmentalism in much of the world for geopolitical reasons, led the US to press for open trade and financial deregulation with single-minded devotion in the 1990s and 2000s.

Financialization and the neoliberal focus of the IMF, World Bank, and WTO had the most deleterious effects on the poorest nations. As Harvey rightly notes, "borrowers are forced by state and international powers to take on board the cost of debt repayment no matter what the consequences for the livelihood and well-being of the local population. If this requires the surrender of assets to foreign companies at fire-sale prices, so be it" (2005: 29). Yet this is just a high-tech version of gunboat diplomacy. Weak governments and their citizens have always been forced to open themselves to looting by powerful states and their capitalists. The methods and supporting ideology have changed, but the consequences for citizens' living standards remain dire. Stuckler et al. (2009) document a significant rise in mortality following privatization of state firms in Eastern Europe, even though, as we have noted, social benefits remained in place. In countries where social programs have never been enacted, citizens forced off the land congregate in vast slums without water, sewer, or transportation systems (Davis 2006). Government funds are applied to debt repayment rather than infrastructure, health, or education. Where national states and indigenous capitalists are weak and disorganized, neoliberal policies can be forced on countries. Psychological shock or ideological conversions are superfluous under those conditions.

Finally, China's transformation since 1978 is difficult to understand within the rubric of neoliberalism. Most Chinese never received social benefits, which were largely granted to urban workers through their employment in state firms. As those firms were privatized, the benefits largely disappeared. But, otherwise, state officials retain close control over firms, even if they share the profits with a new class of capitalists and with foreign investors. Despite membership in the WTO since 2001, China's currency remains regulated and "private" banks are closely controlled by the state in ways that combine corruption with policy goals.

Harvey (2009) points out that China, because of state control over banks and the existence of agencies capable of carrying out vast infrastructural projects, will be able to adopt Keynesian policies to overcome the economic crisis of 2008, while the US, which has withdrawn from regulation and reduced public works and which is hampered by an ideology that views state spending as "socialist" (hardly an issue in what is still officially communist China), will be less successful at mounting a Keynesian recovery. Harvey's astute comparison of 2009 counters his view that neoliberalism is a political and ideological tide that has washed away state regulation and social benefits worldwide. Instead, its adoption and effects vary depending on the strength and structure of the state, the organization of domestic capitalist and working classes, and their position in the world economic and geopolitical system.

Neoliberalism is not the primary cause of state weakness. Rather, neoliberalism is most powerful in already weak states. How states weaken and break down is the topic of the next chapter.

6

State Breakdowns

States, as they gather resources and powers and as they become the sites for the contestation, adjudication, and legitimation of property, authority, and ideology, become ever more permanent and unassailable. State breakdowns are rare events in the modern world. Unlike ancient empires or feudal kingdoms, which amassed territory, fielded armies, built cities, organized networks of commerce, and then disappeared, leaving decentralized polities rather than large-scale successors, most modern states once established achieve, at least from the perspective of today, permanence. Border changes are rare, especially when states are bounded by other states. Revolutionaries, even as they plot and achieve the destruction of states, work to replace those they overthrow with new states that they hope will have even greater control over civil society than the old regimes.

Social revolutions and catastrophic defeat in war are the main causes of state breakdowns both historically and in the contemporary world, while post-colonial states often are weak from the outset and prone to breakdown. My goal here is not to explain why revolutions occur or why states fight and lose wars. Those topics would each require a book of its own, and have been the subject of many. Rather, my concern in this chapter is with the consequences of revolutions, colonialism, and military defeats on states. I examine the range of ways in which states have been affected, and attempt to account for those variations. I am especially concerned with evaluating the claim that modern states are less likely to suffer breakdown than their historical counter-parts. Theda Skocpol, in 1979, wrote "it seems highly unlikely that modern states could disintegrate as administrative-coercive organizations without destroying society at the same time, a modern social revolution would probably have to flow gradu-ally, not cataclysmically, out of a long series of 'non-reformist reforms'" (p. 293). Since her book was published, there have been revolutions in Iran and Nicaragua (both in 1979) and a decade later in Russia and Eastern Europe. More recently, states have disintegrated in various countries, mainly in Africa. Thus, we need to account for the renewed vulnerabilities of states in recent decades.

Revolutions

Revolutions are more than extra-constitutional changes of gov-ernment. Revolutions transform state structures, turn colonies into independent nations, replace monarchies with republics, or turn dictatorships into democracies or vice versa. Skocpol (1979: 4) distinguishes "social revolutions," which combine "the coinci-dence of societal structural change with class upheaval; and the coincidence of political with social transformation" from "politi-cal revolutions," which "transform state structures but not social structures, and . . . are not necessarily accomplished through class conflict."

My goal is not to construct a typology to which we can assign every change of government over the past 500 years. Rather, we need to acknowledge that such changes are arrayed over a con-tinuum. At one end are the social revolutions that fundamentally disrupted the structure of states and their capacity to sustain a ruling class, such as the French monarchy and aristocracy in 1789, China's state and the landlords and foreign capitalists in 1949, or the communist states and parties of the Soviet bloc in 1989. In the middle are the political revolutions that left in place basic social relations, even as the state system was transformed and many of the personnel of both the state and the ruling class were killed, exiled, or retired. Examples include the English Revolution and Civil War of 1640–9, the American Revolution of 1776–83, most of the Latin American independence wars of the early nineteenth century and the numerous independence struggles of the post-1945 era, South Africa in 1994, and the "color revolutions" of 2000–5 in Yugoslavia, Georgia, Ukraine, Kyrgyzstan, and Lebanon. At the other end are coups that are like political neutron bombs: they destroy the people staffing the government but leave the institutions and the government's structural relation to groups in civil society largely intact. Bolivia's 193 coups between 1825 and 1981 had virtually no effect on social relations in that country or on the structure and policies of the state.

Civil wars can fall anywhere along the continuum of governmental change. Civil wars occur when a revolution or coup remains unresolved. The old government is able to fight on for a period that can stretch into years. The Bolshevik Revolution was challenged by old regime remnants in a civil war that lasted until 1921. Had the White Russian forces won, there would have been no social revolution and the state would have returned to the status quo ante. The Confederacy's defeat in the US Civil War opened the way for a social revolution in the South, even as social relations remained stable in the rest of the nation. The Nationalist coup in Spain in 1936 sought to reverse a partial political revolution that began with the left's electoral victory that year. Over the years of the war the Republicans became radicalized and, had they won, Spain might have undergone a partial social revolution. The Nationalist victory was a political revolution that removed the left from Spanish government for forty years. Virtually all the civil wars since 1945 have been along ethnic and regional lines, and almost all have failed. If Biafra had succeeded in winning independence from Nigeria, it would have divided the state in two, creating two separate political elites. At the outset of the war, the rulers of Nigeria and Biafra governed similar states with similar class bases of support. The war did nothing to significantly change state structures or political coalitions on either side. Biafran victory would not have been a social revolution.

All revolutions, social and political, cause at least temporary state breakdowns. Coups, like elections, can be merely epiphenomenal: changing top personnel and policies, while government agencies maintain operations, and relations between the state and civil society remain substantially the same. In the long-term, social revolutions increase state capacity. Political revolutions vary in their effect, while coups lead to state weakness and in extreme cases state breakdown. Let us see why that is so.

Social revolutions are propelled by class mobilization. While the key contemporary theorists of revolution (Skocpol 1979; Paige 1975; Wickham-Crowley 1992; Goldstone 1991; Goodwin 2001; Foran 2005) disagree on who mobilizes to oppose the old regime and why, they agree that once mass mobilization has occurred the revolutionary leadership needs to adopt policies to satisfy and pacify the mobilized forces. Revolutionary leaders often are uncertain of what steps to take to respond to the anger and violence from below, as we saw in the previous chapter, in Markoff's (1996b) analysis of the interactions between mobilized peasants and the National Assembly during the French Revolution. Even when a revolution is led by a party vanguard, which claims to be certain of the interests and desires of its followers, party programs can be revised in the face of continuing violence and of the need to build coalitions to defeat remaining enemies. Lenin and the Communist Party made concessions and adapted its program during the years it fought the Civil War and even after as it consolidated power. Even where revolutionaries quickly and non-violently took power, as in Eastern Europe in 1989, the need to contest and win elections forced the revolutionaries to revise and expand their original platforms.

Revolutionaries offered widely differing concessions and programs, depending on the classes and factions that were mobilized and the sorts of coalitions they sought and were able to build. Obviously, there is a world of difference between what the French Revolutionary state of the 1790s accomplished and the program of Communist China, between Nicaragua in 1979 and Hungary in 1989. Yet all those new regimes shared a substantial expansion of state capacity. Peasants could be satisfied and neutralized only when the state gained the capacity to depose landlords and to establish new mechanisms to provide farmers with inputs and to market their surpluses. Industrial workers relied upon the state to replace capitalists and ensure the operation of factories. Thus, revolutionary upheaval only ended once the new states achieved the organizational capacities needed to meet the demands of mobilized forces. Women participated in the Nicaraguan Revolution as guerillas, as well as being non-violent organizers, to an extent never recorded in any previous revolution. These women mobilized largely through autonomous women's organizations (Kampwirth 2004). Those organizations were incorporated into the Sandinista state and became the mechanisms through which the Nicaraguan state created the capacity to regulate gender relations, offer services to women and families, and provide for women's interests in a range of settings. The vast extension of state capacities in the realms of gender and family happened because women remained mobilized and had the organizational base to make demands on the state.

The 1989 revolutions are the great exception to the relationship between mass mobilization, social revolution, and gains in state capacity. The revolutions in Eastern Europe were directed against state capacities: above all, the state's ability to control its subjects' behavior in civil society, combined with state ownership and control of enterprises. Yet even those revolutions created new state capacities to regulate the privatized economies, and, as we saw in the previous chapter, the state retained its capacities to provide social benefits.

Political revolutions have a much more varied effect on state capacities. The first of those revolutions were anti-monarchical, and in the twentieth century most were anti-colonial. The post-revolutionary states were shaped by the forces that overthrew the old regimes. Those forces' cohesion and capacities, in turn, were largely determined by the nature of the monarchies and colonial regimes that ruled those polities. We saw in chapter 2 how the English Crown's efforts to create a horizontal absolutism had the inadvertent effect of surrendering county-level power to cohesive gentries. As a result, when Charles I was overthrown in the English Civil War, and his allies were removed from office in parliament and in county and town governments, new cohesive elites took office. They were able to expand governmental capacities at each level. Parliament formulated and was able to implement a new, far more aggressive foreign policy that laid the groundwork for empire (Brenner 1993), and county elites became far more effective at regulating the poor (Somers 1993; Lachmann 2000: 190–4). The nineteenth-century anti-monarchical revolutions in Europe had varying effects. The bourgeoisies of continental Europe were far less cohesive than that of England, and their victories were either short-lived, as were all the 1848 revolutions, or yielded weak regimes that gave way to counter-revolutions, as in Spain in 1874. Revolutions that were led by weak classes or fragmented coalitions often were just the first act in a sequence leading to state breakdown. The weak Spanish monarch of 1874–1931 was succeeded by the Second Spanish Republic, which rested on a coalition of internally divided classes that were in conflict with one another. The Republic lacked the capacity and cohesion to organize its own citizens or to field a cohesive army with the resources to counter Franco's forces.

Post-colonial States

Colonization leaves a legacy of political disorganization and weak administrative structures which anti-colonial political revolutions rarely overcome. Imperial powers almost always conquer territories with forces that are tiny in relation to the populations they control, and the staffs left in place to govern are smaller still. Colonial rule is backed with the threat of extreme violence, but it operates on a daily basis through clever stratagems designed to recruit collaborators and divide local populations. The ways in which colonial regimes organized their subjects decisively shaped the post-colonial states. Scholars of colonization are only beginning to engage in the sorts of fine-grained case and comparative studies that will allow us to determine how the objectives and capacities of imperial states interacted with the collaborators and resisters in the colonies to shape regimes that in turn structured post-colonial states. Van Onselen (1982) is exemplary in showing how the stratagems adopted by the precariously independent South African Republic of the late nineteenth century to fend off British domination, build an autonomous economy, satisfy its agrarian political base, and profit from foreign investment in the newly discovered gold fields, created class relations and state capacities that fostered apartheid a half-century later. Steinmetz (2007), whom we discussed in chapter 3, makes the significant contribution of identifying divisions among colonial officials that, in the German colonies, resulted in genocide in Southwest Africa, an only lightly disruptive rule in Samoa, and a complex effort at restructuring and collaboration in the Germans' leasehold colony of Qingdao. Steinmetz is concerned with determining German policy and so only looks at the interaction between colonial rule and indigenous resistance in so far as it affected Germans. Yet his analysis, if extended into the post-colonial era and especially if used as a template for scholars of other nations' colonization, can provide a theoretical and empirical basis for understanding differences among post-independence polities.

India and the Congo are polar opposites along the continuum of imperial influence. We examined the Congolese extreme in earlier chapters. Belgian colonists were able to destroy pre-colonial political structures and the brief independence movement created only a thin and divided national political elite. The new state lacked the capacity to administer services or even to assert authority beyond the capital. Regional elites also were weak and gained the strength to challenge the national government only with foreign support. Neither the national nor regional Congolese governments were able to take any military or organizational initiatives without support from foreign sponsors. Since foreign powers had an interest in preventing the development of state capacities that would reduce their ability to extract resources, and Congolese classes were disorganized, state capacity never developed beyond the low level with which it was left at the moment of independence.

India was quite different from the Congo and indeed from most of Africa. It was, in the centuries before British conquest, alternately an empire and a set of coherent polities. Britain ruled by sustaining and coopting indigenous elites, both in the princely states and in areas of direct rule. The British disrupted some local elites and advanced others through their patronage, but throughout India coherent provincial governments were sustained and their capacities enhanced to allow collaborators to control the population, foster commerce, and funnel revenues to London. The long twilight of British rule created an opening for the Congress Party to link together provincial elites into a nationwide bloc that manned a coherent state after independence. Congress was a mass movement but its leadership knit together Indian civil servants employed by the British, professionals, and an Indian capitalist class formed under British hegemony. Only in those areas where the British encouraged a Muslim counterweight in an effort to weaken Congress did a national elite fail to emerge (Brown 1999). When those areas became Pakistan, they were left with autarkic provincial elites only weakly held together into a nation. The lack of a Muslim equivalent to Congress shapes the Pakistani state and politics sixty years later, as provinces looted by local elites (such as the Bhuttos of Sindh) remain only nominally under national control. The Pakistani state's capacities to extract revenues, administer, and deliver services remain low.

Colonies fell closer to the Indian or Congolese poles, depending on: (1) the strength of the pre-conquest polities; (2) the extent to which the conquerors used violence to disrupt and kill off indigenous elites; and (3) the degree to which an autonomous domestic capitalist class developed under colonial rule. Stronger states, like India, Singapore, and Malaysia among British colonies, and French Côte d'Ivoire, all had relatively well-developed polities which survived conquest partly intact. The British in India were highly violent, but the depth and resilience of many of the polities into which the subcontinent was divided left more intact elites than in some weaker polities elsewhere in the world exposed to less violence. Further, because of their centrality in imperial trade and manufacture, India, Singapore, and Malaysia developed strong bourgeoisies. Côte d'Ivoire had less commerce in absolute terms but became a center for French Africa. Most of Africa, and other colonies elsewhere, endured the destruction of local elites and had little capitalist development.

British settler colonies in North America, Australia, and New Zealand, and the Spanish ones in Chile, Argentina, and Uruguay, were formed on lands cleared of the aboriginal peoples whom the settlers largely exterminated. Settlers created new indigenous elites, and all developed capitalist classes. Upon independence, all had states with capacities that rivaled those of their former rulers. By contrast, settler states, where large indigenous populations survived conquest and/or were supplemented with large slave populations, failed to develop cohesive elites and bourgeoisies and were left with weak post-independence estates. The US Southern states escaped that fate because of their incorporation within the United States.

The clear correspondence between colonial regime and post-independence state was disrupted by two intervening forces: prolonged independence movements and post-independence meddling by foreign powers. Independence movements – such as India's Congress Party, South Africa's ANC, Nicaragua's FSLN, Iran's Islamists, and Communist Parties almost everywhere – are able to knit together local elites into a cohesive national bloc that can strengthen the new state's post-independence capacities. Independence movements that are based in single ethnic groups and exclude others create weak and corrupt states, as in much of Africa. Where a minority ethnic group is dominant economically, and the independence movement reaches an accommodation rather than attempting to overwhelm the minority, then a higher-capacity state with political stability (but not necessarily much democracy) emerges, as in Singapore, Malaysia, and post-apartheid South Africa.

Many states became independent without significant anti-colonial struggles. Britain and France's decisions to cede independence to many colonies before armed movements developed reflected financial weakness and post-1945 military exhaustion in the metropole. However, it was also a generally accurate judgment by the British and French on their ability to select docile rulers and to manipulate and dominate the new governments.

The states that emerged out of such soft and managed transitions were weak and prone to remain that way because post-independence rulers were able to remain in power through foreign backing, and therefore lacked the need or autonomy to develop their own capacities to deliver services or build a domestic base of support. Such regimes became "sultanistic . . . an extreme form of patrimonialism in which authority is solely based on personal rulership exercised without restraint, unencumbered by law, values, ideology or custom, and where loyalty to the ruler signifies total submission based on fear and greed" (Brachet-Marques 2005: 469). We saw in the previous chapter how oil-rich states, primarily in the Middle East, became sultanistic by turning on their imperial sponsors and nationalizing oil. Non-oil regimes became sultanistic as leaders used foreign support to eliminate bases of domestic opposition, enter into an alliance with foreign capitalists, and appropriate domestic resources, undermining the possibility of a cohesive indigenous bourgeoisie that could become a counterweight to the regime. Mugabe in Zimbabwe is the epitome of that model. He took office with international support against the white minority regime. Mugabe adopted a Bonapartist strategy with his victory in the first election. He offered concessions to white farmers and businessmen, and used aid and support from abroad to undermine the Ndebele minority and block the emergence of a black bourgeoisie. In the absence of a viable domestic opposition, Mugabe was able to cement his control over the army and police and pack the government with corrupt retainers. He then turned on his white allies and expropriated their property, turning the regime in a sultanistic direction.

Many personalistic regimes, especially in Latin America, were put in place by the United States to guard American investments and to suppress leftist parties. Brachet-Marques (2005) cites Somoza in Nicaragua, about whom President Franklin D. Roosevelt said, "He's a son of a bitch, but he's our son of a bitch," as a sultanistic ruler, as well as Batista in Cuba, Trujillo of the Dominican Republic, the Shah of Iran, and Marcos of the Philippines. More broadly, weak states, whether sultanistic or wrecked by factional conflict, are easily exploited by imperial or neo-imperial powers. Schwartz (2008) found that US plans for neoliberalism in Iraq, which we discussed in the previous chapter, were facilitated by a military strategy that served to intensify violent conflict among Sunni and Shia. Ethnic violence in Iraq, Schwartz (2008) shows, held back the formation of a nationalist coalition that could demand the withdrawal of US forces and block neoliberal policies.

International Wars

Wars between states have had very different effects from the imperial conquests or engineered coups we have just discussed. Military success in early modern Europe was not additive. In other words, victory in one war and the conquest of territories, in Europe or beyond, did not increase the likelihood of further success against European rivals. The absolute size or rate of growth of state budgets in early modern Europe were poor predictors of state capacities and achievements, whether victories in battle, the conquest of European territories or foreign colonies, or the construction of public works. Revenues did not correlate with military success. Spain, even as it overtook France in revenues in the late sixteenth century, failed to conquer any new lands in Europe or on other continents, and it lost control of the Netherlands, which had a fifth of Spain's budget, and also of its colonies, to Britain, the poorest of the powers. France, the richest of the powers from the 1630s to 1789, conquered almost no territories in that time while losing many of its colonies to poorer Britain. The Netherlands and Britain took colonies in the seventeenth and eighteenth centuries from richer Spain and France. Britain and the Netherlands fought wars with each other and seized colonies from one another. Often the country with the smaller budget at the time was victorious (Lachmann 2009).

Wars affect state capacity mainly by transforming internal political dynamics, above all, as we saw in chapters 3 and 5, by deepening citizen-soldiers' political mobilization within and against the state, which, in turn, strengthens their demands for social benefits. Mobilization and state response can occur in states that lose wars, though usually not with as robust outcomes as in victorious states, and with the risk that mobilization can become revolutionary as it did among the losers after World War I. Skocpol (1979) argues that military defeat was a necessary, though not sufficient, cause of the social revolutions in France, Russia, and China. However, those social revolutions created states that "were stronger and more autonomous within society and more powerful over against foreign competitors within the international states system" than their pre-Revolutionary predecessors (1979: 285).

Military defeat, when it does not lead to social revolution, has much more deleterious long-term consequences for state capacities. It can lead to the splintering of multi-ethnic polities, most notably the Ottoman and Austro-Hungarian Empires at the end of World War I, but also more recently in Iraqi Kurdistan after Saddam Hussein's defeat in the 1991 Gulf War. The fate of the Kurds illustrates the dynamics of ethnic independence in post-war eras. Independence is won only when an ethnic group is organized, often through regional governments established under the old imperial regime, or through long independence struggles. The national or imperial government's defeat in war removes or sufficiently undermines the repressive apparatus that forced the ethnic group to remain within the larger polity. Foreign powers with armed forces in the area are the ultimate arbiter of borders. After World War I, the victorious great powers (the United States, Britain, and France) encouraged independence to undermine the defeated central powers and determined the final boundaries of the new nations. The victorious allies in World War II in contrast decided to preserve the identities, though not the exact borders, of the defeated Axis powers. Kurdistan won autonomy in 1991 only because the US forces in the Middle East decided to restrain Iraq from suppressing the rebellion. Yugoslavia splintered in 1991 during a moment when Russia was too weak to preserve Serbian dominance and NATO was able to project force there to guard each ethnicity's claim to nationhood.

Wars, then, do not have uniform effects, nor are the consequences of victory and defeat necessarily different. Rather, we need to look at the internal dynamics of each combatant's pre-war polity to trace the effects of militarization. Invasion and even occupation are transformative only over the long-term and mainly when a country at the center of the world system subdues one at the periphery. Colonization, as we discussed above, has a far more profound effect on social relations than the occupations of one advanced capitalist country by another. The Nazis left piles of bodies in the countries they occupied but virtually no social change (Aly 2005). Japan's greatest influence in East Asia was on Taiwan and Korea, which it occupied well before the start of World War II.

Napoleon had a transformative effect on some of the countries he occupied, as did the US on Germany, Japan, and South Korea after 1945, because in defeating their enemies France and the US wiped out specific elites and set in motion political and social structural realignments. It was Napoleon's defeats of aristocracies in parts of Italy and Germany that created progressive change, while his occupation of Spain and the Low Countries did little to realign social relations and left little trace on those states' functions and capacities (Lynch 1989; Israel 1995: 1122–30). The political systems and liberal constitutions the US imposed on Japan and Germany ratified and institutionalized political realignments set in motion in the course of those Axis powers' years at war. Hitler, as he centered power in the Nazi Party and mobilized resources for war, undermined the landlords and capitalists who had played the fatal roles in undermining Weimar democracy. The occupying powers' de-Nazification was secondary to Hitler's wartime destruction of a political base for a post-war authoritarian regime. Defeat in war discredited and shattered the class forces that backed the military regime in Japan and that collaborated with the Japanese occupation in Korea. US occupation forces had a harder time controlling the workers and peasants unleashed by the destruction of their class enemies than in removing militarists from office. The solutions the US devised in those two distinct polities produced contrasting liberal and authoritarian regimes in Japan and Korea.

War's transformative, or often epiphenomenal, effects can be understood only in terms of the specific social structure of each combatant. The designs and capacities of occupying powers are secondary. That is why schemes of state-building often cannot be realized, and why efforts to translate the "lessons" of seeming success from one nation to another fail. US achievements in democratizing post-war Germany and Japan cannot be reproduced in Iraq or Afghanistan, not because of a lack of resources or will but because the US arrived in each country at a particular moment in their distinct sequences of contingent structural change.

The Disintegration of States

Most state breakdowns are temporary. Polities that have been destroyed by social revolution, overthrown, or suffered catastrophic military defeat are replaced by new regimes. Some parts of the world, however, have become essentially stateless. The pre-state political world we examined in chapter 2 has been revived in much of Africa, growing parts of Pakistan and Afghanistan, and portions of the Philippines. Governments there lack a monopoly on the use of force, and must defer in much of their nominal domains to local rulers who command territories in which they share few revenues and little authority with the state. Those local rulers finance themselves by exploiting the lands and people they control and establish trade networks that are based on long-distance appetites for goods, often drugs or natural resources, and services, which can include slaves (Bales 2004) and sex workers, produced in their local realms.

The question we must answer is why, after centuries of growing state power, has that process been reversed in some parts of the world. Is it merely that the end of the Cold War led the US and Russia to withdraw support from regimes that without external backing had little capacity to actually rule their territories? That view (see Clough 1992 for an early statement) assumes that the superpowers, like the colonial powers before them, were bringing modern political institutions to what had been a decentralized collection of tribal polities. That image of Africa is more literary conceit, presented in different forms by Chinua Achebe in *Things Fall Apart* and Jean de Brunhoff in his *Babar* books,[1] than historical reality. It also glides over the ways, discussed above, in which foreign powers disordered rather than strengthened polities in their colonies and dependencies. Thus, foreign withdrawal has a variety of effects, and even in Africa some states have been strengthened by the decline of foreign manipulation and meddling.

Charles Tilly rightly turns the focus to dynamics that are internal to states. He argues that just as state formation and democratization were propelled by the integration of trust networks into national polities, so efforts by "the already rich and powerful [to] withdraw their trust networks, install inequalities, and create autonomous power centers" can undermine democracy and weaken state capacity (2007: 195). Tilly is clear on the advantages to elites of life outside the state, in "gated communities and private schooling" (p. 204), but he doesn't explain how elites are able to get away with placing themselves and their resources beyond state control in some places and times but not others. The only motivating factor he identifies is "the rise of religious fundamentalism across the world [which] encourages people to withdraw religiously bonded networks from public politics, that momentous change should promote widespread dedemocratization in regions of religious zealotry" (p. 204). That description fits Afghanistan, parts of Pakistan, Yemen, and Islamic sub-Saharan Africa, and may be a harbinger for Egypt, but certainly not for Iran whose state is stronger under an Islamic republic able to block US interference than it was under the more secular Shah, who was dependent on and manipulated by the US.

Elsewhere, Tilly (1995b) describes the decline of "worker power and union densities" around the world since 1980 and rightly points out that "capitalists caused the shifts in question, deliberately creating transnational structures to evade control by any particular state and its organized labor" (pp. 18, 19). But, as we saw in chapter 5, supposedly global neoliberal forces have different effects, depending on the existing strength of the state and the degree of class and elite mobilization. Worker rights and social benefits have not declined universally. In any case, Tilly is unable to explain how capitalists have gained control over transnational institutions and why those entities switched from policies that foster development to ones that propel financialization.

Elite self-interest and religious fundamentalism, like colonialism and neoliberalism, operate in existing polities whose internal dynamics determine elites' interest in, and capacities to withdraw, assets and powers from states. Tilly's concern is that elite withdrawal creates categorical inequalities and that in turn makes it easier for those elites to exist without government services. But, while gated communities may be new, the rich in the US have always purchased private education, security, health care, and various other services provided by the state in Europe. In that way, the US is closer to the third world pattern, but, as we saw in our discussions of social benefits and neoliberalism in chapter 5, changes in state policies to increase or decrease control over capital allocation, and to create or reduce social benefits, are the result of direct demands upon the state by elites or popular forces. Unilateral decisions by groups to withdraw resources or participation can be blocked by strong states. In places where states are weak, tax avoidance, walled compounds, private security forces, and religiously based polities are symptoms not causes of state breakdown.

Some authors contend that all states are being weakened, and the regions of state breakdown are harbingers of the future rather than pathological outliers of the present. Friedman (2005), whom we encountered in the Preface, believes that technology allows the flow of goods, people, and capital in ways all states are incapable of controlling. Markoff (1996a: 130–9) argues that globalization weakens states mainly as it operates through transnational organizations, but the states most vulnerable to the IMF and its ilk are weaker states to begin with. Global economic and organizational forces, like waves of religious fundamentalism, affect states differently in ways that can be predicted and understood in terms of those states' capacities and structural positions.

World systems theorists look to different sources of state weakness: in the functioning of the system itself and from "antisystemic movements." Peripheral zones, as we saw in chapter 4, have weaker states than the core and semi-periphery. Thus, in Wallerstein's (1974–89) and Arrighi's (1994; 2007) analyses, zones with weak state capacity are integral to the world system, and they widen as the hegemon falters. Just as neither author offers adequate explanations of why particular states rise out of the periphery, so they fail to analyze why particular states lose capacity. They are content to note that the US as current hegemon is losing capacity both domestically and as regulator of the world system as a whole. And they do not explain why world system chaos affects some peripheral states more severely than others.

The other main consequence of world systemic crisis, in Wallerstein's (2003) view, is the intensification of anti-systemic movements. Wallerstein is careful to distinguish between anti-systemic and anti-state. He argues that nineteenth- and twentieth-century movements, whether socialist, nationalist, or some combination, were properly focused on taking state power, even though their promises of fundamental transformation on a world scale once in power went unfulfilled. However, in the current "age of transition – a period of bifurcation and chaos – . . . it is clear that the issues confronting antisystemic movements pose themselves in a very different fashion . . . The two-step, state-oriented strategy [take power, then transform the world] had become irrelevant" (2003: 269). Wallerstein is properly modest in his predictions and prescriptions for contemporary movements, and therefore he does claim that current anti-systemic movements can account for the weakening of state power in either core or periphery.

State breakdowns have particular causes specific to each nation. Extreme collapse requires multiple causes: long-term disruption of political networks and of classes' capacities for mobilization by colonial and post-colonial intervention, economic weakness and exploitation, and then wars, revolutions, and civil wars can shatter weakened states. Worldwide forces and structures – the dynamics of the world system, globalization, or social movements – and historical events, of wars, revolutions, coups, or colonization, affect each state in particular ways. Generalizations require systematic comparisons of states and analysis of sequences of temporal change. They cannot be imputed to social forces that occur, and have different consequences, in each era and location.

Skocpol's predictions, which we presented at the outset of this chapter, are partly valid. While she was wrong that revolutionary overthrows of states were impossible because they necessarily would destroy societies, she was correct that modern societies still need states. Where a concatenation of causes has left regions stateless and ruled by local elites, modern social order is impossible. However, such conditions are not a harbinger of a coming world future of statelessness, but instead the legacy of particular forces that were concentrated in certain peripheral regions of the world. We need to look elsewhere for the social forces that will affect strong states and their societies in the future. That is the task for our conclusion.

7

The Future

As we know, there are known knowns.
There are things we know we know.
We also know there are known unknowns.
That is to say we know there are some things
We do not know.
But there are also unknown unknowns,
The ones we don't know we don't know.

Donald Rumsfeld, US Secretary of Defense, 2001–6

Let us distinguish two ways of anticipating any future: extrapolation and if-then prediction. Extrapolation extends past trends into the future on the assumption that the causes of those trends will keep operating in pretty much the same fashion as the years roll on . . . If-then predictions provide less crisp scenarios for coming years, but map out alternative futures.

Charles Tilly (2007: 203–4)

There are two rooms, one in Beijing, the other in Tokyo. In those two rooms sit the men in charge of investing their nations' trade surpluses. At the beginning of 2009, China had $1 trillion in US government bonds and Japan had three-quarters of that. The men know two things. One is that they don't want to sell those bonds because, if they do, their massive holdings will ensure that the value of the dollar will crash, interest rates in the US will rise, the American economy will slump further, and much of the value of their remaining bonds will be lost. In other words, both governments are trapped in their holdings. However, those men also know that it would be even worse to sell their bonds *after* the men in the other room do. Therefore, the men in both rooms watch for signs that the men in the other room, or the men in similar rooms in Seoul, Taipei, London, or New York are selling. So many bonds trade each day that it is hard to know for sure when normal trading has become a concerted effort to dump US holdings. The easiest plan is to hold the bonds and hope for the best. The danger is that some decision by the US government – yet another expensive bank bailout, an indication that future Federal deficits will never be brought below the $1 trillion annual level – will convince the men in one room that prospects are so dire that the men in the other room must have decided to sell. Then the catastrophic events feared by the men in both rooms would actually come to pass.

This is one potential scenario for the near future, based on extrapolation of current trends in US political economy. How such a financial collapse, which would be far worse than the market crash of 2008–9, would affect the world economy and American social stability requires much vaguer if-then predictions that can be only loosely based on the range of outcomes such collapses have had on states and societies in the past.

Just as we can't be confident about predicting an American or global future after such a collapse, we also can't be sure such a collapse actually will occur. If I had written this book fifty years ago I would have described two different rooms, one underground in Nebraska (which is the setting for the climactic scene in *Dr Strangelove*), and a similar one in the Soviet Union. Americans, Russians, and indeed people throughout the world worried more that the men in either room would launch a nuclear attack by accident than in a deliberate attempt to anni-hilate the population of its opponent. With missiles capable of reaching their targets in under an hour, there was little time for careful consideration of what the other side's latest maneuver, or a faulty signal light, actually meant. In those hair-trigger con-ditions, war was most likely to come through miscalculation or fear.

Over the last fifty years, all those who predicted nuclear war had extrapolated from the massive build-up of nuclear weapons, and were wrong. They failed to account for popular opposition to nuclear weapons, which forced the US and Soviet governments to restrain their plans and to negotiate arms reductions (Wittner 1993–2003). They also failed to recognize how American and Soviet political and military leaders' fear and their essential humanity held them back from exploiting weaknesses and launching attacks, most notably in the Cuban Missile Crisis.

Both these extrapolations minimize human agency. Neither pay much attention to states in the way that we have throughout this book, as sites where elites and classes can mobilize to further their interests. The "ifs" of human agency filter through state structures that are themselves the products of previous human agency. Only by analyzing those structures can we determine the "thens," the probable results of nuclear arms build-ups or the accumulation of US debt in Asia.

If the Cold War and decolonization were the world-shaping developments of the second half of the twentieth century, and US economic and geopolitical decline that of the current moment, then the ecological catastrophes that will result from overpopulation and global warming likely will have the most fundamental effects on human society in the twenty-first century. This chapter seeks to address, or at least provide a framework for addressing, the following questions:

1. Is the decline of US economic and military power inevitable?
2. Will US hegemony be replaced by that of China or of another power, or will the world, for the first time in 500 years, enter an era with no hegemon?
3. Can any state, set of states, or international agencies protect populations from environmental disasters or from nuclear proliferation and non-conventional forms of warfare including terrorism?
4. What benefits will states provide for their citizens in the future, and how will citizens be able to make demands on states?

The Decline of the United States

American decline is visible along almost every dimension. Productivity growth, which is the best long-term indicator of future income, wealth, and governmental revenue, has declined in each decade since the 1960s. The dramatic increase in the 1995–2000 period "was driven by the US stock market bubble," which was not sustainable. NASDAQ companies, "home to the New Economy," suffered losses for the 2000–1 fiscal year that were more than the combined profits from the preceding *five* years. "As one economist pithily put it, 'what it means is that with the benefit of hindsight, the late '90s never happened'" (Brenner 2003: 293, 295). Nor did productivity growth revive with the real estate bubble of the 2000s.

US governmental capacity to plan and carry out public works has declined both absolutely since the 1980s and even more so relative to European and East Asian states. US industrial policy also has weakened since the 1980s, and is concentrated in areas (weapons, aeronautics, pharmaceuticals, and computers) in which the government itself is the dominant customer (Block 2008). Except in information technology, government sponsorship has encouraged products that are rising rather than falling in price over time, hardly the hallmarks of dynamic and sustainable industries.

The military is the realm in which American supremacy appears most dramatic. The US in 2008 spent 41 percent of the world's total military expenditures, more than the next fifteen biggest spenders as measured at market exchange rates, and more than the next nine biggest spenders as measured in purchasing power parity exchange rates (Stockholm International Peace Research Institute 2008). This is a margin far greater than that enjoyed by any of the European states that preceded the US as hegemon of the world capitalist system, and appears to be the greatest margin ever. Yet, by the end of 2003, six months into the occupation of Iraq and a year into the occupation of Afghanistan, both relatively small countries with very weak militaries, US military forces were "almost fully engaged" and current and retired generals believed the capacity to fight another war had degraded significantly (Mann 2003: 20 and passim). This was before the US military had to face an actual insurgency in Iraq and the total cost of that war (including future benefits for veterans) escalated past $1 trillion.

Much of the ample current United States military budget goes "to produce weapons that are too expensive, too fast, too indiscriminate, too big, too unmaneuverable and too powerful to use in real-life war. It makes even less sense to design weapons whose development costs are such that they can only be produced on condition that they are sold to others; particularly since lead times are now so long – ten to fifteen years – as to make it likely that some of the buyers will have become enemies" (Van Crevald 1991: 210). The costs of fighter and bomber planes, for example, have escalated from $50,000 each during World War II, when the US purchased 75,000 per annum, to $100,000,000 for the F-15I and $2 billion for the B-2 in 1995 when "the United States Air Force bought exactly 127 aircraft . . . including helicopters and transports." At such prices "there are simply no targets worthy of the risk" (Van Crevald 1999: 345–6), nor are such weapons suited to attacking terrorists of any stripe or to subduing populations in countries identified as dangerous by the United States (Mann 2003).

The interests of highly consolidated military contractors propel the continued development of such Cold War weapons systems and ensure their export. Despite campaigning, twice, on a platform of military restructuring, President George W. Bush succeeded in canceling only the Army's Crusader Artillery system. All other Cold War weapon systems inherited from previous administrations continued in production.

US hegemony, if we extrapolate from current trends, is doomed. The falling rate of productivity, alongside the declining capacity of the US government to foster industrial innovation and to build physical infrastructure, will lead to the loss of US dominance in more sectors. The shrinking US lead in university attendance means that innovations are more likely to be made elsewhere in the world in the future than they were in the decades after World War II. The US's failure to achieve its goals in Iraq and Afghanistan, and widespread domestic opposition to American casualties, means that both the US government and its potential opponents abroad realize that any American foreign policy objective that requires the risk of significant US casualties cannot be pursued in the foreseeable future.

Can US decline be reversed? Numerous proposals have been issued for strategies to restore economic, technological, or military leadership. The key question is whether the American government could adopt and implement such plans. To use Tilly's rubric, the constraints on US efforts to sustain hegemony are in the "ifs." No matter how likely those policies are to achieve their goals, if they cannot be implemented, then US decline is inevitable.

US policy, as we have seen in earlier chapters, is limited by elites' capacity to veto any initiatives that would challenge their particular control over the government agencies that regulate and subsidize their interests. As a result, a continually growing portion of the budget is allocated to the long-standing claims of existing elites that also enjoy the right to shelter portions of their incomes and assets from taxation. Current examples include: (1) subsidies, water rights, and access to Federal lands for the overproduction of agricultural commodities; (2) the commitment of a sector of the Federal budget to a Medicare drug plan that pays prices significantly higher than anywhere else in the world for drugs developed mainly in Federal or university labs, or for copycat drugs, designed to extend patents, with no medical advantage over older generic drugs; (3) free access to Federal lands for mining, ranching, and logging, with no obligation to pay for environmental effects which are then borne by public funds and health; and (4) Federal tax and direct subsidies for the export of technology and capital to foreign subsidiaries and customers.

Together, these claims and immunities ensure either growing deficits or, even in times of fiscal stability as in the late 1990s, an inability to finance new public projects for either infrastructure or the development of human capital. The combination of elites' ability to shelter much of their income through special provisions in the tax code, and popular opposition to general tax increases, acts as a further fiscal constraint on new government programs.

If we extrapolate from the existing structure of US politics, reforms will remain limited, and steps that could plausibly slow or reverse decline will not be attempted at the magnitude necessary. Any possibility of a significant turn from the present trajectory would require an unanticipated popular mobilization that would compel the state to redistribute resources, restructure administration and regulation, undertake new social investments, and reduce military and imperial ambitions. So far, the level of mobilization that led to the election in 2008 of the first African-American president has not yielded significant pressures for reforms along any of those lines, nor has the state on its own initiative adopted such policies. Elite capacities to preserve their privileges and block reforms remain unchallenged.

A New Hegemon?

Declining hegemons do not resign themselves to their own loss of primacy. They pursue strategies designed to preserve their economic and geopolitical power. The hegemon's decline, and struggle to reverse decline, along with rising powers' efforts to supplant the hegemon, combine to affect weaker states' freedom of maneuver in the world system and their capacities to change internal policies. "In all instances, hegemony has involved a fundamental reorganization of the system and a change in its properties" (Arrighi and Silver 1999: 26 and passim). US hegemony led to at least nominal independence for virtually every European colony within two decades of the end of World War II, and to the integration of those states into an American-led system of trade that became increasingly financialized and mediated by US-dominated international agencies. Since 1989, the former Soviet bloc and China have become part of that world systemic architecture.

The financial crisis of 2008, which capped decades of declining industrial production, falling non-financial profits, and rising indebtedness by the US, made obvious that hegemon's inability to sustain world consumer demand and to act as a safe harbor for world financial capital. A continuation of current trends would produce the sort of financial panic and dollar crash sketched at the outset of this chapter. Whether that happens, or if the worst is averted through coordinated efforts by the major industrial powers to stimulate demand elsewhere in the world and re-regulate the international flow of capital, US control over the world economy certainly will be weakened in coming years.

How then will other states respond to the space for maneuver, competition, and innovation that will be created by the loss of US hegemony? If the pattern of every previous transition is followed, a single power would emerge triumphant after a war. However, such an outcome is merely an extrapolation of past patterns. It has no more predictive power than assuming a batter will get a hit, based on the pitcher's previous record of striking-out left-handers. Nor can we assume a new hegemon will emerge because it "can be very useful to capitalist firms, particularly if these firms are linked politically with the hegemonic power" (Wallerstein 2004: 58). Although firms have great leverage over states, it is not always in their interest to have their state take the steps and incur the costs needed to achieve hegemony, and capitalists may not realize that they would benefit years down the line from being located in the hegemon. Even when capitalists understand the benefits of hegemony and are able to compel the state to pursue those policies, or when capitalists are the unintended beneficiaries of an aggressive foreign policy by self-interested rulers, states often lack the capacity to prevail over rivals. The rulers of a putative hegemon must be able to enlist domestic support and overcome resistance for the human and material sacrifices necessary to vie for world dominance. They must be able to convince or compel subjects to serve and die in the military, and to mobilize the financing needed to fund wars, foreign aid, and a continuing presence in the lands that aspiring hegemon dominates around the world.

The two potential contenders for twenty-first-century hegemony, China and the European Union, appear highly unlikely to be able to mobilize what is needed. Neither has a military that can challenge or supplant that of the US. Europe's voters will not approve the fiscal cost, or tolerate the casualties, that would allow a European military to intervene in significant wars, as evidenced in its limited commitment to wars in the Balkans in the 1990s or Afghanistan in the 2000s. The meager response by the EU to the travails of its new Eastern European members since the 2008 financial crisis is a sign that the EU would not make investments of the magnitude that previous hegemons did to stabilize a world economy under their leadership.

China's ability to draft and deploy soldiers almost certainly is greater than that of the US and the EU, although the regime hasn't tested popular reaction to war since its 1979 invasion of Vietnam. China's almost total lack of foreign military intervention since the 1949 Revolution (the Korean War of 1950–3 in which 200–400,000 Chinese died, and its invasion of Vietnam which resulted in 20,000 deaths, are the only significant exceptions) is an indication of its rulers' judgment on the danger to the regime of fighting a foreign war. China's ability since the late 1990s to divert funds for investment abroad was based on its ability to generate a massive surplus from sales of consumer goods to the US. To the extent that America can no longer buy so much from China, the Chinese government will need to divert resources into generating more demand internally. That in turn will reduce China's capacity to fund its policy of displacing the US and Europe as a trading partner and source of aid in the third world.

For all those reasons, US decline is unlikely to result in war with its principal economic and geopolitical rivals, as did the last change of hegemons, from Britain to the United States, which took almost half a century and was accompanied by two world wars, sparked by Germany and Japan's efforts to challenge Anglo-American dominance of the world system. Nor should it echo the previous transitions when Britain cemented its hegemony in the Napoleonic Wars of 1792–1815, as did the Dutch in the 1618–48 Thirty Years War.

In addition, nuclear weapons permanently changed strategic calculations, and just as the US and Soviet Union never went to war, so it is not possible for any of the major nuclear powers to directly confront one another today. In any case, China's advantage is economic and, unlike the strength of Western imperial powers, does not depend on military force for its maintenance and expansion.[1] Arrighi argues that the demise of US hegemony in East Asia after its defeat in Vietnam, and the subsequent reopening of China to world markets, recentered Asian economies around China, initially through networks created by overseas Chinese. US efforts, which culminated after the end of the Cold War, to create "a world market of unprecedented volume and density [gave] the region endowed with the largest supplies of low-price, high-quality labor . . . a decisive competitive advantage. It is no historical accident that this region is East Asia" (2007: 365).

East Asia's advantage presages a shift of wealth from the US to China, but that does not necessarily provide a basis for hegemony, which requires a capacity to impose order and structures on the rest of the world that China, at least for the foreseeable future, will be unable to achieve. Economic regionalism, and a diminution of the vast inequalities between the current rich countries and the rest, would reinforce the loss of a hegemonic center in global geopolitics and open the space for national economic and political autonomy.[2]

The most likely outcome then is that all three potential hegemons – the US, the EU, and China – will be unable to contend for hegemony in coming decades. All three of those great powers will have to settle for less. The US will surrender control of the world economy, and no one else will fill the vacuum. The US will be unable to intervene militarily in the future, stymied by budget crises that will force real reductions in the Pentagon budget, and will be further constrained by the continuing unwillingness of the American public to tolerate significant war deaths. All three powers will be able to exercise dominance only in their regional spheres of influence, and will have to contend with smaller powers, most notably Russia, that command their own "near abroads."

How will other nations react to the opening created by the absence of a hegemon, and its replacement by competition among weaker and less aggressive core countries? The geopolitical underpinnings of the world system and of unequal trade will be undermined. Poorer countries that are not in the immediate orbit of a regional power will be able to play the competing great powers and their blocs against one another to secure better terms of trade, provided their governments are autonomous enough and have the capacity to adopt developmental plans that can benefit from such geopolitical openings. As we have seen in previous chapters, states vary widely in their abilities to develop and implement such policies, and a key factor in the variation is the relationship between indigenous elites and state officials. The decline of US hegemony will weaken capitalists in those countries, most notably those in Latin America and East Asia, which were most closely allied with American firms. As the power of domestic capitalists and their foreign allies is reduced, state autonomy and capacity are likely to increase.

If the world system remains without a hegemon, the balance between state and capital would then move further in the state's favor. Capitalists in core countries would not have state backing for their foreign investments and their threat to relocate capital would be less convincing, since they would have a harder time gaining priority from peripheral states over domestic capitalists there. Existing differences among nations in their domestic elite and class structures, and in the organization of their capitalist firms, would overwhelm the weakening influence of great powers and international agencies, and would therefore become decisive in determining state capacities and policies. The 1930s and 1940s were, for good and evil, an era of experimentation, which ranged from the beginnings of social democracy in Sweden and after 1945 in much of the rest of Europe, to the New Deal in the US, to various forms of authoritarianism and fascism such as the highly redistributionist Peronism in Argentina and the state-managed militarist economy of Nazi Germany. All those regimes enjoyed high levels of autonomy, varying, as we noted in earlier chapters, in whether that autonomy was due to popular support or elite conflicts that created a structural opening to pursue a Bonapartist strategy. States in the coming post-hegemonic era are likely to benefit from a stalemate of elites that have been fragmented and disorganized by foreign intervention and financialization.

Evans argues that, even after the decline of US hegemony, "local private economic elites in the South . . . would . . . choose the same [neoliberal] policies" unless states in the South are forced by "local social movements" to become "progressive actors" (2008:

283). The greatest unknown is whether there will be significant popular mobilization. Such mobilizations strengthen states at the expense of elites, even as they force states to meet popular demands. If Wallerstein (2003) and Arrighi and Silver's (1999: 271–89) predictions that anti-systemic movements would intensify in this, as in all previous hegemonic crises, are correct, the coming years will hold the potential for states to enact strong programs of redistribution and reform, with dramatic increases in state capacity and the extension of social benefits.

Mass mobilization and increased state capacity are likely to be concentrated in certain parts of the world. At the turn of the twentieth century, "the most spectacular trade union growth took place in Britain, and the most violent class warfare erupted in the United States, the most stunning example of working-class party growth was in Germany . . . if past patterns are any guide to the future, then we should expect major waves of industrial labor unrest . . . to occur in those regions that have been experiencing rapid industrialization and proletarianization," above all China (Silver 2003: 135, 169). Silver doubts that worker militancy, and worker leverage over capitalists and states, will be strengthened by "the escalation of interimperialist rivalries and armed conflict [as it was] in the first half of the twentieth century" because of rich states' ability since the 1980s to make "a sharp shift from labor-intensive to capital-intensive warfare" (ibid.: 174–5). In Silver's view, today the US and other rich states can fight wars without needing, and therefore having to make, concessions to win worker-soldiers' consent. Capital-intensive warfare may serve to pre-empt workers' and soldiers' domestic demands, the subject of Silver's study, but in Iraq and Afghanistan that mode of combat has not led to military victory in the absence of massive and extended commitments of US and allied armed forces.

War, Terror and Global Warming

Some states and non-state actors, of course, have been able to mobilize forces and fight long-term highly bloody wars. The

Iran–Iraq War of 1980–8 and the African World War of 1998–2003 are the most prominent examples. The combatants in both wars, especially the former, relied on weapons from abroad, but the troops and their willingness to commit and endure atrocities were homegrown. Outside powers have shown no evidence of being willing to commit sufficient forces to play a significant role in such wars. The one exception, the US invasion of Iraq in 2003, showed how quickly the limits of desire and capacity were reached, making a repeat performance highly unlikely in the Middle East or anywhere else. As a result, future wars will remain regional.

Terrorism also is unlikely to play a significant role beyond countries with weak states and/or civil wars where attacks on civilian non-combatants become one among a set of tactics upon which armed antagonists can draw. Goodwin (2006) argues that terrorists aim their attacks at those civilians whom they, correctly or not, regard as complicitous in state policies that the terrorists oppose. The efficacy of that strategy is determined mainly by the strength of the state that is the ultimate target of terrorist attacks. If the state has the capacity to aim counter-attacks at civilian supporters of terrorist groups and also offer inducements to those civilians, then the groups employing terror become isolated and are defeated (as in Chechnya or Sri Lanka), or are forced by their civilian allies to enter negotiations (as in Northern Ireland). Where the state is unable to protect its civilian allies, as was the case for most settler colonies after 1945, then the colonial power is defeated by armed attacks that include terror, as in French Algeria and British Kenya, regardless of the ferocity of the colonial powers' counter-terrorism.

Terrorism can be prevented as well as combated by strong states. Israel – through the use of a strong security infrastructure (including its wall in the Occupied Territories), its spy networks, and well-trained police, guards, and soldiers – has been able to severely limit the number of attacks launched, not only within Israel but also against Jewish settlements in the West Bank. Similarly, the lack of any attacks within the US after 9/11 2001, and the paucity of such attacks in Europe, speak to the effectiveness of coordinated investigative and police tactics adopted by those states. The great irony of the Bush administration is that its interest in exaggerating the threat from al-Qaeda, to justify the invasion of Iraq and to manipulate public opinion within the US for electoral gains, led it to not publicize its considerable successes in coordination with allies in weakening al-Qaeda through police work rather than military operations.

Terrorists often are sponsored by states or by autonomous agencies within states, such as the Pakistani Inter-Services Intelligence's backing for terror groups that target India, or the Saudi Arabian government's tolerance of its citizens' support for al-Qaeda. Those examples indicate that terrorist groups often act as proxies for governments, just as the Contras who targeted Nicaraguan civilians in the 1980s were a proxy army financed by the US. Terrorism is not a sign of the absence of states, but a tactic of states or factions within a state against one another, of combatants in civil wars, and of liberation movements seeking to establish a state.

The greatest danger of destabilization lies in the looming environmental catastrophe of global warming, caused by the fatal combination of energy-intensive economies in rich countries and the drastic increase in world population which first reached 1 billion shortly after 1800 and will top 7 billion in 2012. Global warming could render parts of the Earth uninhabitable within the next century, through flooding, drought, desertification, and mass species' extinctions.

State capacities to address famines and natural disasters are limited, and have been most successful where hunger is localized and temporary. There is no precedent for long-term relief of the numbers of people in various parts of the world who will be affected by global warming. Nor are states capable of receiving and providing for the huge numbers of refugees that will be created by environmental catastrophes.

Neither governments nor ordinary citizens have been welcoming of large numbers of refugees, regardless of the cause of their flight. No country has yet proven willing to accept large numbers of people fleeing war, genocide, or famine. Almost certainly under such conditions, states would focus on increasing their capacities to hoard natural resources and to repel refugees. Indeed, the first report the US Department of Defense commissioned on the implications of global warming (Schwartz and Randall 2003) projects conflicts over water, oil, and refugees that could lead to wars in many parts of the world. That report highlights dangers but does not address states' varying capacities to insulate themselves and their citizens from the consequences of global disaster.

Governments have long used public works to control water and other natural resources. Examples of such strategies can be found in the huge public works programs undertaken in the United States, especially during the New Deal, to divert rivers to areas of low rainfall. And these strategies have been adopted elsewhere in the world, including Israel, which has hoarded water from the Jordan River and pumped water from aquifers underneath the Occupied Territories, and China, which plans to divert water from Tibetan rivers that now flow into India. The United States has not hesitated to violate treaties and reduce mandated flows of water from the Rio Grande into Mexico. Under sustained drought conditions, states will undertake more public works to capture and divert water, other natural resources, and food.

States also are likely to strengthen border control, building fortified fences, as the United States is doing along the Mexican border. Military and paramilitary forces will be increased to repel refugees. Stricter border controls and national identity cards will be used to prevent illegal immigration and to capture refugees who make it past such controls.

In all those efforts states will be able to count on the enthusiastic support of their citizens. Citizens are likely to rally around any program that would prevent refugees and immigrants from undercutting or overwhelming the social benefits they receive as citizens. States' decades- or centuries-long efforts to instill national identity have succeeded in virtually every country to a great enough degree that citizens will rally behind their governments' measures, however draconian, to repel new arrivals. Already, spontaneous anti-immigrant movements, and others fomented by political parties and governments, have produced vigilante forces, mob riots, and demands for tighter legal restrictions on immigration in many parts of the world.

Ecological disaster is likely to strengthen states and fortify their popular support wherever those states have sufficient capacity to use security forces and public works to manage resources shortages. Where states already are weak or become overwhelmed by environmental disasters on a scale no government could address, capacities to collect taxes and maintain a monopoly on armed force will disappear. The world, if global warming proceeds as it is projected to, will become divided into regions of very strong, increasingly autarkic states and other regions of localized power, amid a Hobbesian war of all against all and massive population decline.

The Future of States

The collapse of US hegemony and the fragmentation of the world into regional power blocs amid resource scarcity and environmental calamity will strengthen states, except in those regions where ecological collapse will overwhelm already weak states. Elsewhere in the world, states will become ever more powerful because they are the only organizations with the capacity to foster economic development, provide social benefits, and shelter their citizens from predatory foreign investors, as well as from the effects of environmental catastrophes elsewhere.

States will not become powerless against transnational capital or international agencies. Nor, except in isolated regions, will they fall into anarchy. They will not merge into a world government, or even surrender further aspects of their sovereignty to either international or regional bodies. The only exceptions to that will be small countries that fall under the influence of regional powers such as China and Russia, or the weaker European states that are and will become more bound to EU dictates, even as the core European states become freer to flout or selectively adopt those rules.

Variations in state policies and capacities will continue to be determined by the structure of relations among elites and classes and the ways in which those relations are institutionalized in partly autonomous states. Throughout this book we have traced the ways in which elite and class conflicts have transformed states and defined the interests and autonomy of state rulers. As state trajectories become ever less likely to be disrupted by external forces, the dynamic of popular mobilization will become the decisive maker of historical change. Popular politics are highly unpredictable, but they, and therefore states, are shaped by human will.

Notes

Chapter 1: Before States

1 Mann 2005a offers a balanced appraisal of the state of archeological research on indigenous societies in the Americas before Columbus. While highlighting evidence for large-scale and complex societies, his descriptions of polities throughout the Americas make clear that central rulers were highly limited in their control over subjects.

2 This section's discussion of the Roman Empire draws on Mann 1986, chapter 9; Anderson 1974a; Ste. Croix 1981; Wells 1984; and Greene 1986. My comparisons to China are based on Scheidel 2009, and the chapters collected in Twitchett and Loewe 1986, and Twitchett 1979.

3 Anderson 1974a offers the best discussion of the importance of Roman law for creating cohesion in the empire, and then in feudal Europe after the fall of Rome.

4 See Lachmann 2000, chs 2 and 6, for a fuller discussion of clerical relations with lay elites and for the historical sources of my analysis.

5 Anderson 1974b, pp. 435–61, makes this point too. See also Bix 1986; Hall 1968; Morishima 1982.

6 Delumeau [1971] 1977 provides the best overview of numerous studies of efforts by Church officials to investigate and reform parish priests' religious knowledge and practices.

7 See Lachmann 2000, ch. 3, for a fuller discussion of the development and limits of city-state political economies and for the sources of my findings.

Chapter 2: The Origins of States

1 His 1997 article is the clearest exposition of his model.

2 Jessop 1982 provides the best overview of Marxists who take such an "instrumentalist" view of the state, although he is careful to note that Marx's *Eighteenth Brumaire* and Poulantzas [1968] 1975 are exceptions in their

attention to how state autonomy, though not state capacity, is created by internal divisions among capitalists.

3 My critique of Anderson does not apply to his analysis of Eastern Europe where bourgeois revolutions did not occur. For that half of Europe, his model is the most useful we have, and I make use of it in my presentation of state formation in Russia and Eastern Europe in ch. 2 of this volume.

4 See Rogers 1995, especially the two chapters by Parker, for a discussion of military innovations in the sixteenth and seventeenth centuries, and the other chapters in that volume for a sense of the varied military innovations of that era, and how they all were dependent on states' uneven abilities to muster resources and to compel once autonomous officers and forces to fight in tandem in a national army.

5 Rosenthal presents aristocrats, non-noble landowners, and merchants as part of a single elite. He argues that differences among those actors can be ignored because all elites are equally open to Crown "bribes and threats" and equally able to engage in "free riding"; Rosenthal 1998, p. 89. Kiser, too, doesn't distinguish among groups of tax-paying subjects. I explore the problems with those assumptions below.

6 The discussion of Spanish state formation in this section draws on Lynch 1991, 1992, 1989; Kamen 1991; Bush 1967; and Flynn 1982.

7 For the sources of my overall argument about France in this section, see Lachmann 2000, p. 262, nn. 28–9.

8 The discussion of Dutch state formation in this section is based on Israel 1995; de Vries and van der Woude 1997; and 'tHart 1993.

9 The discussion of British state formation in this section is based on Lachmann 2000, chs 4 and 6.

10 The discussion in this section is based on Anderson 1974b; Barkey 2008, ch. 3; Downing 1992, ch. 6; Ertman 1997, ch. 6; and Yanov 1981.

11 The discussion in this section is based on Anderson 1974b; Bix 1986; Hall 1970; Morishima 1982; Yamamura 1979.

12 Tilly and rational choice theorists almost entirely ignore the clergy. Spruyt 1994 does discuss the Church's role in medieval politics, but he mistakenly believes the clergy lost power in the medieval era, centuries before the emergence of states. Downing seems to agree with Spruyt since, after claiming that "an account of medieval political history would be incomplete without discussing the role of the Church" (1992: 34), he then has nothing to say about the clergy in his analysis of state formation. Ertman 1997 sees the Church as the source of ideas about government and administration for European rulers, serving in the medieval era a role similar to what Gorski 2003 attributes to Calvinism in later centuries. But neither Ertman nor Gorski, in building on Weber, see the clergy as political actors, just as ideological or organizational role models for lay statesmen.

Chapter 3: Nations and Citizens

1 Collins 1988 and Dessert 1984 provide the best analysis of the political and organizational parameters of tax farming and the financing of state debt in *ancien régime* France. The volumes edited by Bonney 1999 and Ormond et al. 1999 give the most sophisticated overview of the organization of tax collection and state finance in Western Europe from the medieval era to 1815.

2 The Organization for Economic Cooperation and Development is a research and policy organization of the richest industrialized countries in the world.

3 This section draws on Kestnbaum 2002, 2009; Mjoset and Van Holde 2002; Murray and Knox 2001; and Knox 2001.

4 Lack of attention to those other bases of nationalism led Nairn 1977 to mistakenly predict the break-up of Britain.

5 Breuilly 1982 argues that nationalism is mainly a creation of political rulers. He sees cultural nationalism as affecting only elites. The masses, in his view, become involved in nationalism either as a by-product of rulers' efforts to create chains of collaboration among local elites or when such elites attempt to unite to throw off foreign occupation or colonial rule. That is why nationalism developed quite differently in the original European states than it has in states that attained independence in the twentieth century. Breuilly's insights, on the political genesis of nationalism and on the differences between first and third world nationalism, are offered mainly at a highly abstract theoretical level. His case studies and comparisons are too brief to be more than suggestive and, as a result, he is unable to support his claims that non-elites and intellectuals, and their demands and ideas, never were decisive. My goal in this chapter is to draw on other studies, based on more careful historical research, that specify the roles of non-elites and culture in nationalism.

6 That ideal types can have a range of concrete realizations is shown by Canfora who finds "the biggest difference" between Britain and the US, on the one hand, and France, on the other, in that "the former coexisted happily with slavery . . . the latter led directly to the realization that the 'rights of man' meant nothing if they depended on skin color or if – outside Europe – they allowed a mass of cheap, brutalized labor to be condemned to slavery" (2006: 48–9). Canfora recognizes that slavery was not actually abolished in most of the French empire before Napoleon reinstated its legal standing.

Chapter 4: States and Capitalist Development

1 Readers are invited to consult Lachmann 2000, for my take on the origins of capitalism and my evaluation of past work on that topic.

2 Jessop 1982 offers the best review of Marxist instrumentalists. Skocpol 1985 is the key programmatic statement by a non-Marxist.

3 I am grateful to Julia Adams for long-ago research assistance and conversation that helped expand my knowledge and focus my thinking on mercantilism.

This section relies upon the sources cited in Lachmann 2003 and 2009, as well as on Davis 1973; Lynch 1992; and TePaske and Klein 1981 for the discussion of Spain; Deyon 1969; Ekelund and Tollison 1981; Blackburn 1997; and Adams 2005 for France, the Netherlands, and Britain.

4 For Marx's own, and less concise, description, see *Capital* [1867] 1967, vol. 1, ch. 31. Dobb 1947, and of course Wallerstein 1974–89, provide the conceptual foundations of modern Marxist approaches to mercantilism.

5 O'Hearn's 2001 study of Ireland's incorporation in an Atlantic economy, dominated first by Britain and then the United States, is an exemplary analysis of how "the global policies of core states and classes are implemented at regional and local levels to reinforce this hierarchy" of the world system (p. 2).

6 Throughout ch. 4, Wallerstein's terminology is employed and "core" is used to refer to the capitalist states at the apex of global markets, while "periphery" and "semi-periphery" describe the least developed and somewhat more developed colonies and former colonies.

7 Larrain 1989 remains the best survey of the literature on dependency and development from Marx to the late twentieth century. My discussion on pp. 114–15 of ch. 4 draws on his work.

8 Breuilly 1982 recognizes the role of European colonists in shaping indigenous political elites, but underplays the effect of the economic elites, fostered by European colonialism, in the subsequent development of third world nationalism.

Chapter 5: Democracy, Civil Rights, and Social Benefits

1 Similarly broad definitions of democracy are offered by Rueschemeyer et al. 1992; Diamond 1999; and Garrard 2002. Przeworski 2000 argues that elections can mask a sham democracy, such as that of Mexico under the long rule of the PRI. In Przeworski's view "politicians are just PRIstas by nature" (p. 26), and one cannot be sure a regime is under democratic control until it is voted out of office and actually surrenders power.

Canfora 2006 by contrast defines democracy as "not a political system but a form of relations between classes that was biased toward the 'ascendancy of the demos,'" i.e., class equality in the economic as well as political realm (p. 250). Canfora argues that such true democracy is temporary and rare. As a result, he is unable to specify why it emerges in certain places and moments. His main contribution is to explain the strategies oligarchs use to reassert their control after such democratic eruptions. However, he equates all elite regimes and therefore is unable to account for why popular forces were replaced with outright fascism or Bonapartism in some instances, and with liberal or social democracy in others. It is precisely those differences that are the subject of this chapter.

2 Collier 1999, pp. 4–14, offers an excellent review of many of the authors who come down on either side of this question.

3 Anderson 1976 remains the best analysis of those debates, as well as the clearest exposition of Gramsci, whom I discuss on p. 136 of ch. 5.

4 Therborn 1978 offers the most sophisticated Marxist melding of those two positions in recent decades.

5 Tilly (see especially his 1986 and 1995a – synthetic works on France and Britain respectively) devoted much of his career to tracing the ways in which the forms and targets of popular mobilization changed as states and capitalists gained power.

6 Pichardo 1997 offers a summary and critique of this literature.

7 McAdam, Tarrow, and Tilly 2001 is the most sophisticated iteration of social movement theory and reveals the strengths and lacunae of that approach. Kolb 2007 rightly turns attention to the results of social movements. He argues that social movements employ a range of mechanisms – disruption, court suits, voting, mobilizing public opinion – and that each of those mechanisms has different effects on public opinion, state policies, and institutions. However, Kolb's explanation for how each mechanism produces effects is ad hoc and his ability to analyze his main case, the US civil rights movement, is hampered by his limited understanding of US politics. He analyzes elite divisions only in terms of splits between branches of government and fails to discuss how state officials are linked to elites in civil society.

8 This section draws upon Esping-Andersen 1990; and Haggard and Kaufman 2008.

Chapter 6 State Breakdowns

1 For the ultimate critique of Babar, but not of Achebe, see Dorfman 1983.

Chapter 7 The Future

1 Arrighi 2007, pp. 277–89, reviews the key debates in US foreign policy circles around how to deal with China, and explains why China will not resort to military aggression to fortify its position in East Asia or to challenge the US.

2 The US National Intelligence Council 2008 also predicts that by 2025 the world geopolitical "system will be multipolar with many clusters of both state and nonstate actors" (p. 1). However, in contrast to my analysis here, it goes on to predict "nation-states will no longer be the only – and often not the most important – actors on the world stage . . . the relative power of various nonstate actors – including businesses, tribes, religious organizations, and even criminal networks – will grow" (p. 81). The report does not explain how it reconciles state weakness with its other observations that "today wealth is moving not just from West to East but is concentrating more under state

control" (p. 8) and that "perceptions of a rapidly changing environment may cause nations to take unilateral actions to secure resources, territory and other interests" (p. 54), and disasters such as a pandemic could lead to more "internal or cross-border tensions and conflict . . . as nations struggle – with degraded capacities – to control the movement of populations seeking to avoid infection or maintain access to resources" (p. 75).

Bibliography

Abraham, David. 1981. *The Collapse of the Weimar Republic: Political Economy and Crisis*. Princeton, NJ: Princeton University Press.

Abu-Lughod, Janet. 1989. *Before European Hegemony: The World System A.D. 1250–1350*. New York: Oxford University Press.

Adams, Julia. 2005. *The Familial State: Ruling Families and Merchant Capitalism in Early Modern Europe*. Ithaca, NY: Cornell University Press.

Agamben, Giorgio. 2005. *State of Exception*. Chicago, IL: University of Chicago Press.

Aguiar de Medeiros. 2009. "Asset-Stripping the State: Political Economy of Privatization in Latin America." *New Left Review* 55: 109–32.

Alexander, Jeffrey. 2006. *The Civil Sphere*. New York: Oxford University Press.

Allen, Robert C. 1992. *Enclosure and the Yeoman: The Agricultural Development of the South Midlands 1450–1850*. Oxford: Clarendon Press.

Aly, Gotz. 2005. *Hitler's Beneficiaries: Plunder, Racial War, and the Nazi Welfare State*. New York: Metropolitan.

Amenta, Edwin. 1998. *Bold Relief: Institutional Politics and the Origins of Modern American Social Policy*. Princeton, NJ: Princeton University Press.

Amsden, Alice. 1989. *Asia's Next Giant: South Korea and Late Industrialization*. New York: Oxford University Press.

Amsden, Alice. 2001. *The Rise of "the Rest": Challenges to the West from Late-Industrializing Economies*. New York: Oxford University Press.

Amsden, Alice. 2007. *Escape From Empire: The Developing World's Journey through Heaven and Hell*. Cambridge, MA: MIT Press.

Anderson, Benedict. [1983] 1991. *Imagined Communities: Reflections on the Origin and Spread of Nationalism*. London: Verso.

Anderson, Perry. 1974a. *Passages From Antiquity to Feudalism*. London: New Left Books.

Anderson, Perry. 1974b. *Lineages of the Absolutist State*. London: New Left Books.

Bibliography

Anderson, Perry. 1976. "The Antinomies of Antonio Gramsci." *New Left Review* I/100: 5–78.

Arrighi, Giovanni. 1994. *The Long Twentieth Century: Money, Power and the Origins of Our Times.* London: Verso.

Arrighi, Giovanni. 2007. *Adam Smith in Beijing: Lineages of the Twenty-first Century.* London: Verso.

Arrighi, Giovanni and Beverly J. Silver. 1999. *Chaos and Governance in the Modern World System.* Minneapolis: University of Minnesota Press.

Ashford, Douglas. 1982. *British Dogmatism and French Pragmatism: Central-local Policymaking in the Welfare State.* Boston, MA: Allen & Unwin.

Babb, Sarah. 2004. *Managing Mexico: Economists from Nationalism to Neoliberalism.* Princeton, NJ: Princeton University Press.

Bakhtin, Mikhail. [1965] 1968. *Rabelais and His World.* Cambridge, MA: MIT Press.

Bales, Kevin. 2004. *Disposable People: New Slavery in the Global Economy.* Berkeley: University of California Press.

Barkey, Karen. 2008. *Empire of Difference: The Ottomans in Comparative Perspective.* Cambridge: Cambridge University Press.

Beik, William. 1985. *Absolutism and Society in Seventeenth-century France: State Power and Provincial Aristocracy in Languedoc.* Cambridge: Cambridge University Press.

Bix, Herbert. 1986. *Peasant Protest in Japan, 1590–1884.* New Haven, CT: Yale University Press.

Blackburn, Robin. 1997. *The Making of New World Slavery from the Baroque to the Modern.* London: Verso.

Block, Fred. 2008. "Swimming Against the Current: The Rise of a Hidden Developmental State in the United States," *Politics & Society* 36: 169–206.

Bonney, Richard, ed. 1999. *The Rise of the Fiscal State in Europe, c.1200–1815.* Oxford: Oxford University Press.

Brachet-Marques, Viviane. 2005. "Undemocratic Politics in the Twentieth Century and Beyond." In Thomas Janoski et al., eds, *The Handbook of Political Sociology: States, Civil Societies, and Globalization*, Cambridge: Cambridge University Press, pp. 461–82.

Braudel, Fernand. 1977. *Afterthoughts on Material Civilization and Capitalism.* Baltimore, MD: Johns Hopkins University Press, pp. 65–6.

Brenner, Robert. 1993. *Merchants and Revolution: Commercial Change, Political Conflict, and London's Overseas Traders, 1550–1653.* Princeton, NJ: Princeton University Press.

Brenner, Robert. 2003. *The Boom and the Bubble: The US in the World Economy.* London: Verso.

Breuilly, John. 1982. *Nationalism and the State.* Manchester: Manchester University Press.

Bibliography

Brown, Judith. 1999. "India." In *The Oxford History of the British Empire*, vol. 4. Oxford: Oxford University Press, pp. 421–46.

Brown, Norman O. 1959. *Life Against Death: The Psychoanalytical Meaning of History*. Middletown, CT: Wesleyan University Press.

Brubaker, Rogers. 1992. *Citizenship and Nationhood in France and Germany*. Cambridge, MA: Harvard University Press.

Burawoy, Michael and Pavel Krotov. 1992. "The Soviet Transition from Socialism to Capitalism: Worker Control and Economic Bargaining in the Wood Industry." *American Sociological Review* 57: 16–38.

Bush, M. L. 1967. *Renaissance, Reformation, and the Outer World*. London: Blandford Press.

Butters, H. C. 1985. *Governors and Government in Early Sixteenth-century Florence, 1502–1519*. Oxford: Clarendon Press.

Canfora, Luciano. 2006. *Democracy in Europe: A History of an Ideology*. Oxford: Blackwell.

Carruthers, Bruce. 1996. *City of Capital: Politics and Markets in the English Financial Revolution*. Princeton, NJ: Princeton University Press.

Casanova, Pascale. [1999] 2004. *The World Republic of Letters*. Cambridge, MA: Harvard University Press.

Castells, Manuel. 2000. *End of Millennium*. Oxford: Blackwell.

Chandler, Tertius. 1987. *Four Thousand Years of Urban Growth: An Historical Census*. Lewiston, NY: Edwin Mellen Press.

Chang, Ha-Joon. 2002. *Kicking Away the Ladder: Development Strategy in Historical Perspective*. London: Anthem.

Charlesworth, Andrew, ed. 1983. *An Atlas of Rural Protest in Britain, 1548–1900*. Philadelphia: University of Pennsylvania Press.

Chibber, Vivek. 2003. *Locked in Place: State-Building and Late Indusrialization in India*. Princeton, NJ: Princeton University Press.

Chown, John. 1994. *A History of Money from AD 800*. London: Routledge.

Clough, Michael. 1992. *Free at last?: U.S. Policy toward Africa and the End of the Cold War*. New York: Council on Foreign Relations Press.

Collier, Ruth Berins. 1999. *Paths toward Democracy: The Working Class and Elites in Western Europe and Latin America*. Cambridge: Cambridge University Press.

Collins, James B. 1988. *Fiscal Limits of Absolutism*. Berkeley: University of California Press.

Congressional Budget Office. 2006. *Historical Budget Data*. <http://www.cbo.gov/budget/historical.pdf>.

Cronin, William. 1983. *Changes in the Land: Indians, Colonists, and the Ecology of New England*. New York: Hill and Wang.

Davis, Gerald F. and Mark S. Mizruchi. 1999. "The Money Center Cannot Hold: Commercial Banks in the U.S. system of Corporate Governance." *Administrative Science Quarterly* 44/2: 215–39.

216

Bibliography

Davis, Mike. 2001. *Late Victorian Holocausts: El Nino Famines and the Making of the Third World.* London: Verso.

Davis, Mike. 2006. *Planet of Slums.* London: Verso.

Davis, Ralph. 1973. *The Rise of the Atlantic Economies.* London: Weidenfield and Nicholson.

de Gaulle, Charles. [1954] 1955. *War Memoirs: The Call to Arms, 1940–1942.* New York: Viking.

Delumeau, Jean. [1971] 1977. *Catholicism Between Luther and Voltaire.* London: Burns and Oates.

De Roover, Raymond. 1963. *The Rise and Decline of the Medici Bank, 1397–1494.* New York: Norton.

Dessert, Daniel. 1984. *Argent, pouvoir et société au Grand Siècle.* Paris: Fayard.

de Vries, Jan. 1984. *European Urbanization 1500–1800.* Cambridge, MA: Harvard University Press.

de Vries, Jan and Ad van der Woude. 1997. *The First Modern Economy: Success, Failure, and Perseverance of the Dutch Economy, 1500–1815.* Cambridge: Cambridge University Press.

Deyon, Pierre. 1969. *Le mercantilisme.* Paris: Flammarion.

Diamond, Larry. 1999. *Developing Democracy: Toward Consolidation.* Baltimore, MD: Johns Hopkins University Press.

Dobb, Maurice. 1947. *Studies in the Development of Capitalism.* New York: International Publishers.

Dorfman, Ariel. 1983. *The Empire's Old Clothes: What the Lone Ranger, Babar, And Other Innocent Heroes Do to Our Minds.* New York: Pantheon.

Downing, Brian. 1992. *The Military Revolution and Political Change.* Princeton, NJ: Princeton University Press.

Eisenstadt, S. N. 1963. *The Political Systems of Empires.* New York: Free Press.

Eisenstadt, S. N. 1968. "Introduction." In *Max Weber on Charisma and Institution Building.* Chicago, IL: University of Chicago Press, pp. xi–lvi.

Ekelund, Robert B. Jr. and Robert D. Tollison. 1981. *Mercantilism as a Rent-Seeking Society: Economic Regulation in Historical Perspective.* College Station, TX: Texas A&M University Press.

Elias, Norbert. [1939] 1978. *The Civilizing Process.* New York: Urizen.

Elias, Norbert. [1939] 1982. *Power and Civility: The Civilizing Process, volume 2.* New York: Urizen.

Elias, Norbert. [1969] 1983. *The Court Society.* New York: Pantheon.

Ellis, John. 1975. *The Social History of the Machine Gun.* New York: Pantheon.

Engels, Frederick. [1884] 1972. *The Origin of the Family, Private Property and the State.* New York: International Publishers.

Ertman, Thomas. 1997. *The Birth of the Leviathan: Building States and Regimes in Medieval and Early Modern Europe.* Cambridge: Cambridge University Press.

Bibliography

Esping-Andersen, Gøsta. 1990. *The Three Worlds of Welfare Capitalism.* Princeton, NJ: Princeton University Press.

Evans, Peter. 1979. *Dependent Development: The Alliance of Multinational State and Local Capital in Brazil.* Princeton, NJ: Princeton University Press.

Evans, Peter. 1995. *Embedded Autonomy: States and Industrial Transformation.* Princeton, NJ: Princeton University Press.

Evans, Peter. 2008. "Is an Alternative Globalization Possible?" *Politics & Society* 36: 271–305.

Farris, William Wayne. 2006. *Japan's Medieval Population: Famine, Fertility, and Warfare in a Transformative Age.* Honolulu: University of Hawaii Press.

Faust, Drew Gilpin. 2008. *This Republic of Suffering: Death and the American Civil War.* New York: Knopf.

Finer, Samuel. 1975. "State- and Nation-Building in Europe: The Role of the Military." In Charles Tilly, ed., *The Formation of National States in Western Europe.* Princeton, NJ: Princeton University Press.

Flora, Peter et al. 1983. *State, Economy, and Society in Western Europe, 1815–1975.* Frankfurt: Campus Verlag.

Flynn, Dennis O. 1982. "Fiscal Crisis and the Decline of Spain (Castille)." *Journal of Economic History* 42/1: 139–47.

Foran, John. 2005. *Taking Power: On the Origins of Third World Revolutions.* Cambridge: Cambridge University Press.

Friedman, Thomas L. 2005. *The World Is Flat: A Brief History of the Twenty-first Century.* New York: Farrar, Straus and Giroux.

Fukuyama, Francis. 1992. *The End of History and the Last Man.* New York: Free Press.

Fulbrook, Mary. 1983. *Piety and Politics.* Cambridge: Cambridge University Press.

Garrard, John. 2002. *Democratisation in Britain: Elites, Civil Society and Reform since 1800.* Houndmills: Palgrave.

Gelete, Jan. 2002. *War and the State in Early Modern Europe: Spain, the Dutch Republic and Sweden as Fiscal-military States, 1500–1660.* London: Routledge.

Goldstone, Jack. 1991. *Revolution and Rebellion in the Early Modern World.* Berkeley: University of California Press.

Goldstone, Jack. 2008. *Why Europe? The Rise of the West in World History, 1500–1850.* Boston, MA: McGraw Hill.

Goodwin, Jeff. 2001. *No Other Way Out: States and Revolutionary Movements, 1945–1991.* New York: Cambridge University Press.

Goodwin, Jeff. 2006. "A Theory of Categorical Terrorism." *Social Forces* 84: 2027–46.

Gorski, Philip. 2003. *The Disciplinary Revolution: Calvinism and the Rise of the State in Early Modern Europe.* Chicago, IL: University of Chicago Press.

Gramsci, Antonio. [1929–35] 1971. *Selections from the Prison Notebooks*. New York: International Publishers.

Greene, Kevin. 1986. *The Archaeology of the Roman Empire*. London: Batsford.

Guilbaut, Serge. 1983. *How New York Stole the Idea of Modern Art: Abstract Expressionism and the Cold War*. Chicago, IL: University of Chicago Press.

Haggard, Stephan and Robert R. Kaufman. 2008. *Development, Democracy and Welfare States: Latin America, East Asia, and Eastern Europe*. Princeton, NJ: Princeton University Press.

Hall, John Whitney. 1968. *Japan from Prehistory to Modern Times*. New York: Delacorte.

Hall, John Whitney. 1970. *Japan from Prehistory to Modern Times*. New York: Delacorte.

Hardt, Michael and Antonio Negri. 2000. *Empire*. Cambridge, MA: Harvard University Press.

Harvey, David. 2005. *A Brief History of Neoliberalism*. Oxford: Oxford University Press.

Harvey, David. 2009. "Why the U.S. Stimulus Package is Bound to Fail." <http://davidharvey.org/2009/02/why-the-us-stimulus-package-is-bound-to-fail/>.

Heckscher, Eli F. [1931] 1955. *Mercantilism*. 2 vols. New York: Macmillan.

Herlihy, David and Christiane Klapisch-Zuber. 1978. *Les Toscans et leurs familles: une étude du catasto florentin de 1427*. Paris: Centre National de la Recherche Scientifique.

Higley, John and Michael Burton. 2006. *Elite Foundations of Liberal Democracy*. Lanham, MD: Rowman & Littlefield.

Hill, Christopher. 1972. *The World Turned Upside Down*. London: Penguin.

Hobsbawm, E. J. 1990. *Nations and Nationalism since 1780: Programme, Myth, Reality*. Cambridge: Cambridge University Press.

Hochschild, Adam. 1999. *King Leopold's Ghost: A Story of Greed, Terror, and Heroism in Colonial Africa*. Boston, MA: Houghton Mifflin.

Ikegami, Eiko. 1995. *The Taming of the Samurai: Honorific Individualism and the Making of Modern Japan*. Cambridge, MA: Harvard University Press.

Israel, Jonathan. 1995. *The Dutch Republic: Its Rise, Greatness, and Fall, 1477–1806*. Oxford: Clarendon Press.

Jansen, Marius B. 2000. *The Making of Modern Japan*. Cambridge, MA: Harvard University Press.

Janssen, Susanne, Kuipers, Giselinde and Marc Verboord. 2008. "Cultural Globalization and Arts Journalism: The International Orientation of Arts and Culture Coverage in Dutch, French, German and U.S. Newspapers, 1955 to 2005." *American Sociological Review* 73: 719–40.

Jenkins, J. Craig and Barbara Brents. 1989. "Social Protest, Hegemonic Competition and Social Reform: The Political Origins of the American Welfare State." *American Sociological Review* 54: 891–909.

Bibliography

Jessop, Bob. 1982. *The Capitalist State: Marxist Theories and Methods.* New York. New York University Press.

Kamen, Henry. 1991. *Spain 1469–1714: A Society of Conflict.* London: Longman.

Kampwirth, Karen. 2004. *Feminism and the Legacy of Revolution: Nicaragua, El Salvador, Chiapas.* Athens, OH: Ohio University Press.

Kennedy, Paul. 1987. *The Rise and Fall of the Great Powers: Economic Change and Military Conflict from 1500 to 2000.* New York: Random House.

Kestnbaum, Meyer. 2002. "Citizen-Soldiers, National Service and the Mass Army: The Birth of Conscription in Revolutionary Europe and North America." In Mjoset and Van Holde, eds, *The Comparative Study of Conscription in the Armed Forces.* Amsterdam: JAI, pp. 117–44.

Kestnbaum, Meyer. 2009. "The Sociology of War and the Military." *Annual Review of Sociology* 35: 235–54.

Kiser, Edgar and Joshua Kane. 2001. "Revolutions and State Structures: The Bureaucratization of Tax Administration in Early Modern England and France." *American Journal of Sociology* 107: 183–223.

Kiser, Edgar and April Linton. 2002. "The Hinges of History: State-Making and Revolt in Early Modern France." *American Sociological Review* 67: 889–910.

Kiser, Edgar and Yong Cai. 2003. "War and Bureaucratization in Qin China: Exploring an Anomalous Case." *American Sociological Review* 68: 511–39.

Klein, Naomi. 2007. *The Shock Doctrine: The Rise of Disaster Capitalism.* New York: Metropolitan.

Knox, MacGregor. 2001. "Mass Politics and Nationalism as Military Revolution: The French Revolution and After." In MacGregor Knox and Williamson Murray, eds, *The Dynamics of Military Revolution, 1300–2050.* Cambridge: Cambridge University Press, pp. 57–73.

Kohli, Atul. 2004. *State-Directed Development: Political Power and Industrialization in the Global Periphery.* Cambridge: Cambridge University Press.

Kolb, Felix. 2007. *Protest and Opportunities: The Political Outcomes of Social Movements.* Frankfurt: Campus Verlag.

Kumar, Krishan. 2003. *The Making of English National Identity.* Cambridge: Cambridge University Press.

Kuzmics, Helmut and Roland Axtmann. 2007. *Authority, State and National Character: The Civilizing Process in Austria and England, 1700–1900.* Aldershot: Ashgate.

Lachmann, Richard. 2000. *Capitalists In Spite of Themselves: Elite Conflict and Economic Transitions in Early Modern Europe.* New York: Oxford University Press.

Lachmann, Richard. 2003. "Elite Self-Interest and Economic Decline in Early Modern Europe." *American Sociological Review* 68: 346–72.

Lachmann, Richard. 2009. "Greed and Contingency: State Fiscal Crises and

Bibliography

Imperial Failure in Early Modern Europe." *American Journal of Sociology* 115: 39–73.

Laclau, Ernesto and Chantal Mouffe. 1985. *Hegemony and Socialist Strategy: Towards a Radical Democratic Politics*. London: Verso.

Lane, Frederic C. 1973. *Venice, a Maritime Republic*. Baltimore, MD: John Hopkins University Press.

Larrain, Jorge. 1989. *Theories of Development: Capitalism, Colonialism and Dependency*. Cambridge: Polity.

Leach, Edmund. 1954. *Political Systems of Highland Burma: A Study of Kachin Social Structure*. Cambridge, MA: Harvard University Press.

Lemarchand, Guy. 1990. "Troubles populaires au XVIIIe siècle et conscience de classe: Une Préface à la Révolution française." *Annales Historique de la Révolution Française* 279: 32–48.

Lenin, V. I. [1917] 1976. *The State and Revolution*. Beijing: Foreign Languages Press.

Lenin, V. I. [1917] 1996. *Imperialism: The Highest Stage of Capitalism*. London: Pluto.

Levine, Lawrence W. 1988. *Highbrow Lowbrow: The Emergence of Cultural Hierarchy in America*. Cambridge, MA: Harvard University Press.

Levy, Marion. J., Jr. 1966. *Modernization and the Structure of Societies*. Princeton, NJ: Princeton University Press.

Lipset, Seymour Martin and Gary Marks. 2001. *It Didn't Happen Here: Why Socialism Failed in the United States*. New York: Norton.

Lo, Clarence Y. H. 1982. "Theories of the State and Business Opposition to Increased Military Spending." *Social Problems* 29: 424–38.

Lukes, Steven. 2006. "Pathologies of Markets and States." Miliband Lecture. <http://www.lse.ac.uk/collections/LSEPublicLecturesAndEvents/pdf/20060316 –Lukes.pdf>.

Lynch, John. 1989. *Bourbon Spain, 1700–1808*. Oxford: Blackwell.

Lynch, John. 1991. *Spain 1516–1598: From Nation State to World Empire*. Oxford: Blackwell.

Lynch, John. 1992. *The Hispanic World in Crisis and Change, 1598–1700*. Oxford: Blackwell.

McAdam, Doug, Sidney Tarrow and Charles Tilly. 2001. *The Dynamics of Contention*. New York: Cambridge University Press.

McMichael, Philip. 2004. *Development and Social Change: A Global Perspective*. Thousand Oaks, CA: Pine Forge Press.

Mahoney, James and Matthias vom Hau. 2005. "Colonial States and Economic Development in Spanish America." In Matthew Lange and Dietrich Rueschemeyer, eds, *States and Development: Historical Antecedents of Stagnation and Advance*. New York: Palgrave, pp. 92–116.

Mann, Charles. 2005a. *1491: New Revelations of the Americas Before Columbus*. New York: Knopf.

Bibliography

Mann, Michael. 1986, 1993. *The Sources of Social Power*. Vols 1 and 2. Cambridge: Cambridge University Press.

Mann, Michael. 2003. *Incoherent Empire*. London: Verso.

Mann, Michael. 2004. *Fascists*. Cambridge: Cambridge University Press.

Mann, Michael. 2005b. *The Dark Side of Democracy: Explaining Ethnic Cleansing*. Cambridge: Cambridge University Press.

Markoff, John. 1996a. *Waves of Democracy*. Thousand Oaks, CA: Sage.

Markoff, John. 1996b. *The Abolition of Feudalism: Peasants, Lords, and Legislators in the French Revolution*. Pittsburgh: Pennsylvania State University Press.

Martin, Isaac William. 2008. *The Permanent Tax Revolt: How the Property Tax Transformed American Politics*. Stanford, CA: Stanford University Press.

Marx, Karl [1846] 1970. *The German Ideology*. New York: International Publishers.

Marx, Karl. [1852] 1963. *The Eighteenth Brumaire of Louis Bonaparte*. New York: International Publishers.

Marx, Karl. [1867] 1967. *Capital*, vol. 1. New York: International Publishers.

Meeropol, Abel. 1943. "The House I Live In." <http://www.songfacts.com/detail.php?id=2306>.

Mennell, Stephen. 2007. *The American Civilizing Process*. Cambridge: Polity.

Meyer, John et al. 1997. "World Society and the Nation-State." *American Journal of Sociology* 103/1: 144–81.

Mizruchi, Mark S. 2004. "Berle and Means Revisited: The Governance and Power of Large U.S. Corporations." *Theory and Society* 33: 579–617.

Mjoset, Lars and Stephen Van Holde, eds. 2002. "Killing for the State, Dying for the Nation: An Introductory Essay on the Life Cycle of Conscription into Europe's Armed Forces." In Mjoset and Van Holde, eds, *The Comparative Study of Conscription in the Armed Forces*. Amsterdam: JAI, pp. 3–94.

Modelski, George. 2003. *World Cities: –3000 to 2000*. Washington, DC: FAROS2000.

Mohlo, Anthony. 1971. *Florentine Public Finances in the Early Renaissance, 1400–1433*. Cambridge, MA: Harvard University Press.

Moller, Stephanie et al. 2003. "Determinants of Relative Poverty in Advanced Capitalist Democracies." *American Sociological Review* 68: 22–51.

Moore, Jr., Barrington. 1966. *Social Origins of Dictatorship and Democracy*. Boston, MA: Beacon.

Morishima, Michio. 1982. *Why Has Japan "Succeeded"?: Western Technology and the Japanese Ethos*. Cambridge: Cambridge University Press.

Muchembled, Robert. [1977] 1985. *Popular Culture and Elite Culture in France, 1400–1750*. Baton Rouge, LA: Louisiana State University Press.

Murray, Williamson and MacGregor Knox. 2001. "Thinking about Revolutions in Warfare." In Knox and Murray, eds, *The Dynamics of Military Revolution, 1300–2050*. Cambridge: Cambridge University Press, pp. 1–14.

Muto, Giovanni. 1995. "The Spanish System: Center and Periphery." In Richard Bonney, ed., *Economic Systems and State Finance*. Oxford: Clarendon Press, p. 231–59.

Nairn, Tom. 1977. *The Break-up of Britain: Crisis and Neo-nationalism*. London: New Left Books.

Neal, Larry. 2004. "The Monetary, Financial and Political Architecture of Europe, 1648–1815." In Leandro Prados de la Escosura, ed., *Exceptionalism and Industrialisation: Britain and Its European Rivals, 1688–1815*. Cambridge: Cambridge University Press, pp. 173–90.

Needham, Joseph et al. 1954–2004. *Science and Civilization in China. Volumes 1–7*. Cambridge: Cambridge University Press.

O'Brien, Patrick K. 1988. "The Political Economy of British Taxation, 1660–1815." *Economic History Review* 41/1: 1–32.

OECD (Organization of Economic Cooperation and Development). 2006. *Revenue Statistics, 1965–2005*. Paris: OECD.

O'Hearn, Denis. 1998. *Inside the Celtic Tiger: The Irish Economy and the Asian Model*. London: Pluto Press.

O'Hearn, Denis. 2001. *The Atlantic Economy: Britain, the US and Ireland*. Manchester: Manchester University Press.

Ó Riain, Sean. 2004. *The Politics of High-Tech Growth: Developmental Network States in the Global Economy*. Cambridge: Cambridge University Press.

Orloff, Ann and Theda Skocpol. 1984. "Why Not Equal Protection: Explaining the Politics of Public Social Spending in Britain, 1900–1911, and the United States, 1880s–1920." *American Sociological Review* 49: 726–50.

Ormond, W. M., Bonney, Margaret and Richard Bonney, eds. 1999. *Crises, Revolutions and Self-Sustained Growth: Essays in European Fiscal History, 1130–1830*. Stanford, CA: Shaun Tyas.

Paige, Jeffrey. 1975. *Agrarian Revolution: Social Movements and Export Agriculture in the Underdeveloped World*. New York: Free Press.

Paige, Jeffrey. 1997. *Coffee and Power: Revolution and the Rise of Democracy in Central America*. Cambridge, MA: Harvard University Press.

Pichardo, Nelson. 1997. "New Social Movements: A Critical Review." *Annual Review of Sociology* 23: 411–30.

Piven, Frances Fox and Richard Cloward. 1971. *Regulating the Poor: The Functions of Public Welfare*. New York: Vintage.

Poggi, Gianfranco. 1978. *The Development of the Modern State: A Sociological Introduction*. Stanford, CA: Stanford University Press.

Porter, Bernard. 2004. *The Absent-Minded Imperialists: Empire, Society, and Culture in Britain*. Oxford: Oxford University Press.

Porter, Bruce. 1994. *War and the Rise of the State: The Military Foundations of Modern Politics*. New York: Free Press.

Poulantzas, Nicos. [1968] 1975. *Political Power and Social Classes*. London: Verso.

Prasad, Monica. 2006. *The Politics of Free Markets: The Rise of Neoliberal Economic Policies in Britain, France, Germany, and the United States.* Chicago, IL: University of Chicago Press.

Prechel, Harland. 2000. *Big Business and the State: Historical Transitions and Corporate Transformation, 1880s–1990s.* Albany, NY: SUNY Press.

Przeworski, Adam et al. 2000. *Democracy and Development: Political Institutions and Well-Being in the World, 1950–1990.* Cambridge: Cambridge University Press.

Putnam, Robert. 2000. *Bowling Alone: The Collapse and Revival of American Community.* New York: Simon & Schuster.

Putnam, Robert et al. 1993. *Making Democracy Work: Civic Traditions in Modern Italy.* Princeton, NJ: Princeton University Press.

Quadagno, Jill. 1984. "Welfare Capitalism and the Social Security Act of 1935." *American Sociological Review* 49: 632–47.

Quadagno, Jill. 2004. "Why the United States Has No National Health Insurance: Stakeholder Mobilization Against the Welfare State, 1945–1996." *Journal of Health and Social Behavior* 45: 25–44.

Robb, Graham. 2007. *The Discovery of France: A Historical Geography from the Revolution to the First World War.* New York: Norton.

Rogers, Clifford J. ed. 1995. *The Military Revolution Debate: Readings on the Military Transformation of Early Modern Europe.* Boulder, CO: Westview.

Rokkan, Stein. 1970. *Citizens, Elections, Parties.* New York: David McKay.

Rosenthal, Laurent. 1998. "The Political Economy of Absolutism Reconsidered." In Robert Bates et al., *Analytic Narratives.* Princeton, NJ: Princeton University Press, pp. 64–108.

Rostow, W. W. 1960. *The Stages of Economic Growth.* Cambridge: Cambridge University Press.

Rueschemeyer, Dietrich et al. 1992. *Capitalist Development and Democracy.* Chicago, IL: University of Chicago Press.

Sabine, B. E. V. 1966. *A History of Income Tax.* London: George Allen & Unwin.

Scheidel, Walter. 2009. "From the 'Great Convergence' to the 'First Great Divergence': Roman and Qin-Han State Formation and its Aftermath." In W. Scheidel, ed., *Rome and China: Comparative Perspectives on Ancient World Empires.* New York: Oxford University Press, pp. 11–23.

Schmitt, Carl. [1922] 1985. *Political Theology.* Cambridge, MA: MIT Press.

Schwartz, Michael. 2008. *War Without End: The Iraq War in Context.* Chicago, IL: Haymarket.

Schwartz, Peter and Doug Randall. 2003. "An Abrupt Climate Change Scenario and Its Implications for United States National Security." Global Business Network. <http://www.edf.org/documents/3566_AbruptClimateChange.pdf>.

Scott, James. 1998. *Seeing Like a State: How Certain Schemes to Improve the Human Condition Have Failed,* New Haven, CT: Yale University Press.

Seeley, Hart. 2003. "The Poetry of D. H. Rumsfeld: Recent Works by the Secretary of Defense." *Slate*, April 2, 2003. <http://www.slate.com/id/2081042/>.

Silver, Beverly J. 2003. *Forces of Labor: Workers' Movements and Globalization Since 1870*. Cambridge: Cambridge University Press.

Skocpol, Theda. 1979. *States and Social Revolutions: A Comparative Analysis of France, Russia and China*. Cambridge: Cambridge University Press.

Skocpol, Theda. 1985. "Bringing the State Back In: Strategies of Analysis in Current Research." In Peter Evans, Rueschemeyer Dietrich, and Theda Skocpol, eds, *Bringing the State Back In*. Cambridge: Cambridge University Press, pp. 3–37.

Skocpol, Theda. 1996. *Boomerang: Clinton's Health Security Effort and the Turn Against Government in U.S. Politics*. New York: Norton.

Skocpol, Theda. 1999. "Advocates without Members: The Recent Transformation of American Civil Life." In Theda Skocpol and Morris P. Fiorina, eds, *Civic Engagement in American Democracy*. Washington, DC: Brookings Institution Press and Russell Sage Foundation, pp. 461–509.

Skocpol, Theda. 2003. *Diminished Democracy: From Membership to Management in American Civic Life*. Norman, OK: University of Oklahoma Press.

Skocpol, Theda and Edwin Amenta. 1985. "Did Capitalists Shape Social Security?" *American Sociological Review* 50: 572–5.

Sombart, Werner. 1906 [1976]. *Why is there No Socialism in the United States?* London: Macmillan.

Somers, Margaret. 1993. "Citizenship and the Place of the Public Sphere: Law, Community and Political Culture in the Transition to Democracy." *American Sociological Review* 58: 587–620.

Somers, Margaret. 2008. *Genealogies of Citizenship: Markets, Statelessness, and the Right to Have Rights*. Cambridge: Cambridge University Press.

Spruyt, Hendrik. 1994. *The Sovereign State and its Competitors: An Analysis of Systems Change*. Princeton, NJ: Princeton University Press.

Ste. Croix, G. E. M. de. 1981. *The Class Struggle in the Ancient Greek World: From the Archaic Age to the Arab Conquests*. Ithaca, NY: Cornell University Press.

Steinmetz, George. 2007. *The Devil's Handwriting: Precoloniality and the German Colonial State in Qingdao, Samoa, and Southwest Africa*. Chicago, IL: University of Chicago Press.

Stockholm International Peace Research Institute. 2008. "The 15 Major Spending Countries in 2008." <http://www.sipri.org/research/armaments/milex/resultout put/15majorspenders/?searchterm=15%20major%20spender%20countries. html>.

Stuckler, David, King, Lawrence and Martin McKee. 2009. "Mass Privatisation and the Post-communist Mortality Crisis: A Cross-national Analysis." *The Lancet* 373: 399–407.

TePaske, John J. and Herbert S. Klein. 1981. "The Seventeenth-century Crisis in New Spain: Myth or Reality?" *Past and Present* 90: 116–35.

Bibliography

'tHart, Marjolein, C. 1993. *The Making of a Bourgeois State: War, Politics, and Finance during the Dutch Revolt*. Manchester: Manchester University Press.

Therborn, Goran. 1978. *What Does the Ruling Class Do When it Rules?* London: Verso.

Tilly, Charles. 1975. "Western State-Making and Theories of Political Transformation." In *The Formation of National States in Western Europe*. Princeton, NJ: Princeton University Press, pp. 601–38.

Tilly, Charles. 1986. *The Contentious French*. Cambridge, MA: Harvard University Press.

Tilly, Charles. 1990. *Coercion, Capital, and European States*. Oxford: Blackwell.

Tilly, Charles 1995a. *Popular Contention in Great Britain, 1758–1834*. Cambridge, MA: Harvard University Press.

Tilly, Charles 1995b. "Globalization Threatens Labor's Rights." *International Labor and Working Class History* 47: 1–23.

Tilly, Charles. 2004. *Contention and Democracy in Europe, 1650–2000*. Cambridge: Cambridge University Press.

Tilly, Charles. 2005. *Trust and Rule*. Cambridge: Cambridge University Press.

Tilly, Charles. 2007. *Democracy*. Cambridge: Cambridge University Press.

Timberlake, Richard H. 1993. *Monetary Policy in the United States*. Chicago, IL: University of Chicago Press.

Time. 1973. "Lyndon Johnson: 1908–1973." *Time*, February 5, 1973.

Tocqueville, Alexis de. [1835–40] 2000. *Democracy in America*. Chicago, IL: University of Chicago Press.

Twitchett, Denis. 1979. *The Cambridge History of China, volume 3, Sui and Tang China, 589–906, Part I*. Cambridge: Cambridge University Press.

Twitchett, Denis and Michael Loewe. 1986. *The Cambridge History of China, volume 1, The Ch'in and Han Empires, 221 B.C.–A.D. 220*. Cambridge: Cambridge University Press.

US National Intelligence Council. 2008. "Global Trends 2025: A Transformed World." <http://www.dni.gov/nic/PDF_2025/2025_Global_Trends_Final_Report.pdf/>.

US National Science Foundation. 2008. "Endangered Languages." <http://www.nsf.gov/news/special_reports/linguistics/endangered.jsp>.

Van Crevald, Martin. 1991. *The Transformation of War*. New York: Free Press.

Van Crevald, Martin. 1999. *The Rise and Decline of the State*. Cambridge: Cambridge University Press.

Van Onselen, Charles. 1982. *Studies in the Social and Economic History of the Witwatersrand 1886–1914*. 2 vols. Harlow: Longman.

Vovelle, Michel. 1993. *La découverte de la politique: Géopolitique de la Révolution française*. Paris: Editions de la Découverte.

Wade, Robert. 1990. *Governing the Market: Economic Theory and the Role of Government in East Asian Industrialization*. Princeton, NJ: Princeton University Press.

Walder, Andrew. 2003. "Elite Opportunities in Transitional Economies." *American Sociological Review* 68: 899–916.

Wallerstein, Immanuel. 1974–1989. *The Modern World System*. vols 1–3. New York: Academic.

Wallerstein, Immanuel. 2000. "The Agonies of Liberalism." In *The Essential Wallerstein*. New York: New Press, pp. 416–34.

Wallerstein, Immanuel. 2003. *The Decline of American Power*. New York: New Press.

Wallerstein, Immanuel. 2004. *World-Systems Analysis: An Introduction*. Durham, NC: Duke University Press.

Walzer, Michael. 1965. *Revolution of the Saints*. Cambridge, MA: Harvard University Press.

Weber, Max. [1916–17] 1958. *The Protestant Ethic and the Spirit of Capitalism*. New York: Scribner's.

Weber, Max. [1922] 1978. *Economy and Society*. Berkeley: University of California Press.

Weber, Max. [1927] 1981. *General Economic History*. New Brunswick, NJ: Transaction Books.

Wells, Colin. 1984. *The Roman Empire*. Stanford, CA: Stanford University Press.

Wickham-Crowley, Timothy. 1992. *Guerillas and Revolution in Latin America*. Princeton, NJ: Princeton University Press.

Williams, Raymond. 1977. *Marxism and Literature*. Oxford: Oxford University Press.

Wittner, Lawrence. 1993–2003. *The Struggle Against the Bomb* (3 vols). Stanford, CA: Stanford University Press.

Yamamura, Kozo. 1979. "Pre-Industrial Landholding Patterns in Japan and England." In Albert Craig, ed., *Japan: A Comparative View*. Princeton, NJ: Princeton University Press, pp. 276–323.

Yamamura, Kozo. 1986. "The Meiji Land Tax Reform and Its Effects." In Marius B. Jansen and Gilbert Rozman, eds, *Japan in Transition: From Tokugawa to Meiji*. Princeton, NJ: Princeton University Press, pp. 382–99.

Yanov, Alexander. 1981. *The Origins of Autocracy: Ivan the Terrible in Russian History*. Berkeley: University of California Press.

Zeitlin, Maurice. 1984. *The Civil Wars in Chile, or, The Bourgeois Revolutions that Never Were*. Princeton, NJ: Princeton University Press.

Index

Index

232

Index